UN-MAKING A MURDERER

The Framing of Steven Avery and Brendan Dassey

SHAUN ATTWOOD

For Dolores and Allan Avery
and Barb Tadych

ACKNOWLEDGEMENTS

This book would not have been possible without the generous help of Tracy Keogh (copy editing), Penny Kimber (proof reading), Stephen Walker (cover design), Jane Dixon-Smith (typesetting and cover formatting) and everyone who has contributed information

SHAUN'S BOOKS

English Shaun Trilogy
Party Time
Hard Time
Prison Time

War on Drugs Series
Pablo Escobar: Beyond Narcos
American Made: Who Killed Barry Seal?
Pablo Escobar or George HW Bush
We Are Being Lied To: The War on Drugs (Expected 2017)
The Cali Cartel: Beyond Narcos (Expected 2017)

Life Lessons

Two Tonys (Expected 2017)
T-Bone (Expected 2020)

GET A FREE BOOK

Sign Up For Shaun's Newsletter:

http://shaunattwood.com/newsletter-subscribe/

CONTENTS

Intro   1

THE ART OF FRAMING INNOCENT PEOPLE   7
   Strategy 1:   Trigger Emotional Reactions   9
   Strategy 2:   Conceal Other Suspects   24
   Strategy 3:   Coerce False Confessions   43
   Strategy 4:   Plant Evidence   85
   Strategy 5:   Pay Expert Witnesses to Lie   122
   Strategy 6:   Ensure Public Defenders Work
                  for the Prosecution   144
   Strategy 7:   Neutralise Honest Witnesses   180
   Strategy 8:   Procure Dishonest Witnesses   191
   Strategy 9:   Hire Sociopathic Prosecutors   215
   Strategy 10: Rig the Jury   236

Who Killed Teresa and Planted Evidence?   253
What You Can Do for Steven and Brendan   261
Get A Free Book   263
Social-Media Links   264
Shaun's Books   265
Shaun Attwood's True-Life Jail Experience   266
Other Books by Shaun Attwood   273
About Shaun Attwood   277

INTRO

In December 2015, *Making a Murderer* broke my heart in many ways. It featured the story of Steven Avery, a Wisconsin resident who in 2003 was exonerated of a rape and attempted murder for which he'd spent 18 years in prison. Two years after his release, he was on the verge of receiving $36 million in compensation when he was accused of the brutal rape, murder and dismemberment of 26-year-old Teresa Halbach. Eventually, as the state worked hard to build its case against Steven, his nephew, 16-year-old Brendan Dassey was brought in for police questioning. Highly suggestible and intellectually challenged, Brendan was coerced by investigators into admitting helping Steven rape and murder Teresa. Steven and Brendan both received life sentences.

Their plight was compounded by the suffering of their family members, especially Steven's parents, Dolores and Allan Avery, and Brendan's mother, Barb Tadych. Watching the documentary made me want to help Steven and Brendan. Being familiar with the Department of Corrections' procedures, I posted some YouTube videos advising people how to send letters and money to them without violating the prison rules. The avalanche of positive responses was overwhelming.

Some of the millions who watched *Making a Murderer* went online to express their outrage at the blatant injustice. The villains in the documentary were attacked in Facebook posts, Tweets and reviews. The Manitowoc County Sheriff's Office received bomb threats and hundreds of online reviews such as this one: "you don't deserve the ground you walk on!!! scum scum scum hope you all get your heads blown off for what you have done."

Since *Making a Murderer* premiered, many activists have continued to campaign online. I joined forces with *Making a*

Murderer warriors, and, in the UK, we had a demonstration outside the US Embassy in London organised by Belinda Wilson and Kayleigh Brandon, which I attended in an orange jumpsuit. I have written to Steven and Brendan, liaised with some of their family members and corresponded with people close to the case.

After learning about ex-special prosecutor Ken Kratz's book and reading the two books by the Wisconsin prosecutor Michael Griesbach, I was outraged by their efforts to continue to manipulate the public. I felt compelled to write this book with two goals. Firstly, to expose how easy it is in a broken justice system to convict innocent people. Secondly, to help raise money for charity. Half of the profits from this book will be going to Steven and Brendan via their lawyers: Kathleen Zellner & Associates; Laura Nirider and Steven Drizin of the Centre on Wrongful Convictions of Youth. The other half will be spent on free book donations to school children and prisoners. Unlike Kratz and Griesbach, I'm not out to profit from the tragic death of Teresa Halbach.

Ken Kratz – the *Making a Murderer* supervillain – and a minority of people have criticised Netflix for its favourable treatment of Steven and Brendan. Kratz claimed that Netflix left out crucial evidence that would have convinced viewers of their guilt. The more I researched the case, the more material I discovered that strengthened my belief in their innocence. That material is in this book.

I live in London, so this book was written in British English, hence USA readers may notice some spelling differences with American English.

On September 6, 2015, Ken Kratz – the Calumet County District Attorney and lead prosecutor on Steven's second wrongful conviction – sent Steven a letter in an attempt to manipulate Steven into confessing to crimes he had not committed, for the purpose of helping Kratz write a book:

KRATZ LAW FIRM

RE: I'm Sorry That You Are Not Interested

Dear Mr Avery:

I got your letter dated August 28, 2015, wherein you tell me that your visitor list is full, and ask if I checked out other fingerprints found on Teresa Halbach's car, telling me that these people could have "set you up" for this.

I apologize for misunderstanding your letters from a couple years ago, as I thought you were interested in being honest about what happened and finally telling the whole story to someone. Since I'm the person who probably knows more about your case than anyone else, I hoped that you would choose me to tell your story to.

Unfortunately, you only want to continue your nonsense about being set up. That's too bad, because you had ONE opportunity to finally tell all the details, but now that will never happen.

By the way, the difference between you and famous convicted murderers from the past is that they told their whole truthful story to someone, who then wrote a book about what actually happened and people got to understand both sides. I was willing to do that for you... but if you are going to continue to lie about what happened between you and Ms Halbach, I am not interested.

If you change your mind, and want to tell your story someday, please contact me.

Sincerely yours,
Kenneth R. Kratz
Attorney & Counselor of Law

On September 6, 2016, I sent Kratz a letter asking him to contribute to this book:

Shaun Attwood
Author and Activist
London, UK
Email: attwood.shaun@hotmail.co.uk

RE: I'm Appalled That You Framed Two Innocent People

Dear Mr Kratz,
I reference your letter dated September 6, 2015, wherein you attempted to lure Steven Avery into admitting guilt to crimes that originated in the depths of your depraved mind, in the greedy hope that Steven would contribute towards your book *Avery: The Case Against Steven Avery and What "Making a Murderer" Gets Wrong.*
If you are interested in being honest about what happened and finally telling the whole story of how you framed two innocent people, including an intellectually challenged teenager, I'm hoping that you might choose to tell me your story for inclusion in my book: *Un-Making a Murderer: The Framing of Steven Avery and Brendan Dassey.*
Unfortunately, it is with an embarrassing narcissism that you have chosen to continue your charade even though anyone with a jot of common sense – with the exception of Nancy Grace – has seen through your pretence and views you with ridicule and contempt. I'm offering you ONE opportunity to come clean.
For your information, the difference between you and other circus ringleaders from days of old is that they promoted hoaxes before the advent of DNA testing, so that people were never privy to the truth. I am willing to put the truth out there for you, Ken, however if you are going to

continue to lie about what happened in the face of Kathleen Zellner's DNA evidence, I am not interested.

If you change your mind and you'd like the opportunity to tell your story someday, please contact me. I am not the douchebag you referred to me as on Facebook. Just be honest with me, Ken, I have your best interests at heart – just like your buddies Fassbender and Wiegert who pretended to help Brendan Dassey get back to school and home to watch *WrestleMania*. Come clean and bring down all of Manitowoc County with you. You'd better do it soon before they throw you under the bus. An admission of guilt with some feigned tears, remorse, blame-shifting to your Xanax addiction and Samuel Barber's *Adagio for Strings* playing in the background might help mitigate your prison sentence.

If you do ever end up in an orange jumpsuit, Ken, hold onto that soap very carefully. In the event that it slips from your hand in the shower and you must bend over, try to remember the ordeals of your multiple sex-pest victims, including the vulnerable women you were meant to serve and protect.

Sincerely yours,
Shaun Attwood

THE ART OF FRAMING INNOCENT PEOPLE

STRATEGY 1: TRIGGER EMOTIONAL REACTIONS

Framing Steven Avery and Brendan Dassey was easy, but the culprits could never have foreseen that a ten-part docuseries produced by Netflix would expose their deeds to a global audience.

The most powerful technique to manipulate a jury's perception is to trigger emotional reactions. A jury in a hyped-up state will accept things from a prosecutor that have no basis in reality. By keeping their focus on the source of the surge of emotion – such as the grotesque description of a crime – jurors are more likely to lose their peripheral vision and be blinded to the facts, such as the absence of DNA evidence or statements from alibi witnesses.

To trigger emotional reactions, prosecutors wield words, gory photos and re-enactments as weapons that assault the senses. The more dramatic, the better the effect. Setting Steven up twice was simple because a court is not a place where justice is administered. A court is theatre. The side with the most money puts on the best show. In Steven's case, that was the State of Wisconsin backed up by billions of dollars of taxpayers' money.

With a lack of credible evidence linking Steven to both the assault on Penny Beerntsen and the Teresa Halbach murder, prosecutors began their offences by triggering emotional reactions. They opened their dramatizations with vivid grotesque accounts of the crimes, and they continued to layer in similar details throughout the trials.

With considerable cunning, prosecutor Ken Kratz employed this strategy at a law enforcement press conference held on March 6, 2006. Bespectacled and in a dark suit, portly Kratz, with his greying hair swept back, spoke in a low coaxing effeminate tone:

"I know that there are some news outlets that are carrying this live, and perhaps there may be some children that are watching this. I'm gonna ask that if you're under the age of 15, that you discontinue watching this press conference. We have now determined what occurred sometime between 3:45 pm and 10:00 or 11:00 pm on the 31st of October.

"Sixteen-year-old Brendan Dassey, who lives next door to Steven Avery in a trailer, returned home on the bus from school about 3:45 pm. He retrieved the mail and noticed one of the letters was for his uncle, Steven Avery. As Brendan approaches the trailer, as he actually gets several hundred feet away from the trailer, a long, long way from the trailer, Brendan already starts to hear the screams. As Brendan approaches the trailer, he hears louder screams for help, recognizes it to be of a female individual and he knocks on Steven Avery's trailer door.

"Brendan says that he knocks at least three times and has to wait until the person he knows as his uncle, who is partially dressed, who is full of sweat... opens the door and greets his 16-year-old nephew. Brendan accompanies his sweaty 43-year-old uncle down the hallway to Steven Avery's bedroom. And there they find Teresa Halbach completely naked and shackled to the bed. Teresa Halbach is begging Brendan for her life.

"The evidence that we've uncovered... establishes that Steven Avery at this point invites his 16-year-old nephew to sexually assault this woman that he has had bound to the bed. During the rape, Teresa's begging for help, begging 16-year-old Brendan to stop, that "you can stop this." Sixteen-year-old Brendan, under the instruction of Steven Avery... cuts Teresa Halbach's throat... but she still doesn't die."

As if Steven and Brendan had already been convicted, the news reporters supported Kratz:

First male reporter: "The horrible picture of how Teresa Halbach died, painted by a 16-year-old boy who couldn't keep his terrible secret any longer."

Second male reporter: "Investigators from here at the Calumet County Sheriff's Department and from the Wisconsin

Department of Justice interviewed Brendan Dassey twice this week. They used his statements like instructions to put together pieces of a sick puzzle. According to this complaint, Dassey and Avery are accused of choking Teresa Halbach and then dragging her lifeless body outside, throwing her in the burn pit and shooting her in the head and in the stomach."

Female reporter: "Today's development [is] certainly on the minds of many. Here is what some people in the Fox Valley had to say."

To stamp public approval on the media's verdict, the opinions of three men were aired:

"I'm a little surprised by the age of him, but I wasn't... wasn't surprised there was somebody else involved."

"I think he did help him out. I don't think he was the master behind it, but I think he helped him out."

"You know, I believed him at first and now it's the other way around..."

By seamlessly crafting together and broadcasting snippets from hours of coerced testimony from Brendan Dassey, an intellectually limited and highly suggestible teenager, Kratz turned the majority of the public against Steven and Brendan without presenting a shred of valid evidence. The press conference was so impactful that it even turned people against Steven who'd previously supported him. It tainted the jury pool across Wisconsin and stacked the odds in favour of a guilty verdict.

When *Making a Murderer* broadcast the conference, many viewers, including myself, started to wonder whether Steven and Brendan had actually committed the crimes. But as the episodes unfolded, Netflix showed the bigger picture of Brendan being spoon-fed by two manipulative detectives. With Kratz's illusion exposed, it began to fall apart, causing considerable outrage among the viewers.

The strategy of triggering emotional reactions employed by Kratz was a carbon copy of that used by prosecutor Dennis

Vogel in Steven's first wrongful conviction. The trial commenced with Vogel extracting dramatic details from the victim Penny Beerntsen. It was an assault on the hearts of the jurors.

Penny and her husband, Tom, owned and ran an ice cream and candy store in downtown Manitowoc. High school sweethearts, they had married during their third year at arts school in Illinois. Tom's work at the YMCA had taken them from state to state. During these relocations, Penny had a baby girl, followed by a boy. After ten years, the couple had returned to Manitowoc in 1983 to operate the candy store, which Tom's grandparents had opened in 1932.

After work, Penny and her family sometimes went to Neshotah Park to swim in Lake Michigan. On July 29, 1985, Penny, Tom and their 11-year-old daughter arrived at the park without their 10-year-old son who was with a friend. On the beach, Penny started to read a book about Lizzie Borden, a woman who had been tried and acquitted for the 1892 axe murders of her father and stepmother.

"I can't believe I'm reading such a gruesome book on a beautiful day," Penny said. "I'm going for a jog." Due to the heat, she set off in her swimsuit at 3 pm.

She jogged north into Point Beach State Forest, a public area of the beach with homes. She reached a point where, about ten yards away from her, she came upon a bearded man with a black leather jacket slung over his shoulder. He seemed out of place.

"It's a great day," he said.

"Yes, it's a beautiful day for a jog." Penny continued past the man. She jogged three miles north and reversed course, hoping to re-join her family by 4 pm.

A couple of minutes after 3:50 pm, she spotted the man in the leather jacket. He emerged from underneath a half-fallen poplar tree, close to the water. Knowing that she would have to jog past him filled her with dread.

Approaching him, she thought, *I have to get away from this guy.* She swerved towards the water. The man attempted to grab her, but failed. Wading through the water slowed her down. The man homed in, clasped her upper body with his arms and pulled her ashore. A chokehold silenced her screams.

"We're going to go for a little walk in the woods," he said.

Terrified, Penny thought, *I have to stay calm. I have to get a really good look at this guy. I need to study him to see what he looks like.*

As she was pushed over sand dunes, her top came off. Despite her brave resistance, including attempts to twist free and escape, the man manoeuvred her to the edge of the woods. He undid his jeans and revealed his penis. Pushing her into the woods, he managed to take off the rest of her swimsuit. "Do what I tell you. I have a knife." He touched her breasts. He sucked one and bit it. "Make me hard."

"I've been gone too long. My husband will be worried and he'll come looking for me."

"Make me hard."

"No!"

He pushed her down, pinned her shoulders to the ground and knelt over her. Several times he strangled her until she almost lost consciousness. "Now, are you going to do it?" Every time she refused, he strangled her again. She was threatened with a knife and forced to touch his penis. He grabbed her breasts. "Play with yourself."

Penny took her hand off his penis to use on herself.

"Now put your mouth on my penis."

"No."

"Put your fucking mouth on my penis. You're really fucking this up. Spread your legs. Spread your goddamned legs. You're fucking this up." The man responded to Penny's resistance by beating her endlessly in the face.

She kicked him where it hurts.

"Now I'm going to kill you. Now you're gonna die, bitch." With her skull getting smashed into the ground against either a rock or a tree root, she braced to get stabbed to death. He grabbed her nose, yanked it to the side and she heard a bone crack. When she was on the verge of losing consciousness, the man paused. "Now, are you going to do it or not?"

"OK. I'll do it," Penny said, trying to regain her strength. "But I'm sure my husband is looking for me. I've been gone too long."

Her response provoked another round of violence, which lasted several minutes.

Expecting to die, Penny was sad because she hadn't kissed her son goodbye that morning and told him that she loved him and she assumed that her daughter's last memory of her would be her bloodied strangled corpse and her husband would have to raise two children on his own.

After strangling her until she became unconscious, the man took off into the woods.

Eventually, Penny's eyes opened. Flat on her back, she saw what she assumed was his blood on her hand. She thought, *Oh, I didn't think I scratched him, but maybe I did. This is evidence. I've got to preserve this.* During the assault, she had attempted to leave scratches on his face, so that he could be identified. Her vision was too blurred to see her watch.

Fearful of her attacker returning, Penny attempted to stand, but fell. On her hands and knees, she crawled towards the water, while maintaining her palms upwards to preserve the blood evidence. Disorientated, she thought she was heading straight for the shoreline, but she was zigzagging across the sand. Every so often, she lost consciousness, only to revive and resume crawling.

At the shoreline, naked, huddled into a ball, she spotted a couple north of her. She cried for help, but the words didn't come out right, as if she had suffered a stroke.

The couple wrapped her in a towel. "Do you think you can walk with our help?"

"Yes." They headed south along the beach.

In the meantime, Tom had realised something was wrong – such as his wife drowning – after Penny hadn't returned on time. He'd driven to a convenience store and called the police. He'd arranged for his father to come and pick up his daughter. He'd sent guys on jet-skis searching for Penny.

Heading north on the beach, Tom spotted Penny and the couple.

"A man tried raping me, Tom. He tried to kill me."

Tom picked Penny up and ran back to where an ambulance was waiting. Penny was rushed to a hospital.

In court, prosecutor Vogel asked Penny to detail what had happened after she'd kicked the assailant in the groin.

"He was shaking me up and down so hard that my head and upper back were hitting the ground. Both his hands [were] around my neck, my windpipe, and he was kneeling over me. He was grabbing me so tight I couldn't breathe. He kept saying, 'Now are you gonna do it? Are you gonna do it?' I remember thinking he was going to kill me if I didn't cooperate, but I couldn't say anything because I couldn't get any air."

Asked how she felt after the man had gone into the woods, Penny replied, "I was bruised. I was bloody. I was unable to move. It felt like my arm and legs were made of lead. I was dazed. I was humiliated."

To trigger an even bigger emotional reaction from the jury, Vogel switched from Penny's testimony to an actual re-enactment. "Penny, what I'd like to do is just have you get up out of your chair. Mr Beerntsen, why don't you come up here? Can you do that? What I'd like to do is go back and have you show the jury a couple things in terms of how you were grabbed. Have your husband grab onto you. Have him take his arms or whatever and show how you were first grabbed as you were jogging."

"Put your right arm there and your left arm here," Penny told her husband. "OK. Initially, his hand was on my shoulder. When I twisted to holler to the sailboat, he did exactly what my husband just did. He grabbed my neck and cut off my windpipe... You can let go now."

"For the record," Vogel said, "you're demonstrating your husband has his left arm around you. His right hand would be on your right arm. Is that a fair statement?"

"That's correct."

"Show me how you were being held when you were halfway into the woods, when the top of your swimsuit... was removed."

"OK. With this arm, OK, he removed his left hand and then undid, I don't know, the top or the back first. At this point, I twisted. He again put his left arm around my neck and said, 'Do what I tell you. I've got a knife.'"

"When you were in the wooded area or close to the wooded area, you told us about the conversation about touching his penis and so forth. Could you just show me in which position you were at that time?"

"OK. We were face-to-face."

"Penny, turn the other way so we can both see... You indicated before that you did touch his penis. How did you do that?"

"With my right hand."

"You indicated he pushed you down on the ground. Show me how he did that."

Penny directed her husband where to grab her shoulders. "He grabbed both my shoulders like this. OK. My arms were pressed against my body, and then he pushed me down onto the ground."

"OK. Can we just slowly do that? How was he over you? That's what I want to know."

"OK. I was lying on my back like this."

"Can everybody see OK?" Vogel said to the jury. "If you can't see, stand up."

Penny had her husband adjust his knees back further. She confirmed that the assailant's jeans were open and his penis exposed.

With the physical re-enactment ending, Vogel moved on to a third medium: photos. "I'm showing you what's been marked as Exhibit 9. Do you recognise that?"

"Yes," Penny said. "It's a photo of the area of Neshotah Beach. This is the tree where my assailant was standing. I'm looking northbound here."

"How about Exhibit 10?"

"That's a close-up of the tree, looking north."

"Exhibit 11?"

"The same tree, only this time looking south."

"Exhibit 12?"

"That's the same area of the beach with the tree, looking southbound. I'm standing in the water approximately at that point where I began to jog into the water. My husband is standing in the shadow of the tree where Mr Avery was standing."

"What's Exhibit 8?"

"The incline of the sand dune area that Mr Avery pushed me up?"

"Thirteen?"

"OK. This is a picture of the wooded area where I was assaulted, and I'm standing approximately on the spot where the assault occurred."

"Fourteen?"

"This is a close-up of the wooded area where I was assaulted. I'm standing on the spot where I was assaulted, where I was lying on the ground."

The trial had barely begun, and Vogel had already convinced the jury of Steven Avery's guilt by appealing to their emotions on three levels: verbal, physical and visual.

Attempting to minimise the damage done so far, Steven's lawyer tried to prevent the introduction of a photo of Penny's beaten face taken in the emergency room. "The issue isn't how badly the victim was beaten. It's who committed this brutal assault. The photograph appeals to sympathy for the victim and disgust for whoever assaulted her. That's the only reason the state wants it in front of the jury, Judge."

"I don't believe there's any better way," Vogel said, "to show the nature and extent of the victim's beating than using the photographs. The extent of the beating is critical in this case, and this photograph corroborates it. It corroborates the victim's testimony."

"With respect to the photographs of the injuries," the judge said, "the court believes they're reasonable and valuable evidence to the jury. And while they're not exactly the most pleasant things to look at, I believe it's reasonably necessary for the state to use those photographs to demonstrate the nature and extent of the attack. Therefore, the objection is overruled."

With an emergency room doctor on the stand as a witness, Vogel said, "I'm showing you what's been marked as Exhibit 1. Is this a photograph of the way Penny looked when you saw her at the hospital that night?"

"Yes, it is," the doctor said.

The judge granted Vogel permission to show an enlarged photo to the jury. Creeping along the front of the jury box, Vogel took his time, allowing the jurors to absorb the full impact of Penny's battered and bloodied face. "Do you have an opinion to a reasonable degree of scientific certainty, Doctor, as to whether or not the bruise at the base of Penny's neck would be consistent with someone choking her?"

"It very well could have been."

"The degree of force required, Doctor, to cause that sort of bruising: do you have an opinion to a reasonable degree of scientific certainty as to the amount of force required to cause that?"

"It's relatively hard to cause the breaking of the blood vessels there to cause that kind of bruising."

"Do you have an opinion to a reasonable degree of scientific certainty as to how much force would be required to cause bruising to her back the way you saw it, to a reasonable scientific certainty, that it would be consistent with Penny being shaken or pushed on the ground up and down several times?"

"Could very well have been, yes."

Vogel's strategy was so effective that despite sixteen alibi witnesses stating that Steven was with his family at locations too far away from the scene of the crime for him to get there and back, the jury still found him guilty of rape and attempted murder. He was sentenced to 32 years.

On January 29, 1986, Steven Avery wrote a letter to the judge:

Dear Judge Hazlewood,

I am writing in regards to my case. I truly believe I did not get a fair trial. Why on god's green earth would I go out and hurt a woman I don't even know and when I am Happily married and my wife just got out of the Hospital with our twins the day before. Why should My Wife have to raise our children alone, and Why should my kids have to grow up without a father, especially when I did not do this and I am an innocent man.

I pray every night to god that the guy who did this would turn himself in as I don't have a life setting up here and I have to worry about my Wife and 5 kids out there alone With that guy Still running around out there.

I really feel sorry of Mrs Beerntsen as I Would not want anyone to have to go through something like that. I know I have done some bad things in my past, but I started to realize it after I pulled an empty gun on Sandy Murphy that I Went about it in the Wrong Way and I started to turn my life around. I had heard that Sandy Murphy wanted to drop the charges against me but Mr Vogel won't. Why is everybody against me, am I really that bad?

I was wondering if you could please help me and my family as our future is in your hands. I am scared shitless as to the outcome of my case and I am also scared for my family. I am not lieing with god as my Wittness. Please help me in any way you can I would Really appreciate it.

Thank you for your time. Please help me thank you Judge.

Sincerely,
Steven Avery

The judge never responded.

With no evidence linking Brendan Dassey to the murder of Teresa Halbach, Ken Kratz, in his opening statement to the jury, started by describing the victim:

"I'm going to introduce you to a lovely young woman. This is Teresa Halbach. Ms Halbach was 25 years old on Halloween of 2005. You're going to hear evidence in this case that Ms Halbach was single. That Ms Halbach was a college graduate. Ms Halbach was a freelance photographer. She was a daughter. She was a sister. She was a friend. And she had her whole life ahead of her.

"You're also going to hear evidence that all of that came to an end on Halloween of 2005. This story, this case, begins at about 8:12 am on Halloween Day of 2005, when the plan was set into motion to take this young woman's life. The plan was set into motion to rape and to kill and to mutilate this 25-year-old innocent young woman."

Kratz stated that Teresa was a photographer for *Auto Trader*, whom Steven Avery had lured – using his sister's name and phone number – to a salvage yard, under the auspices of taking a picture of a car that he wished to sell. The Avery Salvage Yard was forty acres of junked cars. The four trailer residences on the property included Steven's, which was next to the one owned by Brendan Dassey's mother in the north-west corner of the property. The other two belonged to Steven's parents and his brother Chuck. After Teresa was reported missing, a citizens' search conducted at the salvage yard had located her vehicle.

Kratz started layering in details about Teresa's blood:

"On Monday... the 7th the Crime Lab... make a startling discovery. Remember the SUV of Teresa was taken to the... Crime Lab for processing. They found male blood in six different locations in the SUV and they found a great deal of female blood in the back or what's called the cargo area of Teresa's SUV. These were the first results they had gotten. They didn't get any DNA results back yet, but they could tell it was male blood. They could tell that it was female blood."

After the blood, Kratz focused on the bones:

"And the third and most chilling discovery, on the 8th, the evidence will show is this burn area... a few feet behind the garage of Steven Avery. You're going to hear evidence that within this burn area, obvious human bone fragments were found. You're going to hear that the Crime Lab came to process this scene, that arson investigators came to process the scene. They recovered, at least on that first day... as many of the bones that they could recover... This is a photo that just assists you and explains why it took until Tuesday to find these human remains in that area. All right?

"... the recovery of those bones, you will hear, were in very, very small size. They were also very degraded. They were charred. But they were all examined by a forensic anthropologist. We'll talk about that little bit later in the case. What you need to know on Wednesday is that they were able to say that they're human bones and that they're from an adult female."

Then he got down to the business of provoking emotional reactions:

"But let me also warn you, because it's fair for me to do this, that some of the details may be disturbing... Now, we have to give you those details...

"Brendan Dassey, in, again, sometimes graphic detail, will talk about approaching Uncle Steve's trailer, and before he even knocks on the door, he hears screaming. He hears screaming from inside of the trailer, and he knocks on the door...

"You're going to hear that Steven Avery answers the door. You're going to hear that he's sweaty, and that he tells Brendan Dassey that he has raped this woman that he has in the back of his bedroom. These are difficult hard images to kind of wrap your mind around. But this is the version that Brendan Dassey gave on the 31st of October.

"Brendan actually sees Teresa tied up. He sees her shackled with handcuffs and leg irons to the back bed in the back bedroom. And here, when we talk about decisions, Mr Avery himself asks Brendan if he wants to have sex with the woman that's been restrained in the bedroom now.

"Some of the language is very graphic... They don't use the word, do you want to have sex. All right? They use some very, very crude degrading language towards any woman, but certainly towards a young woman, uh, who is in this trailer already.

"When we talk about those decisions that Brendan gets to make at this point, Brendan says, 'Yes, I want to do that.'

"You're going to hear that Brendan Dassey rapes Teresa Halbach. You hear that he walks into the bedroom while Teresa's restrained on the bed, and, by force and by violence, and with the use and threat of a weapon, he had sexual intercourse with this woman without her consent.

"After the rape, Steven Avery praises his nephew, and says, 'That's how you do it.' These are explanations again from Brendan. The repulsive expression, lack of empathy, lack of any kind of moral fibre, any kind of moral compass at all, for an uncle to tell a nephew, 'That's how you do it.'

"Then Steven and Brendan discuss if they should and how they should kill Teresa Halbach. Again, the decision tree. What does Brendan decide to do? Steve says, 'Will you help me?' Brendan says, 'Yes.' You'll hear testimony about Steven and Brendan going into the bedroom. Steven Avery stabs the victim. Brendan Dassey, handed the knife by Uncle Steve, cuts Teresa Halbach's throat.

"You're going to hear that they take, um, this 25-year-old woman, unclothed, to the garage. They place her on the floor. Dassey waits with Teresa Halbach, who is not yet dead, laying on the floor, as Mr Avery retrieves his .22 calibre Marlin Glenfield semiautomatic rifle, and Brendan says Uncle Steve shoots her ten times, at least twice in the head, including on the left side of her head."

Kratz then detailed the mutilation and burning of the corpse.

With the jury being played Brendan's confession in court – which I deal with in detail in Chapter 3 – the teenager didn't stand a chance. Despite no DNA or physical evidence linking him to the crime, he was convicted of being party to first-degree murder, mutilation of a corpse and second-degree sexual assault.

He was sentenced to mandatory life in prison with a possibility of parole set for November 1, 2048.

Steven and Brendan were doomed because the decision-making of the jury wasn't logical: it was based on emotion. Knowing that, all the prosecutors had to do was to keep the jury focused on the gruesome details and distracted from the absence of any evidence. In Wisconsin's Alice in Wonderland justice system, theatre usually triumphs over facts. But on the off-chance that this strategy had failed to sway the jury, the authorities employed numerous other dirty strategies.

STRATEGY 2: CONCEAL OTHER SUSPECTS

In 1985, Steven Avery was languishing in custody for the rape and attempted murder of Penny Beerntsen. The case was closed as far as Manitowoc County Sheriff Tom Kocourek was concerned. As a friend and neighbour of the Beerntsens, Kocourek had shown up in the emergency room twenty minutes after Penny's arrival. He promised to move heaven and earth to apprehend the culprit.

In the emergency room, Kocourek asked Penny for a description of the suspect. She described a stocky man about 30 years old, approximately five foot six or seven, with long sandy hair and a scruffy beard. He was wearing a black leather jacket with buttons or studs and jeans. He had brown eyes.

Despite Steven Avery having blue eyes, Deputy Judy Devorak concluded that Steven had committed the crime. Having arrived at the hospital first, Devorak had questioned Penny about the assault. Devorak lived close to Steven and despised him. Working as a guard at the County jail, she'd encountered Steven, whom she later described as dirty and in need of an immediate shower because "the stench was that bad."

With Steven already in trouble for running off the road his cousin, the wife of a deputy sheriff, Sheriff Kocourek and Deputy Devorak figured they had their man.

But some members of the District Attorney's office were convinced that another suspect had committed the assault on Penny. Gregory Allen was a sexual predator under police surveillance, whose crimes had become increasingly violent. Due to his predatory behaviour on the beach, Allen had been nicknamed the Sandman by deputies.

On August 2, 1983, Allen had assaulted a victim walking a

dog on the same beach where Penny had been attacked. Wearing a tank top and blue shorts, he'd run over sand dunes to approach his victim from behind. He'd dropped his shorts and started masturbating. He'd attempted to grab the victim, but she'd twisted free and escaped.

The victim told police that she knew the assailant was Gregory Allen, a customer in the convenience store where she worked. The terrified victim moved to Green Bay, but Allen discovered her location and called her. She reported the call to the police.

On January 26, 1985 at 6:30 am, a woman contacted the police about a man in a ski mask in her neighbour's backyard, peeping into the bathroom. The police discovered that a teenager had been in the bathroom. She had emerged from the shower, seen Gregory Allen and screamed. Weeks earlier, she had told her parents that someone was watching her in the bathroom, but they had dismissed her claim. From police photos, the teenager identified Gregory Allen. An assistant district attorney refused to file charges against Allen for this crime, so the investigating officer cited Allen for prowling, but the city attorney dismissed the charge.

On June 23, 1985 at 4:30 am, a bartender who had been working late was in her kitchen when someone tapped on a window. The man outside, who had a red T-shirt wrapped around his head, was masturbating. In a panic, she sprinted to lock the front door, just beating Allen to it. Unable to get in, he continued masturbating. He asked her to display her breasts. She declined.

"What difference would it make?" Allen said. "You'll never see me again."

"Get out of here. I'm calling the police."

Before disappearing, Allen promised to return the next day. She contacted the police, who told her to call them if he returned.

On June 26 at 2:31 am, someone knocked on her front door. After getting off the sofa, she saw Allen, wearing a red T-shirt around his head and masturbating. He'd opened the screen door and attempted to enter the premises. She screamed so loudly that he fled.

Ten minutes later, the police stopped Allen on his motorbike in her neighbourhood. He was wearing a red T-shirt and had in his possession two screwdrivers with which he had removed twelve screws from her window frame. As a T-shirt had been wrapped around his head, she was unable to identify him.

Certain it was Allen, a detective filed a report that ended with: "It would appear that this is getting very serious in regard to the suspect Gregory Allen. He is in all probability the suspect involved; however, at this point the victim could not make a positive identification. Allen will have to be caught in the act as he is starting to become very bold."

On July 14, 1985, shortly after 3 am, a 17-year-old awoke to a naked man in her bedroom with her bathing suit wrapped around his head. He put a knife to her throat. With her parents away from home, she was helpless.

"Say anything and I'll kill you." He sat on her and covered her mouth with a hand. He fondled a breast. "Take off your clothes or I'll kill you."

Crying and pointing at a heating pad below her, she said she was on her period.

The Sandman touched the heating pad. "Where's your younger sister?"

"Up north with my parents."

He guided her hand to his penis and forced her to touch him until he ejaculated. Holding a knife to her throat, he dragged her by an arm towards a door. "Call anyone and I'll come back and kill you." He disappeared into the night.

Noticing a white stain on her nightgown, she rushed to the bathroom and vomited. She attempted to call the police, but Allen had cut the line. Terrified to emerge from her home, she surveyed the area for any signs of Allen. She ran to her car and drove to the police station.

She described the assailant as approximately five foot eight with a strong build and possibly a beard that had been obscured by her bathing suit wrapped around his head. Neighbours told the police about the activity of a man on a motorbike, who had been lurking around her house for the past month.

Once again, no charges were filed against Allen.

A detective wrote, "This department has compiled several complaints recently concerning prowling, window peeping, indecent exposure and sexual assault, ranging from January 1985 through July 14, 1985. In each case, Gregory Allen has been listed as a suspect. Past record and intelligence concerning Gregory Allen reveals he is a dangerous individual with a potential for violence."

Twelve days later, Penny was attacked.

On the day of Penny's assault, Kathy Sang was sailing near the shoreline. At 3:30 pm, she and her boyfriend saw Penny jogging in her swimsuit. They also saw a man with a beer belly, wearing long trousers and a black shirt. On the same day, Kathy gave a statement to a sheriff's deputy. Her statement and description of the suspect – whom she later claimed was not Steven Avery – went missing and no records of them exist to this day.

Two days after getting assaulted and with Steven Avery in jail, Penny received a call at home.

"Hello," she said.

"What are you doing?"

"Who do you want?"

"I want you."

The caller revealed details of the assault that hadn't been reported in the news.

After hanging up, Penny called her husband and the police. Sheriff Kocourek stationed deputies outside Penny's house and attempted to trace any future calls. In jail, Steven Avery was banned from making phone calls, so the sheriff knew that Steven hadn't contacted Penny.

On October 17, 1985, two teenagers aged 13 and 15 told their parents that a man had been peeping at them in the bathroom. Checking outside, their father saw a block of wood under a bathroom window that didn't belong there. Gregory Allen was the main suspect.

Among hundreds of documents in Steven Avery's file, a file on Gregory Allen was discovered by prosecutor Michael Griesbach on September 3, 2003. The prosecutor on Gregory Allen's August 1983 attempted assault on the dog walker had been Denis Vogel. Before Steven's arrest for the assault on Penny, Vogel had known about the predatory habits of the Sandman.

Three women working in the district attorney's office had approached Vogel in 1985, and said that they believed Allen had assaulted Penny. Their conclusion was based upon Allen's criminal history and interactions with the justice system in the preceding six months for charges that included stalking, window peeping and stealing underwear.

Vogel told the women that Allen couldn't possibly have assaulted Penny because he was on probation in Door County. Vogel claimed to have called Allen's probation officer, who had supposedly informed Vogel that Allen had been in Sturgeon Bay on the day of Penny's assault. To keep Steven incarcerated, Vogel had lied.

To conceal the main suspect, Vogel had crossed a line by manufacturing an alibi for Allen. Vogel knew that he could get away with it because consequences rarely arise for prosecutors who commit crimes, as we shall see in a later chapter with the sex-pest behaviour of Ken Kratz. Years later, when interviewed by Wisconsin Department of Justice investigators, Vogel stated that he didn't specifically recall any of his staff asking him about the Avery case.

Just prior to Steven Avery's release for his first wrongful conviction, prosecutor Michael Griesbach contacted Denis Vogel, who had relocated and was working for a law firm in Madison, Wisconsin. Griesbach informed Vogel that he'd sent an innocent man to prison for 18 years. Vogel expressed no surprise or remorse. A week later, they spoke again. Vogel blamed Steven's conviction on the hair analysis performed by Sherry Culhane at the crime lab.

"Is there anything on Allen in the [Avery] file?" Vogel said.

Knowing that Vogel was attempting self-preservation, Griesbach responded that he'd turned the file over to the attorney general.

With Steven incarcerated, Gregory Allen was free to continue his spree of sexual crimes. On June 27, 1995, he entered a house and raped the occupant, whose daughter was asleep in an adjacent room. He ended up sentenced to 60 years for burglary, kidnapping and second-degree sexual assault while possessing a bullet-proof garment.

I wonder if Allen's victim was aware that if Denis Vogel had not concealed the main suspect in the Beerntsen assault to frame Steven Avery, she would never have been subjected to her terrifying ordeal.

Vogel wasn't alone in protecting Allen. Detective Tom Bergner of the City of Manitowoc Police Department had Allen under surveillance. At the time of Penny's assault, Allen had slipped off their radar. Bergner told Sheriff Kocourek that Steven Avery hadn't assaulted Penny and that Allen matched the description of the assailant given by Penny. He asked the sheriff if he was aware of the escalating danger of Allen's crimes, from peeping Tom activity to attempted rapes. The sheriff said that he had ruled Allen out.

In later years, Kocourek denied the conversation had occurred with Bergner. He told Attorney General's Office investigators that in 1985 he was unaware of Gregory Allen. But in the sheriff's files, the investigators found a copy of the criminal complaint against Allen for the incident on the beach prior to the assault on Penny.

Kocourek had also lied to Penny about Allen. A week after she had been attacked, Penny had received a call from Bergner, who stated that his department had a suspect that matched the description of her attacker, but was not Steven Avery.

"Had you noticed anybody watching you when you were jogging?" Bergner had asked.

"No."

"Had you noticed a strange car parked outside of your home or somewhere on the block?"

"No."

"Had you noticed anyone watching you when you taught fitness classes at the YMCA?"

"No."

Penny had got off the phone thinking, *Oh my God. Maybe the guy's still out there.*

On top of receiving harassing phone calls while Steven was in jail, Penny was starting to have doubts about Steven being the assailant. Concerned about her and her family's safety, she told Sheriff Kocourek about the call from Bergner. Kocourek assured her that she had nothing to worry about; he would check out the suspect and that the Manitowoc County Sheriff's Department had jurisdiction over the case, not the City of Manitowoc Police Department. A few days later, Kocourek repeated the lie manufactured by Vogel. Kocourek stated that the suspect had an alibi: his probation officer, whom he had been with at the time of the attack.

Ten years later, the strategy of concealing other suspects in Steven Avery's case was still being employed by the Manitowoc County Sheriff's Office. A Green Bay detective called the Manitowoc County jail and stated that an inmate in the Brown County jail had admitted to assaulting a female jogger on a beach in Manitowoc County, and that an innocent person was serving time for his crime. The call was received by Andy Colborn, who was then a corrections officer at the Manitowoc County jail. Colborn told Sheriff Kocourek, who told both Colborn and the Green Bay detective to stay out of it because they had already incarcerated the correct guilty person.

When Steven Avery turned the tables on Manitowoc County after his release for the first wrongful conviction, a report was issued by the Wisconsin Department of Justice, which stated:

"Penny Beerntsen received harassing phone calls following her assault, even after Steven Avery was arrested. Many of the phone calls were of a sexual nature, some of which occurred five minutes after she would return home, indicating she might be being watched. Such stalking behaviour and post-crime contact was consistent with Gregory Allen's history."

The report blamed Steven Avery's wrongful conviction on poor communication between law enforcement agencies. As usual, neither Vogel nor Kocourek was held accountable. When they both ended up on the deposition list in Steven Avery's lawsuit, there was a slight chance that justice would be dealt out. But after Steven was arrested for the murder of Teresa Halbach, his lawsuit deflated and Vogel and Kocourek no longer had anything to worry about.

On January 23, 2016, I published a YouTube video that was the fifth in my "What Kratz Left Out" series. The subject was "No Other Suspects."

In the video, I pointed out that in a murder investigation the standard procedure is first to interview the victim's family and friends as the murderer is usually someone whom the victim knew. Not only did the Sheriff's deputies not investigate the ex-boyfriend, but he was allowed to lead and coordinate the search effort, which is a strategy killers sometimes use to camouflage their activity.

"Teresa's roommate didn't report her disappearance for four days," I said, "yet he was never investigated as a suspect. With voicemails suspiciously deleted from Teresa's phone service after she'd gone missing, the ex-boyfriend and roommate should have been suspects. Instead, Deputies Colborn and Lenk immediately interviewed Steven and proclaimed he was guilty. Then Fassbender and Wiegert coerced Brendan Dassey by telling him he'd be able to go home if he'd just confess to raping and killing Teresa with Steven Avery. Case closed."

On March 4, 2016, I contributed to a *Daily Mirror* article by the journalist Siobhan McFadyen, who helped expose the corruption in the Steven Avery case by publishing stories read by millions worldwide. Entitled "Making a Murderer's Steven Avery named as 'killer' just 154 minutes after Teresa Halbach reported missing,' the article established that Steven was deliberately targeted as the lone suspect two and a half hours after Teresa was reported missing.

Teresa had disappeared on Halloween 2005. Her boss at *Auto Trader* had contacted her family after she missed work for two days. She was reported missing on November 3 2005 at 4 pm by her mother, according to local newspapers.

Legal documents obtained by activist Skipp Topp under Freedom of Information laws showed that Steven was accused of homicide at 6:34 pm on November 3, only 154 minutes after the police had opened a missing persons' case. At that stage of the investigation, the police could not have known that she was dead because her bone fragments were not located until November 8.

Hours later, a search party instigated by Teresa's brother and her ex-boyfriend targeted the salvage yard owned by the Averys, where Teresa's vehicle was found among forty acres in record time by a civilian with a convenient background as a private investigator, who later claimed to have been guided by God.

During Steven's first wrongful conviction, the statement made by the witness on the boat who reported Gregory Allen to the police was lost to conceal the main suspect. During Steven's second wrongful conviction, the same thing happened with another suspect.

A woman who'd married a German national reported his suspicious behaviour to the Manitowoc County Sheriff's Office, but they shut the lead down. For various reasons, the wife suspected that her husband had murdered Teresa Halbach.

The German suspect came to my attention shortly after *Making a Murderer* had premiered. As I was blogging in support of Steven and Brendan, strangers started to email me links to various information. One was this blog entry at Convoluted Brian:

While the Search for Teresa Halbach was underway in November 2005, another series of events was beginning in Bonduel, Wisconsin.

A woman was moving from Bonduel, Wisconsin to Maribel. She had rented a house with the lease to start on 1 November, 2005. The house was on a property that included several outbuildings.

In Bonduel, her husband had exhibited bizarre behavior such as sleeping in their attic and sleeping in a fetal position.

She discovered that the labels had been cut from her clothing, and then her underwear was missing. Her husband denied any knowledge. During the week, he said he burned something at their new address and said it was a doll crib. There was a doll crib at the Maribel address, however, it was not burnt...

During the marriage, the citizen found that her husband had attempted to burn himself in the past. He also had previously burnt her clothing. He was diagnosed with personality disorder, narcissistic disorder, depressive disorder, and psychosis, but he refused to take medication.

She found that on 31 October, 2005, he visited the Maribel area and had stopped at the rental before the lease began. He spoke of visiting an auto salvage yard. He commented that a woman wanted to take pictures of the rental property on 31 October while he was there, and he felt that the photographer was "stupid."

During the week, she observed that her husband had scratches on his back and a cut finger that bled intermittently. She was beginning the move while working in Green Bay.

She found her underwear stuffed in an attic closet at the Bonduel home. She also noted a boombox along with cans of Cherry Pepsi Cola near the steps of the Maribel home. Her underwear disappeared again.

On the 5th of November, when they stopped for lunch in

the Maribel area, the husband saw a missing person poster for Halbach and stated dogmatically, "She's dead."

The following evening, her husband's behavior turned worse. He refused to allow her into the Maribel rental. The citizen contacted the Manitowoc County Sheriff's department, and he was arrested on 6 November, 2005. He was charged with disorderly conduct and resisting an officer.

When she returned to the Bonduel home to continue the move, she checked the attic cupboard again for her missing underwear. Instead, she found a pair of yellow lace panties than were not hers. They were about her size and had stains consistent with menstruation. She placed the panties in a plastic bag to ask her husband about them.

About 10 November, 2005 she looked through the outbuildings in Maribel for her missing clothing. She found some of her clothing cut into pieces. She also discovered a can of lighter fluid with a bloody fingerprint.

Unbeknownst to the citizen, her husband had been placed in two separate psychiatric care facilities during his custody. He was released to an outside address in January, 2006. Court records show that address as Glen's Bar and Grill in Manitowoc. The County did not notify the woman that her husband was free and in the community.

Between November and the end of the year, a few odd things happened. Two explicit adult magazines were placed on the property. Also, her dogs found relatively fresh bones somewhere on the property. She discarded the bones.

While attempting to distract the dogs from the bones, the citizen dropped her husband's tool chest in one of the outbuildings. A masons' hammer and a pair of surgical gloves fell from the chest. The hammer had visible dark red flecks.

In January, she noticed a person staring at her home from the gas station/truck stop across the road. She then discovered that her husband had been released as well as his address. When she parked in the parking lot of the bar and grill, he approached her car and insisted that she take him to the Maribel residence and began searching the house. During the search, he struck her. She called the Sheriff's Department, and her husband was rearrested.

The new charges were burglary, intimidation of a witness, criminal trespass, resisting an officer, and bail jumping.

One night she noted a second-floor balcony door was open. She entered the home and secured the door. After that she discovered an opened closet at the base of the stairs with a pair of women's jeans, a top, and a pillowcase stained with red stains.

She contacted the sheriff's department. When a deputy arrived, the citizen explained her findings and wondered if the clothing were connected with the Halbach case. She then discussed the other incidents with the deputy. The deputy stated that she believed the Halbach clothing had been recovered! She collected one magazine and the yellow panties.

If the Halbach clothing had been recovered, it was not information that was released at or after the trial of Steven Avery. If not, then the deputy was fabricating.

The citizen was contacted by Manitowoc County Detective Dennis Jacobs. Jacobs is the child sex investigator for Manitowoc County. He insisted that the panties were from a child despite the staining and size. He wanted the citizen to accuse her husband of pedophilia. He also volunteered that authorities had their suspect in the Halbach case.

She told Detective Jacobs of the cut clothing and a previous incident when her husband had burnt her clothing. His response was that was not a crime.

The woman left Wisconsin for a job in Oregon. On 2 March, 2006 the Manitowoc County prosecutor dismissed the charges of burglary and intimidation against the husband. Charges of disorderly conduct, criminal trespass, and bail jumping were also dismissed. He pleaded no contest to the two resisting officer charges and was sentenced to time served.

She believes that the victim services office in Manitowoc County provided her husband with her new address. He was at her door soon after his release.

She considered the events of the week of 31 October, 2005, and her husband's behaviors and injuries. The citizen believes that there may be a connection with the Halbach disappearance. When she asked her husband about any possible connection, he simply laughed and said no one would believe her if she reported her suspicions.

But, she had developed a distrust of Manitowoc County law enforcement. Her husband was probably correct that the Wisconsin authorities could not accept the concept that someone else did the crime.

Due to the attention garnered from *Making a Murderer* viewers, the blog post was deleted, but I'd already reposted it to my blog, Jon's Jail Journal.

The wife's first contact with the Manitowoc Sheriff's Department was when she called to report her husband as a suspect. She was told that they were too busy and didn't have any time for such nonsense. But she persisted. She ended up providing statements and evidence to two detectives, who didn't follow up her claims. *Making a Murderer* broadcast the voice of one of the detectives at the end of the first episode when he asked, "Do we have Steven Avery in custody, though?"

As well as the disappearance of the blog entry at Convoluted Brian, the wife deleted some of her Reddit comments. I received a comment at my blog: "The ex-wife was set up herself by a neighboring county sheriff's department after having spoken to Dassey's attorney and requesting records from Manitowoc. They stole everything she had, ruined her life and caused her to become physically ill."

Although the German suspect is a much longer shot than Gregory Allen in the first wrongful conviction, the lead had to be suppressed at all costs. If the defence could have convinced the jury that somebody else might have killed Teresa Halbach then it could not be proven beyond a reasonable doubt that Steven Avery had done it.

Police records show that the German was acting up around the time of Teresa's disappearance. On November 6, 2005, the day after Teresa's car was found, the German hit his wife in the head after she had refused to help him get his green card. She called the police. The German resisted arrest.

In a letter, the wife wrote, "The incident, which occurred on November 6, 2005, was not an isolated incident, but rather a continuation of a long history of aggressive and abusive behaviour committed by [the German]. [The German] is a serious and immediate danger not only to me, but also to all women, children and animals."

She documented that the German had put seizure medication, Klonopin, in her food and drink. While she was hospitalised, he liquidated her bank account. In Pittsburgh, he attacked his wife and shattered her eardrum, causing some long-term hearing loss. They were evicted from several apartments, which he had destroyed and damaged. Her pets disappeared or died. Her German Shepherd puppy ended up with a fractured leg.

Jailed and subsequently released, the German tracked his wife down on January 19 at 2:45 am. Violating his bail conditions, he entered the premises and took her digital camera and cell phone. On that winter morning, the police found the German in a field with the camera and a pair of socks. Upon spotting the police, the German attempted to strangle himself with the socks.

In jail, the German engaged in graffiti:

WHAT IS FAIRNESS IN JUSTIFIED – EVER GUILTY
GOD BLESS YOU
DEAD IS FREEDOM

Prosecutor Michael Griesbach wrote in the German's file: "should handle file, dangerous defendant with victim afraid he'll kill her if he's released. Look for Max and/or deportation."

In a memo dated December 29, 2005, a victim witness coordinator documented the wife's allegations against the German:

"[She] has stated that they live approximately 4 to 5 miles from Steven Avery's residence and that there have been some "suspicious" incidents happening, such as, she found a pair of women's panties that are not hers hidden in the house. [The German] told [her] with a suspicious grin that he burnt something. When she asked for an explanation, he said he burnt an old doll crib. She checked the crib and it wasn't burnt. Then she checked the burn barrels outside and they looked like they hadn't been used in a long time."

Terrified of her husband getting released from jail, the wife emailed the authorities: "I have experienced being held as his captive, he first destroys all telephones or cuts the phone line, he disconnects the electricity, and he tortures the victim with physical and mental abuse. If [the German] is allowed to go free, he will certainly hunt me down and hurt me or kill me."

The wife told the authorities much more about her husband and his possible role in Teresa's murder than she had divulged at Convoluted Brian, but nothing was followed up.

After the German suspect theory went viral, his wife retracted her allegations in a long internet post. Here are some excerpts:

I only contacted the sheriff after finding the second porno magazine in the barn doorway, which happened to be opened to a specific page with a woman that had MY middle name, with the same spelling and it was very scary because I had no idea who was doing this.

Yellow panties could be he found them somewhere, or someone else could have put them there, they could have been from the washing machine since that was also a rental in Bonduel with a washer and dryer. I do not know where they came from.

Bones could mean some animal died, someone was hunting and cleaning an animal, someone had a BBQ, again I do not know what kind of bones they were or where they came from.

He said he burned some junk or debris that was on the property. But the previous tenants also had burn barrels and burn pits that had burned items in them.

I think if you lived alone and someone was placing pornographic magazines in a doorway and the second one had your name specifically opened to that page, then you too may begin to see bones and so forth in a different light after hearing a murder had taken place nearby...

Did it seem strange at the time, yes, it did. I don't know where the things came from but after actually learning the facts of the murder case, it does not implicate my ex-husband. Was there anyone else on the property, it appears there was. There were the guys who worked all the farmland around it and one did introduce himself at the time, but I no longer remember his name...

Sometimes things may look a certain way they are not. After going to [the] police and later finding out the woman had been shot in the head, I never thought it had anything to do with my ex and the problem even back then was I could not connect him in any way with that woman, he simply didn't know her. At the time, I went to [the] police, I had no idea who Avery was, who the victim was, nothing. All I knew was that a person I worked with [had] told me [that] I did not live too far away from where a female photographer had been murdered...

The way he was, he would have been capable of seriously hurting a woman, but not a complete stranger. How is he now? I do not know, have not seen him for many years. The whole problem is I didn't see him doing anything. I did not see him put the underwear in the cupboard, did not see him burn anything, etc. he said he was driving around, but I was not there, do not know where he was driving or what he was doing other than what he told me. So the bottom line was I found some things, don't know how they got there and all I had was his narrative telling me where he was and what he was doing. Yes, from all of those you could imagine a scenario, but proving it is something different. That would be a job for [the] police or someone else in that capacity. And for all the things one can imagine match, too much does not match. He had no guns, he didn't know the woman, there is no documentation of what time he was in the area, no proof that he put any bones or underwear or Pepsi cans there, no proof of who the woman was he claimed stopped there or even when. I don't even know if he was telling me the truth about where he was, etc. It's really all just hearsay...

And here's my view on it now. Cops can get a search warrant in a minute. If anything I had given to them had been connected to my husband, they would have combed the place for any other evidence and if they were framing Avery they could have told me they found nothing. I do not believe they would have taken the chance of leaving anything there for someone else to find, such as the next tenant, the owner, the farmers, the realtor...

Whether her about-turn puts the German suspect theory to rest or casts even more suspicion is debatable. On February 18, 2016, I received an email from the German threatening to sue me for blogging about him:

I would take out the piece which you have written, otherwise there will be a lawsuit because of lying. Have you proof that I am that which you accuse me of? Everything is with my lawyer. We are talking of damages with compensation of half a million if you leave it in. There will soon be a notification against you in England, for the lawsuit is next week in London. Then you won't be laughing anymore.

Whether the German was a credible suspect or not, the Manitowoc County Sheriff's Office's efforts to suppress any further investigation shows that they had adopted the strategy of concealing other suspects.

Ken Kratz took this strategy into the courthouse. In the State of Wisconsin v Kent A Denny, Denny complained that he was denied his constitutional right to present a defence when the trial court refused to allow evidence suggesting that any one of several third parties had the motive and opportunity to murder Christopher Mohr. In 1984, the Wisconsin Court of Appeals ruled that the defence can introduce evidence that suggests that another person or other people might have committed the crime:

…as long as motive and opportunity have been shown and as long as there is also some evidence to directly connect a third person to the crime charged which is not remote in time, place or circumstances, the evidence should be admissible. By illustration, where it is shown that a third person not only had the motive and opportunity to commit the crime but also was placed in such proximity to the crime as to show he may have been the guilty party, the evidence would be admissible.

To prevent other suspects from being named in court, Kratz filed a Motion Concerning Third-Party Liability. In January 10, 2007, Steven's lawyers – Jerry Buting and Dean Strang – attempted to introduce other suspects by filing a Statement on Third-Party Responsibility.

One of them was Andres Martinez, who frequented the Avery lot to get parts for his car. With a history of sexual abuse and burglary, Martinez had served plenty of prison time. On November 5, 2005, Martinez went to his ex-girlfriend's house and tried to axe her to death. With a hatchet from the pantry, he struck her in the back of her neck, and in her arm, which she had raised to shield herself. When the dog tried to protect her, Martinez struck the dog. He also attacked his ex-girlfriend's children.

Martinez was sentenced to 60 years. In prison Visitation, he approached Brendan Dassey's mother and said, "I know Brendan and Steve didn't do this. Brendan doesn't belong here."

In the Statement on Third-Party Responsibility, Buting and Strang named everybody who had anything to do with the salvage yard around the time of the crime. On January 30, 2007, the judge ruled, that although the suspects had the opportunity to kill Teresa, they lacked any motive, and hence failed the legitimate tendency test under the Denny ruling. The jury never heard anything about Martinez and the other suspects.

Between the police not following up any other leads and the motion filed by Ken Kratz, no other suspects were investigated. The strategy of concealing other suspects squeezed the defence into an extremely tight corner and limited their options.

STRATEGY 3: COERCE FALSE CONFESSIONS

Corrupt investigators prey on the naiveté of the public. They are easy victims in comparison to hardened criminals whose standard procedure when faced with an interrogation is to plead the Fifth. The Fifth Amendment to the US Constitution is part of the Bill of Rights. It allows people to decline to answer questions when the answers might incriminate them, and generally without having to suffer a penalty for asserting the privilege. Defendants cannot be compelled to become witnesses at their own trials.

Confined in a tiny room and deprived of sleep, food and human interaction, many adults will eventually break down under the pressure and will say whatever they think that the investigators want to hear. Their own words are then used to convict them even in the absence of physical evidence.

The 2011 case of day-care worker Melissa Calusinski provides an example. At a day-care centre in 2009, a 16-month-old was found unresponsive, and pronounced dead an hour later. The police interviewed several employees. A medical professional determined that the baby had died from a skull fracture that was equivalent to an injury resulting from a one- to two-storey fall that occurred "30 minutes to three hours before his death."

Trusting the police, Melissa waived her right to remain silent and never asked for a lawyer. She was interviewed for nine hours. During the first six hours, she denied – seventy-nine times – having anything to do with the baby's death. By maintaining pressure on Melissa, investigators broke her down. She confessed to "slamming the boy's head to the ground out of frustration."

After the jury heard Melissa's coerced testimony, it was all over for her. The facts that the boy had a prior skull injury and the medical professional's initial determination was erroneous were irrelevant. In November 2011, 28-year-old Melissa was convicted of first degree murder. She was sentenced to 31 years and is still serving time.

Studies of wrongful convictions show that children and adolescents falsely confess with startling frequency; indeed, children are two to three times more likely to confess falsely than adults. In a study documented by Professors Steve Drizin and Richard Leo of 125 proven false confessions, 63% of the confessors were under the age of 25 and 32% were under 18, a strikingly disproportionate result. Another study of 340 exonerations found that 42% of juveniles had falsely confessed, compared with only 13% of adults. A laboratory study found that most youthful participants complied with a request to sign a false confession without uttering a single word of protest.

Over the years, the art of extracting false confessions has been refined by the application of various methods. A popular one is the Reid Technique, which consists of a three-phase process beginning with the Fact Analysis, followed by the Behaviour Analysis Interview – a non-accusatory interview designed to develop investigative and behavioural information – followed when appropriate by the Reid Nine Steps of Interrogation:

1: Direct confrontation. Advise the suspect that the evidence has led the police to the individual as a suspect. Offer the person an early opportunity to explain why the offence took place.

2: Try to shift the blame away from the suspect to some other person or set of circumstances that prompted the suspect to commit the crime. That is, develop themes containing reasons that will psychologically justify or excuse the crime. Themes may be developed or changed to find one to which the accused is most responsive.

3: Try to discourage the suspect from denying his or her guilt.

4: At this point, the accused will often give a reason why he or she did not or could not commit the crime. Try to use this to move towards the confession.

5: Reinforce sincerity to ensure that the suspect is receptive.

6: The suspect will become quieter. Move the theme discussion towards offering alternatives. If the suspect cries at this point, infer guilt.

7: Pose the "alternative question," giving two choices for what happened: one more socially acceptable than the other. The suspect is expected to choose the easier option, but whichever alternative the suspect chooses, guilt is admitted. There is always a third option, which is to maintain that they did not commit the crime.

8: Lead the suspect to repeat the admission of guilt in front of witnesses and develop corroborating information to establish the validity of the confession.

9: Document the suspect's admission or confession and have him or her prepare a recorded statement (audio, video or written).

The formulaic application of the Reid Technique allows even low-IQ investigators to get innocent people to confess to heinous crimes. As we shall see with Brendan Dassey's case, children are highly susceptible to the technique. Due to the amount of false confessions and wrongful convictions that the Reid technique produces, it has been banned in several European countries, but it is the most widely used interrogation technique in America, with approximately two thirds of officers trained in it. Wisconsin investigators employ it wholeheartedly on adults and children.

For the officials of Manitowoc County, nailing Steven Avery a second time around earned them the conviction of the century and saved them from paying out $36 million in a civil lawsuit. Investigators who cracked the case won recognition, promotions and awards. It made their careers. At their annual conference, the Wisconsin Association of Homicide Investigators presented the Meritorious Service Award to Thomas Fassbender and Mark Wiegert – the co-lead investigators on the Avery case who coerced most of the false confession from Brendan Dassey – and the Wisconsin State Patrol. The award is given to a group of members or a team of investigators from a department or from assisting departments who demonstrate the highest degree of professionalism in their respective positions during an investigation or during a multijurisdictional investigation. The Wisconsin State Patrol's Technical Reconstruction Unit was recognised for their work involving the forensic mapping of the scene.

With Steven maintaining his innocence and no credible evidence against him, the authorities swooped down on the easiest target they could manipulate: Steven's 16-year-old nephew Brendan Dassey, a vulnerable and highly suggestible teenager.

Brendan was born to Barb and Peter Dassey in Manitowoc County. He has three brothers: Bryan, Bobby and Blaine, and a half-brother, Brad. His parents had divorced. Brendan lived with his mother and brothers on a large family property near to Steven Avery's residence on the Avery Salvage Yard, where he enjoyed helping Steven with work on cars.

At the time of Teresa's murder, Brendan was a quiet sophomore at Mishicot High School. His other interests included *WrestleMania*, animals, video games such as Pokémon and books in the mystery, fantasy and anime genres. His favourite wrestler: John Cena. He liked to eat hamburgers and chocolate-chip granola bars, preferably washed down with orange juice. Enrolled in a selection of special-education classes, Brendan had demonstrated an IQ in the borderline deficiency range.

Early in the investigation, Brendan made some statements, which were recorded in a police report dated November 6, 2005:

Det. [detective] Baldwin and myself met with and spoke to Brendan Dassey. It was told to us that both Dasseys had borrowed their uncle's car so as to go to the convenience store to buy some soda.

I asked Brendan if he would sit and talk with Det. Baldwin and myself in my unmarked squad car. While in my car I informed Brendan that he was not under arrest and that he was free to leave at any time. Brendan agreed to talk to us.

During the interview Brendan told us that he lives with his mother on Avery Road next to his uncle Steven Avery. He told us that he had never seen Teresa Halbach nor her Toyota SUV at their property on Avery Rd. When I asked Brendan specifically about seeing either Halbach or her vehicle on Monday October 31stt 2005 he again told us that he had not seen either.

I had been informed by Agent Skorlinski that Law Enforcement also involved in this investigation had interviewed the school bus driver that would have dropped off Brendan and his brother Blaine at the end of their driveway in Two Rivers Wisconsin on Monday October 31st 2005 at about 3:45 PM and that the driver had reported seeing both Halbach and her vehicle on the Avery property and that she was taking photos of a vehicle for sale close to the road where the boys were dropped off (Steven Avery's Blazer).

When I confronted Brendan about seeing Teresa Halbach when he had gotten off the bus with his brother on that Monday, Brendan now said that he had seen Teresa Halbach and her vehicle and that he did not tell us because he did not want to go to jail. When I asked Brendan as to what he had seen of Teresa, Brendan said that while he was walking down the driveway with his brother they had moved off to the side of the driveway to allow the Toyota SUV go by. Brendan told us that the vehicle had been traveling out of the driveway toward the road and that it had only been on the property for five minutes.

When asked again as to if he had seen Teresa out of the vehicle by the van by his and his uncles home Brendan now told us that while he was in his home after walking down the driveway to his home, from the kitchen by the kitchen sink window Brendan had seen his uncle Steven Avery and the girl taking pictures by the van parked in front of his home.

Det. Baldwin and myself provided transportation for Brendan to the Avery cabin located on Highline Road without incident.

On February 22, 2006, two of the biggest villains in *Making a Murderer* – Mark Wiegert and Tom Fassbender – showed up at Brendan's school, extracted him from his class without his mother's permission or knowledge, isolated him in a room and started to interrogate him using the Reid Technique. Here's how they began to extract a false confession:

Fassbender: Mark's obviously laying out a tape recorder on the table. We'd like to tape the interview. Um, OK, no problem with that, if that's all right? Um, you're not under arrest. You know that. You're free to go at any time you want. Ah, just listen to us: you don't have to answer any questions if you don't want to and stuff like that. OK... I would really appreciate if you would just kind of relax and open up with us. We're not here to... jump in your face or get into you or anything like that. I know that may have happened before and stuff like that... We're not here to do that. We're here more to maybe let you talk or talk to you a little about how you've been feeling lately and stuff. I... have a feeling there's some things on your mind and I just want to give you that opportunity to talk... about what you're thinking about, feeling maybe. I know something's bothering you, and you know that, and it's got to be laying real real heavy on you.

    Wiegert: You've had a tough go of it lately I'd imagine, huh?

    Brendan: Yeah.

    Wiegert: We definitely understand that.

    Fassbender: We're not here to hurt anyone. We just, you know, if you... got a chance to meet Teresa's mother and stuff, you've got to know them a little and you'd know that they were decent people, too, and just like I think your brothers are and your mom is, and people don't realise that because all the bad press and stuff. And that's all we're... thinking about, just to bring justice, no matter how hard or how much it hurts. Ah, for... Teresa. This feels pretty awkward, but go ahead and tell us what's been bothering you.

    Brendan: That he's... gone and I can't see him.

    Fassbender: That Steve is gone. You're pretty close with Steve?

Brendan: I helped him fix his cars and that.

Fassbender: Mm-huh. I kind of figured that was part of it. Were you probably the closest to him as opposed to like your brothers and stuff?

Brendan: Well, I and Blaine were...

Fassbender: Yeah, Blaine would hang around Steven a lot, too. Have you been able to go up and visit him at all?

Brendan: Well, I tried, but I... couldn't get in 'cause I didn't have my like identity cards.

Fassbender: Oh. You talk to him on the phone much?

Brendan: No.

Fassbender: How's your mom doing?

Brendan: Pretty good.

Fassbender: Anything else bothering you?

Brendan: Not really.

Fassbender: No, Brendan, we know that [on] Halloween and stuff you were with him and... helped him tend to a fire and stuff like that behind the garage and stuff... Anything that you saw that night that's been bothering you? And if you built the fire, and we believe that's... where Teresa was cooked. And if you were out there by the fire and stuff, and by your own words you went and got that... seat out of a − the vehicle seat, remember that one? − brought it over and someone put it on the fire. Did you put that seat on the fire or him?

Brendan: We both did.

Fassbender: What? Did you both grab it and put it... in the fire? What did you see in the fire?

Brendan: Some branches... a cabinet and some tires...

Fassbender: Mm-huh. Did you see any body parts? You know if you think you saw something in the fire, and it's... starting to bother you, or you're feeling bad about it, the only way it's ever gonna end is if you talk about it. I gotta believe you did see something in the fire. You wanna know why I believe that? Because Teresa's bones were intermingled in that seat. And the only way her bones were intermingled in that seat is if she was put on that seat or if the seat was put on top of her. As I said, we're not gonna say you did and we're not gonna say you didn't... We're here to give you the opportunity to come forward, to talk to us about what you did see, encountered out there that night. We want to know. A lot... of the reason that we're doing this is because – how old are you 16, 17? You're a kid, you know, and we got, we've got people back at the sheriff's department, district attorney's office, and they're looking at this now, saying there's no way that Brendan Dassey was out there and didn't see something. They're talking about trying to link Brendan Dassey with this event. They're not saying that Brendan did it. They're saying that Brendan had something to do with it or the cover up of it which would mean Brendan Dassey could potentially be facing charges for that. And Mark and I are both going, 'Well, ah, he's a kid, he had nothing to do with this, and whether Steve got him out there to help build a fire and he inadvertently saw some things that's what it would be. It wouldn't be that Brendan actually helped him dispose of this body.' And I'm looking at you Brendan, and I know you saw something and that's what's killing you more than anything else. Knowing that Steven did this, it hurts. Whether it was an accident that Steven did it by, however it happened, he's... gotta deal with that. Truthfully, I don't believe Steven intended to kill her. I don't know how it happened. Only Steven knows how it happened, and potentially you. Do you know how it happened? What did you see in that fire?

Brendan: ...some black... some garbage bag on there.

Fassbender: Um-hm. And what was in the garbage bag?... and they were plastic? Plastic melts pretty quick, right?

Brendan: Well, I would burn the garbage.

Fassbender: Where did you get those bags from?

Brendan: ...from his garage... He was saving it for a bonfire.

Fassbender: Mm-huh.

Brendan: 'Cause we invited some friends over but they cancelled.

Fassbender: Yeah, I know how hard this is. You know that you saw him put some garbage bags on, but I can, look, I can't see in your eye, but by your look I can tell you know of something, you saw something or somebody, something's laying heavy on you. We wouldn't be here bothering you if we didn't know that. We've gotten a lot of information and you know some people don't care, some people back there say, 'No, we'll just charge him.' We said, 'No. Let us talk to him, give him the opportunity to come forward with the information that he has, and get it off of his chest.' Now make it look… Tell us what you know. That way you don't have to feel bad for Steven. You have to tell the truth. You have no choice in that. Someone has killed someone, and like I said, I don't think Steven intended to do it, but it happened. He still has to pay the price for that… I hope you understand that. He didn't do the right thing. How are you going to live with yourself the rest of your life knowing what you know? And I've got… kids somewhat your age. I'm looking at you and I see you in him and I see him in you. I really do, and I know how that would hurt me, too. I know how much he would hurt because of what he did know, and how… he felt for the person and what he saw and what he knows… I'm here to give you the opportunity to get this off your chest. Mark and I, yeah, we're cops, we're investigators and stuff like that, but I'm not right now. I'm a father that has a kid your age, too. I wanna be here for you. There's nothing I'd like more than to come over and give you a hug 'cause I know you're hurting. Yes, I do wanna give justice to… this and to the Halbachs, too. You wanna tell me what you saw and what you heard 'cause I know that something is, it's intensely bothering you? Talk about it. We're not just going to leave you high and dry. We're gonna talk to your mom after this and we'll deal with this the best we can for your good. OK. I promise I will not leave you high and dry. I'll stand behind you.

Wiegert: We both will, Brendan. We're here to help you.

Fassbender: …I'm more interested in what you probably saw in that fire or something. We know she was put in that fire. There's no doubt about it. The evidence speaks for itself. And you were out there with him. And unfortunately, I'm afraid you saw something that you wished you never would have seen. You know, I mean, and that's what we need to know. We get that off your chest and we can move forward. That's the important thing we need to... get out right now for you. 'Cause you're having a tough go of it, and it's not just 'cause you can't see Steve, but what you saw. Did you see a hand, a foot, something in that fire? Her bones? Did you smell something that was not too right?

Brendan: Well, we weren't there for long... picking up the stuff.

Fassbender: You were both there, you and Steven? Was it just you going around with the cart to get the stuff?

Brendan: Yeah.

Fassbender: ...when you... got home from school and stuff, were you there when the fire started or did you come out after the fire was going pretty good?

Brendan: He had it started...

Fassbender: And then were there tires on it before you got out there?

Brendan: No just branches...

Fassbender: And then what time did you go in the house that night about?

Brendan: About ten.

Fassbender: And was he still out there then?

Brendan: He was out there till like... my brother came home and said he...

Fassbender: And what brother is that?

Brendan: Blaine.

Wiegert: You said you went in at ten.

Brendan: Ten.

Wiegert: All right.

Fassbender: And that same night, did you help him push a vehicle somewhere, too?

Brendan: Yeah, I did...

Fassbender: And what did you do with that, was that a Suzuki? And where did you push that?

Brendan: He had it outside. I just pushed it into the garage.

Fassbender: His garage?

Brendan: Yeah.

Fassbender: And what else was in that garage at that time?

Brendan: His moped.

Fassbender: He had a moped in there? Anything else?

Brendan: Snowmobile... His lawn mower.

Fassbender: No other vehicle? Can you tell me some other things? You saw? Didn't see anything in that fire?

Wiegert: What was in the garbage bags?

Brendan: Paper plates, soda bottles.

Wiegert: Were they heavy?

Fassbender: Did you help carry them out, or?

Brendan: ...I carried one out.

Fassbender: Out of the house or garage?

Fassbender: What else is bothering you?

Brendan: Trying to find a girlfriend.

Fassbender: Mm-huh...

Brendan: Tried to get a hold of ... girlfriend.

Fassbender: Did you just breakup?

Brendan: ...she broke up with me.

Fassbender: Did she say why? Nothing to do with this, is it? Well, I hope you're getting over that. Just a girl. You'll find others, right? Talk to your mom about it at all? Did she say the same thing, find other girls?

Brendan: My mom told me that times heal.

Fassbender: True, time will... heal.

Wiegert: Brendan, we know that Steve told you to say certain things when the police came and talked to you. OK. I know that. We've been told that. What did Steve tell you to tell us?

Brendan: ... not to say stuff

Wiegert: What kind of stuff?

Brendan: Like don't talk.

Wiegert: Did he tell you what to say? I heard that he did. I heard, and I was told, Brendan, Steve told you what to say and what not to say because it was you and him out by that fire. I know you and he knew what was going on there. It's really important that you be honest here. OK. Everybody gets an opportunity with Tom and I... and we want to give you that opportunity to be honest. We want to help you through this. Obviously, it's bothering you. This whole thing is bothering you and the rest of your family, but you'll never ever get over it unless you're honest about it 'cause this will bug you 'til the day that you die, unless you're honest about it. But we wanna go back and tell people that, 'You know, Brendan told us what he knew.' We wanna be able to tell people that, 'Brendan was honest. He's not like Steve. He's honest. He's a good guy. He's gonna go places in this life.' But in order for us to do that, you need to be honest with us, and so far, you're not being 100% honest. OK. Tom and I have been doing this job a long, long time, longer than you've been alive, and our experience and our knowledge in this job tells us that you're not being totally honest with us, and there's no way that you're going to get over this and move on in your life without being honest.

Fassbender: You know Steven said there wasn't a fire that night. He denied that... until enough witnesses came forward and said that they had seen a fire... You know that.

Wiegert: Steve doesn't care about you right now. He cares about himself.

Fassbender: Unfortunately, that's all Steven cares about. He left you to hang out to dry. He told you what to say when you got off the bus and what you saw. You know what you saw... You're the only one that we talked to between the other brothers – Blaine, Bobby, Bryan – that is inconsistent with what they said. Part of it's... 'cause you like Steven. You're trying to help him, but you're misguided that way and you're trying to help him out with what you know happened and did see. I think you're starting to be honest with us about some things right now.

Brendan: Well, when we were up north... he was trying to hide when the cops came and grandpa...

Wiegert: What else did he tell you?

Brendan: That he said he was gonna get in the car and try to get away as far as he could.

Fassbender: ...anyone else by the fire by you that night? ...I think there's a reason for that like Steven felt he... could trust you to not say anything... and asked you to... using your love, and taking advantage of that.

Wiegert: To cover up for hurting that girl. That girl didn't do nothing. How would you feel if that was your sister? That burn pit, Brendan, was no bigger than this table. OK. You know how big it was. I find it quite difficult to believe that if there was a body in that, Brendan, that you wouldn't have seen something like a hand or a foot, a head, hair, something. OK. We know you saw something. And maybe you've tried to block it out, but it's really important that you remember. Think back.

With Brendan unable to state that he had seen any body parts in the fire, Wiegert fed Brendan the exact body parts that Brendan later confessed to seeing in the fire. This is how the crucial details of crimes are transferred from the investigators to the suspect. Brendan had started to believe the fake offers of help the investigators had repeated. He reasoned that the only way he could save himself was by telling them what they wanted to hear.

Fassbender: ...by the garage, by the house, by the fire pit, I know you saw something... Mark and I both can go back to the district attorney and say, 'Ah... Dassey came forward and finally told us. Can you imagine how this was weighing on him?' They'll understand that.

Wiegert: We'll go to bat for you, but you have to be honest with us.

Fassbender: Tell us the truth, exactly. Can you get close... to telling us the truth?

Wiegert: It's OK to tell us.

Fassbender: It's OK. It's a big step... a step toward feeling better about yourself, to recovery, to not crying at night because of this stuff happening... what you saw. I promise you, I'll not let you hang out there alone, but we've gotta have the truth. The truth is gonna be terrible... your mom...

Wiegert: We're not gonna run back and tell your grandma and grandpa what you told us or anything like that. OK.

Wiegert: Let's talk about it.

Fassbender: Talk to us Brendan if you want this resolved.

Brendan: ...some clothes, like a blue shirt, some pants...

Wiegert: Where did he get the clothes from?

Brendan: His garage.

Wiegert: Where in the garage were they?

Brendan: ...in the back...

Wiegert: Back and on the side?

Fassbender: Was her car still in there when you went in there? Tell us the truth. OK. Did you see some undergarments or anything like that? Bra?

Wiegert: How about any shoes? Was there blood on those clothes? Be honest, Brendan. We know. We already know you know. Help us out. Think of yourself here. Help that family out.

Fassbender: It's gonna be all right. OK.

Wiegert: Was there blood on those clothes?

Brendan: A little bit.

Wiegert: OK. Where was the blood?

Brendan: Like...

Wiegert: Blood on the shirt?

Fassbender: You're starting to... get it out now. OK. It'll be all right... Get it all out. It doesn't do any good to get half of it out.

Brendan: ...the fire... said he was gonna bury it and start...

Fassbender: When the fire pit got full, he was gonna bury that whole pit and start... Did he have somewhere else? Where? Oh. So, you had to move it from behind the garage to behind the house. Did he say why? Did you know why?

Wiegert: Where did he tell you those clothes came from?

Brendan: He said that they were...

Wiegert: You kind of knew better though, don't you?

Fassbender: You now know better. They were girl clothes, weren't they?

Wiegert: Were they in a bag or anything?

Brendan: They were... bag.

Fassbender: ...pants and shirt and anything else you saw... Had blood on the shirt?

Wiegert: Where on the shirt was the blood? Was it a button-down shirt?

Fassbender: Remember what kind of pants? Were they blue-jean pants, or?

Wiegert: What else did he get out of the garage? Be honest. OK.

Brendan: ...he had a shovel—

Wiegert: OK.

Brendan: —and a rake... He took...

Fassbender: Go ahead. What did he do with the shovel? ... got a feeling that you saw something in the fire that you're trying to just...

Wiegert: It's not your fault. Remember that.

Fassbender: Yeah, it's not your fault... Like I said, Mark and I are not going to leave you high and dry. I got a very... important appointment at three today. Well, I ain't leaving for the appointment until I'm sure you're taken care of... telling the truth... get this off your chest and get it out in the open ... so go ahead and talk to us about what you saw in the fire... You've got to do this for yourself. I know you feel that it's gonna hurt Steven, but it's actually... gonna help Steven come to grips with what he needs to do. More important, this could help you... You know we found some flesh in that fire, too. We know you saw some flesh. We found it after all that burned. I know you saw it... Tell us. You don't have to worry about... you won't have to prove that in court. Tell us what you saw. You saw some body parts... You're shaking your head... tell us what you saw... You, all right? You, all right? What other parts did you see?

Brendan: Toes.

Fassbender: ...part of a foot, too? What other parts of the body? Did you see part of the arm, the legs? I know. It's all right... Did you see part of her head? Skull?

Brendan: I seen…

Fassbender: OK… a human body… Did you say anything to Steven? …. Was he hoping you didn't see that or what? Where? The body parts that you saw: were they on top of tires or underneath the tires, or?

Brendan: …bottom of tires.

Fassbender: Underneath the bottom of the tires. Could you smell them?

Brendan: No…

Fassbender: All right. We got… a lot of important stuff out there now. Take a breath. Let's go over the parts that you mentioned. OK. So, you mentioned toes, fingers, parts of hand and feet and then what you thought maybe was stomach area or midsection or torso. Did you see any parts of the legs… or arms? You sure you didn't see her…? Now this is very hard. It's not easy, but it's easier to say you saw a toe or a finger, but when you start saying to me, 'I saw a head or a face or hair,' or you know stuff like that, that's when it hurts though, but I find it very hard that you didn't see a skull or the head. Did you see part of the head or face or skull?

Brendan: …somewhat.

Fassbender: Somewhat?

Wiegert: I know this is hard, Brendan, but can you describe what you saw when you mean somewhat?

Brendan: Like her forehead.

Wiegert: Did you see any hair?

Fassbender: When you say her forehead, was it white bone already or was there still flesh on it?

Brendan: …a little bit of flesh.

Fassbender: A little bit of flesh.

Wiegert: Were all the body parts connected yet? Yes? Did you say yes or no? I'm not sure.

Brendan: Yeah.

Wiegert: Yes.

Fassbender: So, all the body parts were pretty much connected then when you saw the toes, which means they were probably connected to the feet yet, correct? Which means the feet, foot is connected to both the legs, so I'm just going to ask this question: you're saying that you seen body parts. You're pretty much, you're seeing a body? Is that accurate? You saw her body in there?

Wiegert: Would you say yes or no for me Brendan?

Brendan: Yes.

Fassbender: And then the shovel and the rake were used to do, to do what? Now you can tell me if you actually think... you seen that?

Brendan: Yeah.

Fassbender: But you did. And you never said anything to him. Have you told this to anyone? And is that what's been bothering you a lot?

Brendan: Yes.

Fassbender: And... I understand that. That's normal because you've done nothing wrong.

Wiegert: Brendan, I'm going to ask you a difficult question. OK. Did you help him put that body in the fire? If you did, it's OK.

Fassbender: Was the body in the fire before you got out to the fire?

Brendan: There was like branches...

Wiegert: When did you see it? When you first went out there or when?

Brendan: Like if...

According to his mother, Brendan was interviewed six times, and some of the interviews were not recorded. *Making a Murderer* showed Brendan in a tiny room, sitting on a couch, gazing down nervously, backed into a corner with Fassbender and Wiegert in front of him. As with the above exchange, Brendan was mostly silent or his mumbles and minimalistic answers simply repeated words verbatim that the investigators had spoon-fed to him. The information he provided often didn't add up. He described the colour of Teresa's clothes differently each time. Nevertheless, the investigators relentlessly coerced details by promising Brendan they were on his side, they wanted to hug him as if he were their son, everything would be all right and he'd be able to go back to school, go home and watch *WrestleMania*.

Barb stated: "They say that I gave them permission to interview Brendan. Well, that was a lie. The day they did this at school, I was at work for ten hours. They called me after the fact. They interviewed him for three to four hours, and then first contacted me to come get him. I never gave them permission to do what they did. They did it behind my back. And when they took us to the police station, they told me I couldn't go in with him because he was going to give them a gruesome story that I wouldn't be able to handle, and told me to go have a seat on the chair. That is the truth, and they are lying through their teeth."

Exclusively for this book, Barb spoke out about the family's ordeal:

"At the cabin in Crivitz, Fassbender took Brendan outside for an interview. There is no record of that anywhere. The day they took me, Blaine and Brendan to Two Rivers' police station, they told me that I was not allowed in while they interviewed my sons. They took them to Fox Hills Resort. I was told if I left I would be arrested. They were not allowed to leave Fox Hills. Wiegert and Fassbender kept saying to me, 'It's your brother or the yard.'

"If I had been allowed into the interrogation room, I think things would have been way different because they would have never been able to pump things into Brendan's head like they did. I started to think something was fishy at the Two Rivers Police Department and at Fox Hills when Fassbender and Wiegert said that if I left they would pick me up. Wiegert and Fassbender are scumbags that take innocent people and lie to them and get them to say what they want them to say. Wiegert always said to me that every family has a black sheep in it. Fassbender and [Calumet County Deputy] Wendy Baldwin tried to get me to say bad things about my brother, Steve: that he had sexually molested me."

I asked Barb about the lawyers and prosecutors involved in the case.

"My thoughts on Ken Kratz are not good," Barb replied. "He is a piece of dog shit. Oh no! That was too good for him! I think they should put all of them in prison for what they did to us, including Len Kachinsky, who is not any better than the rest of them. He is a lying douche bag."

"What toll has Brendan's wrongful conviction taken on the family?" I asked. "How stressful has it been? I was in prison for 6 years and my mother had a nervous breakdown and my sister had to have counselling. I can't imagine your family's suffering."

"Brendan's wrongful conviction has taken a toll on all of us. We are heartbroken. We have had counselling for our stress and frustration. Our family has suffered for over 10 years. It hasn't been easy. On Christmas Day, we always try to go see Brendan, but otherwise there isn't much we can do. It is frustrating and heart-breaking to not have him here for the holidays. Brendan passes his time in prison reading, writing, playing cards and going to the library. He makes phone calls, watches TV, listens to the radio and waits for visits from his family. He doesn't have a job in prison. Brendan's mental strength comes from us having stuck by him for all these years."

"How do you feel about *Making a Murderer*?" I asked.

"*Making a Murderer* has done wonders for the family and it has also got the truth out there about the corruption and the liars."

"After Brendan's release, will he need counselling? He's barely ever been an adult in the outside world. Do you fear that he won't be able to cope?"

"Brendan's release, yes, he will probably need counselling for the simple reason to get him reunited with society. Being on the outside, I think he will cope as long as I stand by him until he feels comfortable."

"Is there anything else you'd like to add or say to the world?"

"So this doesn't happen again to anyone else's child, I ask people to please sign the petition out there called the Barbara

Tadych Law, so we can get this passed. And always have someone with you when you are being questioned by the police. Don't let anyone put words in your mouth that aren't true. If you didn't do it, don't say it.

Fassbender and Wiegert ran into a problem after a report came back that Teresa's skull had a bullet wound. Brendan had previously confessed that the cause of death had been stabbing and throat slashing. Here's how they amended the cause of death:

Wiegert: When did he stab her?
    Brendan: When? Before he choked her.
    Fassbender: Are you sure about that?
    Brendan: *(nods)*
    Wiegert: So, she's laying there, handcuffs on, and that's when Steve stabs her?
    Brendan: Mm-huh. *(nods)*
    Wiegert: And then... he chokes her after that?
    Brendan: Yeah.
    Wiegert: Are you sure?
    Brendan: *(nods)*
    Fassbender: Where exactly did he stab her again?
    Brendan: In the stomach.
    Fassbender: Was it the chest or the stomach?
    Brendan: Well, sort of in the ribs.
    Fassbender: And what did he use to stab her?
    Brendan: A knife.
    Fassbender: Where did he get the knife from?
    Brendan: From the kitchen.
    Fassbender: And what, how big was the knife? Show us.
    Brendan: 'Bout like that.
    Fassbender: About that big and he got it out of the kitchen. When he went in there, did he threaten her with the knife? Did he just go right and do it? What did he do?
    Brendan: That he threatened her.

Fassbender: Tell us what he said.

Brendan: That he was gonna kill her by stabbing her and not letting her go.

Wiegert: What else did he do to her? We know something else was done. Tell us, and what else did you do? Come on. Something with the head. Brendan?

Brendan: Huh?

Fassbender: …can't.

Wiegert: What else did you guys do, come on?

Fassbender: What he made you do, Brendan. We know he made you do something else.

Wiegert: What was it? What was it?

Fassbender: We have the evidence, Brendan. We just need you to… be honest with us.

Brendan: That he cut off her hair.

Wiegert: He cut off her hair. In the house?

Brendan: Mm-huh.

Wiegert: Why did he do that? Was she alive?

Brendan: No.

Wiegert: What did he do with the hair?

Brendan: He set it down on the counter.

Wiegert: The counter where?

Brendan: Like a dresser.

Fassbender: What did he use to cut the hair off with?

Brendan: The knife.

Fassbender: Was she alive?

Brendan: *(shakes head)*

Fassbender: Did he say why he did that?

Brendan: No.

Wiegert: OK. What else?

Fassbender: What else was done to her head?

Brendan: That he punched her.

Wiegert: What else? What else?

Fassbender: He made you do something to her, didn't he? So he would feel better about not being the only person, right?

Brendan: *(nods)*

Wiegert: Mm-huh.

Fassbender: What did he make you do to her?

Wiegert: What did he make you do, Brendan? It's OK. What did he make you do?

Brendan: Cut her.

Wiegert: Cut her where?

Brendan: On her throat.

Wiegert: Cut her throat? When did that happen?

Brendan: Before he picked her off the bed?

Wiegert: So, she was alive yet, right?

Brendan: *(nods)*

Wiegert: So, she's alive and you cut her throat?

Brendan: Mm-huh.

Wiegert: Was that before or after Steve stabbed her?

Brendan: After.

Wiegert: It was after Steve stabbed her?

Brendan: *(nods)* Mm-huh.

Wiegert: Was she a – how do you know she was alive? Tell me. When you cut her throat, how do you know she was alive?

Brendan: She was breathing a little bit.

Wiegert: She was breathing a little bit. Did Steve tell you to do that?

Brendan: Yeah.

Fassbender: How'd he tell you to do that? What'd he say?

Brendan: To go across her throat and pull it back.

Fassbender: Did he say why he wanted you to do that?

Brendan: No. *(shakes head)*

Wiegert: Which knife did you use?

Brendan: The same one he stabbed her with.

Fassbender: And how many times did he stab her again?

Brendan: Once.

Fassbender: Are you sure about that?

Brendan: *(nods)*

Wiegert: So, Steve stabs her first and then you cut her neck?

Brendan: *(nods)*

Wiegert: What else happens to her in her head?

Fassbender: It's extremely, extremely important you tell us this for us to believe you.

Wiegert: Come on, Brendan, what else?

Fassbender: We know. We just need you to tell us.

Brendan: That's all I can remember.

Wiegert: All right, I'm just gonna come out and ask you. Who shot her in the head?

Brendan: He did.

Fassbender: Then why didn't you tell us that?

Brendan: 'Cause I couldn't think of it.

Fassbender: Now you remember it?

Brendan: *(nods)*

Fassbender: Tell us about that then.

Brendan: That he shot her with his .22.

Wiegert: You were there though?

Brendan: Yeah.

Wiegert: Where did this happen?

Brendan: Outside.

Wiegert: Outside? Before? Tell me when it happened?

Brendan: When we bring her outside to throw her in the fire.

The investigators had obtained what they wanted, but not quite. Ken Kratz claimed that Steven had shot her in the garage, not outside. But Brendan's inconsistencies were irrelevant. His hours of testimony were a body of work that Kratz whittled down to form a narrative for his incendiary press conference.

Brendan's confession wasn't permitted as evidence in Steven's trial because Brendan had refused to testify against his uncle for something they hadn't done, and a police interpretation would have been inadmissible hearsay. But, courtesy of Kratz, snippets of the coerced confession had found their way into the homes of the public when Kratz generated shock waves across Wisconsin with his press conference. Most of the jurors had seen Kratz on the news, warning them to remove their children from the room.

The press conference convinced them that Steven was guilty. According to Jerry Buting, "Even though Brendan's confession was not used in Steven's trial, the jury questioners made it clear that 99% of the jurors believed that he [Steven] was guilty and that was largely based on the false narrative."

In a weak attempt at remedying the injustice perpetrated by Kratz, the judge instructed the jurors to put what they had heard on the news out of their minds.

Brendan was convicted based on his testimony. The jury had only been privy to the first 3.5 hours, which were the most incriminating. They should have been permitted to have heard Brendan talking to his mother immediately after his confession. Officers Wiegert and Fassbender had told Barb that Brendan had just confessed to the rape and murder of Teresa Halbach. They allowed Barb to go into the room and talk to him. She was unaware that the investigators had coerced Brendan into fabricating the story, and they were withholding the extent of the trouble he was in:

Barb: Oh. *(door opens and closes)* Are you regretting it now? *(pauses)* You had a whole life ahead of you, Brendan. Just because he's so demanding, doesn't mean you gotta do the stuff he says. Right?

Brendan: Where am I going?

Barb: Where do you think you're going?

Brendan: I don't know?

Barb: You're going to juvie [a detention centre for juvenile offenders]. That's where you're going, to a juvie jail. About forty-five minutes away.

Brendan: Yeah, but I gotta question.

Barb: What's that?

Brendan: What'd happen if he says something, his story's different? Wh – he says he, he admits to doing it?

Barb: What do you mean?

Brendan: Like if his story's like different, like I never did nothing or something.

Barb: Did you? Huh?
Brendan: Not really.
Barb: What do you mean not really?
Brendan: They got to my head.

"They got to my head" is Brendan's explanation for why he had falsely confessed. The psychological pressure from his tormentors had overwhelmed him. To alleviate that pressure, he had regurgitated details fed to him by the investigators. Having just been told that her son had confessed, Barb knew something was amiss. But before Barb could get the truth out of Brendan, the investigators rushed back into the room.

Barb: Huh?
Brendan: ...say anything.
Barb: What do you mean by that? *(pauses)* What do you mean by that, Brendan? *(pauses)* I have a question for you two. Is there any way that I can talk to him? Not him, the other one.
Wiegert: As in Steve you mean?
Barb: Yes.
Wiegert: The only way we can have you talk to him is if he calls you or if it's, you know, you go there for visiting.
Barb: I won't go there and visit.
Wiegert: OK. That's the only way. I have no other way of, you know, I can't hook you up to him or anything like that. I'm not allowed to do that. If he calls you, you can do what you want or if you go there for visiting, you know, that's up to you.
Barb: Were you pressuring him?
Wiegert: Who are you talking about?
Barb: Him [Brendan].
Wiegert: What do you mean, pressuring him?
Barb: In talking to him.
Wiegert: No, we told him we needed to know the truth. We've been doing this job a long time, Barb, and we can tell when people aren't telling the truth. And, in my opinion, he'd never be able

to live with himself if he didn't tell somebody. There's no way, he could've lived with that. Nobody could live with that. I think Brendan knows that.

On May 13, 2006, Brendan was at the Sheboygan County jail. He was allowed to call his mother, whom the investigators were still purposefully misleading:

Barb: Steven says that you seen the body in the fire.

Brendan: No

Barb: You know if he killed her?

Brendan: Not that I know of.

Barb: So then how do you know that there was a bullet shell outside of the garage?

Brendan: 'Cause when Mike [Brendan's public defender's private investigator] came up here he had pictures of it.

Barb: They told everybody that you told them that there was bullet shells inside the garage.

Brendan: No.

Barb: That Steven shot her ten times.

Brendan: No. In the picture, they had a bullet right by a crack or something cement.

Barb: Uh. Don't believe those guys what they say.

Brendan: Yeah.

Barb: You don't need to talk to them. It's just that on that Monday when they took you out of class at 10 o'clock, they said that they called me and asked me to talk to you. They never did.

Brendan: Yeah.

Barb: They never called me on that Monday.

Brendan: But I wished I had listened to someone before I went there.

Manipulating Brendan's vulnerabilities, the investigators taunted him with the threat of a 90-year sentence if he failed to confess.

They continued to lie, telling Brendan that Steven was going to place all the blame on him. They cemented that fear by stating that his most trusted advisor, his mother, had told them that Brendan needed to confess the truth – as defined by them:

Some family members of Steven and Brendan had been manipulated by Kratz's press conference, too. They hadn't been privy to the entire coerced confession. That's why there are news clips of them chastising Steven Avery for criminalising Brendan. Some commentators have pointed to these clips as proof of Steven's guilt. However, now that the family members are aware of the extent of Brendan's coerced confession, they support Steven and hold Fassbender and Wiegert directly and fully responsible.

Fassbender and Wiegert stooped so low that they tried to manipulate Brendan into stating that Steven had molested him. Accusing someone of a sex offence is a devastating strategy, but Fassbender and Wiegert couldn't quite pull it off.

Wiegert: OK. Did you and Steve ever have sex?
Brendan: No.
Wiegert: Are you sure? If you did, it's OK.
Brendan: I didn't.
Wiegert: You and Jodi?
Brendan: No.
Fassbender: Now is the time to really get stuff off your chest, too. Mark asked if you and Steven ever had sex and you said no, but, ah, did Steven ever, let's talk about, you know what masturbating is?
Brendan: Yeah.
Fassbender: Did you and Steven ever masturbate together or anything like that?
Brendan: No.
Fassbender: It's all right. Did he ever touch you? You don't need to think about that question. Did he ever touch you? It's all right. Now is the time.
Brendan: What do you mean by touching?

Fassbender: Um, in places that you felt uncomfortable with?

Brendan: Sometimes.

Fassbender: Yeah. And what places were those?

Brendan: My privates and...

Fassbender: You know.

Brendan: You know and there.

Fassbender: OK. And that's all right that you talk about this. This is the time to talk about it 'cause it's important. It's important to know and for the courts and everyone else to know what you've gone through. It makes us feel a lot more for you. OK. And by privates, you mean by, by your penis?

Brendan: Mm-huh.

Fassbender: Did he touch you on your penis?

Brendan: Well, sometimes he was, he would try to grab it.

Fassbender: Ah huh. And, and ah, were [you] unclothed at that time?

Brendan: No.

Fassbender: Then how did he try to grab it?

Brendan: Through the pants.

Fassbender: Oh. OK. And what did you tell him when he did that?

Brendan: I was trying to get rid a, get him off me.

Fassbender: Yeah. Did you ever touch his?

Brendan: No.

Fassbender: Did he ask you to?

Brendan: No. *(shakes head)*

Fassbender: Did he ever show you his?

Brendan: No. *(shakes head)*

Fassbender: You sure?

Brendan: Yes.

Fassbender: Did he ask to see yours?

Brendan: No. *(shakes head)*

Fassbender: Just try to, ah, grab yours through your pants a couple of times or something?

Brendan: Yeah.

Fassbender: Is that accurate?

Brendan: Yeah.

Fassbender: Did he ever say anything when he was doing that?

Brendan: No. *(shakes head)*

Fassbender: And you told him no, or just tried to get him off you.

Brendan: Just trying to get him off me.

Fassbender: By getting him off of you, was he kind of, what was he doing, pushing against or leaning against you or anything like that, or...?

Brendan: Well, it was like wrestling and...

Fassbender: Oh. And he grabbed you down there? Is that all he's ever done?

Brendan: Yeah.

The investigators realised that Brendan was referring to rough-house wrestling in which grabbing the private parts is a tactic to dominate and humiliate. Their plan was to get Brendan to call his mother to confess to crimes against Teresa and to implicate Steven in additional felonies, supporting the picture of deviancy that they were creating around Steven. Anything Brendan said on a recorded line to his mother would be deemed admissible and played in court. With the jurors not having been privy to the coercion that had taken place before the call, it would appear that Brendan was having a totally honest conversation with his mother. The investigators persisted with the touching theme:

Fassbender: 'Cause we need to know now. It's not gonna help to tell us a month from now, two months from now, two years from now, 'cause then they're gonna go, 'Brendan, why didn't you tell the investigators at that time?' Is there anything else he did to you sexually?

Brendan: No.

Fassbender: Was Jodi ever involved in anything?

Brendan: No.

Fassbender: Have you told Mark everything now… truthfully?
Brendan: Yeah.

Having convinced Brendan that it was in his best interest to confess to Teresa's murder, Fassbender and Wiegert encouraged Brendan to call his mother, so that they could use the recorded conversation in court:

Fassbender: Mark mentioned talking to your mom about this and being truthful with her now. OK. If you're truly sorry to the Halbachs, you'll… tell your mother the truth about this. OK.
Wiegert: Are you gonna do that?
Brendan: Yeah.
Wiegert: When you gonna do that?
Brendan: Tonight.
Wiegert: OK. Probably be a good idea before we tell her. That'd be the right thing to do. Your mom deserves to know. OK.
Brendan: Mm-huh. *(nods)*

As with all his post-confession calls to his mother, the investigators had pressured Brendan with the prospect of them telling Barb the details if he didn't.

This call formed part of a brief filed by Brendan's legal team on December 6, 2016: "The Wisconsin Court of Appeals made an unreasonable factual finding when it found that the state had introduced the May 13 telephone call during trial only to cross-examine Brendan, when the state used the call three times, including during closing argument to neutralize Brendan's alibi."

Brendan perceived that he had no choice but to confess. Once again, he told Barb that Steven had committed the crimes and had forced him to help.

Barb: Did he make you do this?
Brendan: Yeah.

Barb: Then why didn't you tell him that?

Brendan: Tell him what?

Barb: That Steven made you do it. You know, he made you do a lot of things.

Brendan: Yeah, I told them that. I even told them about Steven touching me and that.

Brendan had added the touching because the investigators had insisted on him telling Barb everything that he had told them. To this day, there are people who insist that Steven molested Brendan based on that one sentence that Brendan had said to his mother about the touching. These detractors have a blind faith in the investigators and have drawn conclusions without acknowledging the manipulative role of law enforcement in this case or researching any deeper.

One of Brendan's post-conviction lawyers is Laura Nirider, a Clinical Assistant Professor of Law and Co-Director of the Center on Wrongful Convictions of Youth (CWCY) at Northwestern Pritzker School of Law in Chicago. She has spoken out about why Brendan and others falsely confess.

Laura has pointed out that there are hundreds of cases – documented by organisations such as the Innocence Project – of people confessing to brutal crimes who were subsequently convicted. Years later, DNA evidence proved beyond any doubt that they were innocent. In murder cases like Teresa's, false confessions are the most common cause of wrongful convictions. According to the Innocence Project, more than one out of four people wrongfully convicted but later exonerated by DNA evidence made a false confession or incriminating statement. Most false confessions are detailed and sound believable as if the confessors know what they are talking about.

Laura cites several false myths surrounding false confessions:

1: It is obvious when a confession is false. People assume that false confessions are obvious because the confessors couldn't possibly be able to describe the crime. Most false confessions are accurate, detailed and believable.

2: People only falsely confess while under torture or getting beaten. In the hundreds of documented cases, none were the result of physical abuse. They were all derived from psychological interrogation techniques.

3: Only juveniles or people with mental limitations falsely confess. Although it's true that they are more vulnerable to interrogation techniques, each one of us has a breaking point. The question is: when do psychological tactics cross that point?

According to Laura, false confessions are so powerful that 81% of people who falsely confessed, who subsequently stood up for their innocence and took their cases to trial, still ended up wrongfully convicted.

Laura has identified three errors that occur during police investigations that cause false confessions:

1: The misclassification error. This answers the question: How did the wrong person get inside the interrogation room in the first place?

2: The coercion error. Once the investigators have the wrong person in the interrogation room, how is the person convinced to say something so dramatically against their self-interest?

3: The contamination error. Once the investigators have convinced the wrong person into confessing, how does an innocent person know what details to say to the investigators?

To understand the misclassification error, you must comprehend the two stages of police questioning:

1: The interview. This includes a lot of open-ended questions. The police try to gather information. Where were you when the crime happened? Do you know the victim? Why might somebody want to do this to the victim?

2: The interrogation. This is a different stage altogether, which comes later. It is not about information seeking because people are only interrogated if the police suspect them of knowing something or of being the perpetrators. The police dominate the interaction, which is accusatorial. It's about getting a confession statement.

During the interview, questions are asked and information is obtained, but also something different is happening. Law-enforcement officers are trained to detect deception by the way questions are answered. They read body language and notice the choice of words. They make judgements. It is referred to as behaviour analysis. Officers and interrogators are led to believe that they can become human lie detectors via the Reid technique.

Laura is not a fan of the Reid Technique. In her presentations, Laura shows a Reid Technique handout that officers are trained to use. It lists phrases that people who are thought to be lying use such as, "I didn't take that money," and, "I didn't do that to her."

The handout lists truthful denials, which are supposedly indicators of innocence, such as, "I did not rob anyone," and, "I did not rape her."

Laura shows slides used by the president of John E Reid and Associates, during a presentation that he gave at the University of Arkansas showcasing his interrogation techniques. One slide depicted the body language associated with someone telling the truth and the cues that indicate the individual is lying.

Truthful cues include composed, concerned, cooperative, direct, sincere and open. A truthful individual has open palms, maintains frontal alignment and makes smooth posture changes.

People who are lying slouch, lack frontal alignment and put their hands over their mouth or eyes – all of which Brendan did during his interrogations. Liars use responses such as, "I don't know," and, "I can't recall." They refer to God or religion with statements such as, "My God, I would have never committed this crime."

Using these methods of detecting deception, Reid and Associates claim an accuracy rate of 85%, according to Laura. But she has also stated that virtually every independent study of the Reid Technique has concluded that people cannot be trans-formed into human lie detectors. Officers who have been trained in the technique produce results that are no greater than chance when they try to determine whether somebody is telling the truth or lying. They get it right about 45% to 60% of the time, so it's basically a coin toss.

The truth is that there is no human behaviour unique to deception. There is no physiological giveaway that tells when someone is telling the truth or lying, but this is a powerful myth amongst law enforcement. It leads to the misclassification error: making wrong assumptions about whether somebody is lying and therefore guilty based on body language, the choice of words and whether they say, "I don't know." This powerful error can lead to bias in the investigation and it can trigger interrogation.

Another of Brendan's lawyers is Steven Drizin, a Clinical Professor of Law at Northwestern Law School and the founder of the Center on Wrongful Convictions of Youth.

On the Reid Technique, Drizin has stated that investigators spend time during the interview stage evaluating and assessing the body language and verbal responses of the suspect. After determining that the suspect is lying and therefore guilty, their conclusion drives the next part of the interrogation.

Drizin believes that to understand the coercion error, you must comprehend that an interrogation is a guilt-presumptive process. Every interrogation he has seen – especially those using the Reid Technique – began in the same way. There's usually a break, and the interrogator will come in after the interview process. He will make a direct accusation to the suspect that the suspect is guilty. "We're not here today, Brendan, to talk about whether you committed this crime. We already know you committed this crime. We have the evidence."

Oftentimes, they present a file filled with blank paper that they use as a prop, and say something like, "I've been investigating this case for weeks now. I've talked to many many people and everybody and every piece of evidence I've come up with points that you are guilty. What we need to find out today is why you committed this crime."

According to Drizin, at the beginning of an interrogation, innocent people are highly confident of emerging from the process unharmed. What do they have to worry about? Oftentimes, they are there to cooperate. Some just volunteer to come to the police station because they trust law enforcement. But the goal of the interrogation is to collapse that confidence level down to such a low point, such a place of hopelessness, where interviewees no longer believe that their innocence can save them and they are powerless to resist the accusations and demands to confess. When they reach that low point, the Reid Technique is designed to give them an out.

Drizin helped to exonerate Robert Taylor, who stated, "Being interrogated felt like I was choking, like there was no more air left in the room."

After the confrontation phase, the next thing the interrogators are taught is to interrupt the suspect. It's important not to let suspects say that they are innocent because the Reid Technique teaches that the more the suspects assert their innocence then the more they become psychologically attached to the notion of their innocence and the harder it is to get them to confess. At this stage, interrogators may move close to the suspects, knee to knee or within touching distance. Many times, they will touch or pat the suspects, while urging them to confess.

During this process, what Drizin has seen in nearly every case of a false confession are false-evidence ploys, which are lies about evidence such as claims that the police have evidence against the suspects that they don't have. This can trap suspects in a place of panic and desperation. These claims are usually general because if suspects are told that the police have their fingerprints or DNA or a video of them at the crime scene, then innocent suspects know that's not the case and start to doubt the interrogators. Generalisations include telling suspects repeatedly statements such as, "We already know. We just need to hear it." Just like Wiegert and Fassbender did to Brendan.

The police are allowed to lie. They have lied with abandon

since 1969, fuelled by a Supreme Court decision that blessed the practice of using deception during interrogations.

Although police can lie, John E Reid and Associates caution police not to lie under certain circumstances. Deceptive tactics should not be used with individuals who have significant mental limitations or with young children or with youthful suspects of low social maturity. Drizin believes that the Reid manual should have a picture of Brendan Dassey next to those words.

After the suspects have reached a low point, the tactic of minimisation is employed. Suspects are given an out, which is a suggestion that there are only two alternatives, both of which make the suspect guilty. One gives the suspect a face-saving moral legal excuse. The other paints the suspect as a cold-blooded heartless deliberate premeditated killer.

Questions are asked such as, "Did you intend to kill the victim or was it just an accident? Did you plan this act or was it just a temporary loss of self-control? Did you instigate the assault or were you just responding in self-defence? Did you want to participate in the rape or did your uncle force you to do it?" The suggestion is that if the suspects accept the less heinous version, they will be treated with leniency.

Once the suspects admit to some involvement in a crime, the investigators' job truly gets underway as they work to secure convictions. The investigators now require the suspects to reveal intimate details of the crime and crime scene that only the true perpetrators would know. This is a problem for the innocent as they now must embark on guessing tangible details to satisfy their interrogators, such as what was done to Teresa's head; unable to say that she had been shot, Brendan answered that Steven had cut Teresa's hair off with a kitchen knife.

Many false confessions are filled with accurate details. It's a direct result of the contamination error. The most significant source of contamination is fact feeding: leading questions by the interrogators that give the suspects the answers the interrogators are seeking. Suspects adopt those answers and incorporate them into their confessions, such as, "Did you see Teresa's toes in the fire, Brendan?" Sometimes they show the suspects crime-scene photos. Other times they take the suspects to the crime scene, as they did in the Central Park Five case.

In Brendan's case, the three errors – misclassification, coercion and contamination – were prevalent.

Making a Murderer showed Brendan in the police station on March 1, 2006, the day he had confessed to rape and murder. But what *Making a Murderer* didn't show was that interview was the fourth that he had endured over a 48-hour period.

In the early afternoon of February 27, 2006, officers came to Mishicot High School, where the investigators planted the idea of a sexual assault with statements along the lines of, "Brendan, after you saw the fingers and the toes and the forehead in the fire, you must have talked to your uncle about it, and asked him, 'What is this?' And he must have told you that he assaulted this young woman. Isn't that right, Brendan?" Eventually, Brendan was recorded agreeing with the investigators and stating that's what his uncle had told him.

After getting the statement from Brendan at his high school, the investigators immediately took him to the Two Rivers Police Department. Recording Brendan on videotape, the investigators had him repeat the statement that they had worked on in the high school.

Later that evening, there was a third interview at a local hotel. The session was unrecorded, so that nobody knows exactly what was said or how long the interrogation lasted.

Two days later on March 1, 2006, the investigators returned to Brendan's high school. They extracted him from his class and put him in the back seat of a police car. They drove for forty-five minutes to the Manitowoc Police Department. That's where the interrogation shown on *Making a Murderer* happened. It's where Brendan confessed to rape and murder.

Regarding the misclassification error or behaviour analysis, on March 1, Brendan displayed many of the characteristics associated with lying as defined by the Reid manual: slouched, hands over mouth or eyes, rigid and immobile posture, postures with barriers such as hand barriers, and saying, "I don't know," which Brendan did numerous times.

Laura Nirider believes that the investigators were using behaviour analysis to make judgements about Brendan based on his body language, choice of words and the frequency with which he responded, "I don't know."

In Brendan's case, Laura identified a second part of the misclassification error. Laura obtained an email sent by private investigator Pete Bates to Dean Strang and Jerry Buting. The investigator had researched Brendan's background in case Brendan had decided to testify against Steven. The email read:

This kid [Brendan] has had problems since kindergarten particularly in the social area. It's noted from as early as third grade that he can't look an adult in the eye. He is withdrawn. He doesn't function well with others. He has been in special ed classes since grade school. He has trouble understanding vocabulary both to and from him. He has been continually diagnosed as having a learning disability. He is easily intimidated and withdraws into himself in confrontational situations.

Laura believes that Brendan's disability, as described in the email, caused the investigators to make incorrect judgements, which is a misclassification error. Using the Reid Technique, the investigators reduced Brendan to a hopeless state, and offered him an out. He was misled into confessing.

Laura found watching the videotaped confession particularly heart-breaking because Brendan was a child who thought that if he just confessed to rape and murder he could go back to school to complete a project. Brendan was convicted based on his videotaped confession, but the section where he told his mother that the investigators had got to his head was never shown to the jury. Brendan never got to tell the jury why he had confessed. No experts were ever presented to show how false confessions are extracted. The lawyers after Len Kachinsky didn't know how to litigate a false-confession case. In court, they never played Brendan's recantation to Barb.

Drizin and Laura litigated Brendan's case in the Wisconsin state court system by presenting the evidence in Manitowoc, including Brendan's recantation, but the post-conviction relief was denied. The Wisconsin appellate court also denied Brendan relief. The Wisconsin Supreme Court denied Brendan's petition for leave to appeal. With the state remedies exhausted, Brendan's case is now in the federal court system.

A legal document filed in December 2016 with Laura's consent in support of Brendan stated that certified interrogation specialists are using the footage of Brendan's interview as an example of what not to do. The brief pointed out that the investigators in Brendan's case violated the protocol contained in the Reid Technique's investigators tips:

Take special precautions when interviewing juveniles or individuals with significant mental or psychological impairments [sic]. Every interrogator must exercise extreme caution and care when interviewing or interrogating a juvenile or a person who is mentally or psychologically impaired. Certainly, these individuals can and do commit very serious crimes, but since many false confession cases involve juveniles and/or individuals with some significant mental or psychological disabilities, extreme care must be exercised when questioning these individuals and the investigator has to modify their approach with these individuals. Furthermore, when a juvenile or person who is mentally or psychologically impaired confesses, the investigator should exercise extreme diligence in establishing the accuracy of such a statement through subsequent corroboration. In these situations, it is imperative that the interrogator does not reveal details of the crime so that they can use the disclosure of such information by the suspect as verification of the confession's authenticity.

Although the combined strategies of coercing false testimony and triggering emotional reactions were devastatingly effective at the time, those tactics started to unravel thanks to *Making a Murderer* and a federal judge.

In August 2016, Judge William E Duffin found that Fassbender and Wiegert had repeatedly made false promises to Brendan in extracting a confession. Handing down a 91-page decision, the judge ruled that the confession was involuntary. The judge stated that over the course of the interrogation Brendan was "generally responding to the investigators' questions with answers of just a few hushed words [and] a story evolved whereby in its final iteration Dassey implicated himself in the rape, murder and mutilation of Teresa Halbach." The confession happened without a parent or another adult present, and investigators "exploited the absence of such an adult by repeatedly suggesting that they were looking out for his interests."

The decision added that Brendan's "borderline to below average intellectual ability likely made him more susceptible to coercive pressures than a peer of higher intellect." The judge was unimpressed with the investigators' constant reassurances that everything was going to be OK for Brendan and that they already knew about his role in the crime. "No single statement by the investigators, if viewed in isolation, rendered Dassey's statement involuntary," the decision stated. "But when assessed collectively and cumulatively... it is clear how the investigators' actions amounted to deceptive interrogation tactics that overbore Dassey's free will."

The judge summed up how the confession was involuntary: "Especially when the investigators' promises, assurances, and threats of negative consequences are assessed in conjunction with Dassey's age, intellectual deficits, lack of experience in dealing with the police, the absence of a parent, and other relevant personal characteristics, the free will of a reasonable person in Dassey's position would have been overborne. Once considered in the proper light, the conclusion that Dassey's statement was involuntary under the totality of the circumstances is not one about which 'fair-minded jurists could disagree.'"

The judge ordered Brendan's release within ninety days of the ruling unless prosecutors filed an appeal against him. Unfortunately, a new Ken Kratz rose to the occasion by way of Wisconsin Attorney General Brad Schimel, who appealed the judge's decision.

After over a decade of incarceration, Brendan was on the verge of getting released. Probation officers visited his family in preparation for his return. Their excitement mounted as the final hours approached. Convinced he would soon be free, Brendan even gave away his meagre belongings to other prisoners.

But Schimel managed to stop the ninety-day release ruling. He argued that Brendan is a convicted murderer, rapist and a danger to society. Schimel failed to mention that the most dangerous thing Brendan had done in prison was to trade Ramen noodle soup with another prisoner without permission from the prison. Prisoners constantly trade food in violation of the prison rules. Whoever gave Brendan a disciplinary ticket for trading a Ramen noodle soup was either extremely petty or keen to blemish the record of a high-profile prisoner.

In prison, Brendan had watched the media circus that had played out across from Columbia Correctional all week, excited and expectant for his future. Schimel's last minute appeal left Brendan, his family and worldwide supporters devastated.

"Brendan was supposed to have been released in November 2016," Barb said, "but it turned out to be a let-down again from the state and it was very emotional and very heart-breaking again."

I started a #whereistheblood campaign on Twitter. Schimel received Tweets and Facebook messages asking him why there was no blood found at the crime scene or on Brendan's clothes. Schimel offered no explanation.

As of January 2017, Brendan is still inside; however, the 7th Circuit Court in Chicago, with unprecedented speed, set oral arguments for 9:30 am, February 14, 2017. A decision is expected within six to nine weeks from the arguments being heard.

The Wisconsin authorities coerced and convicted Brendan with great urgency, but they are in no hurry to release him due to the millions in compensation that he would be eligible for and the harm it would cause to the reputations of those who framed him.

STRATEGY 4:
PLANT EVIDENCE

Manipulated by experienced investigators, Brendan Dassey told a fantastical story. His compliance came from a need to please the detectives, as all he wanted to do was go back to school to complete a project and go home to watch his beloved *WrestleMania*. The description of events procured from Brendan was so extreme that the crime scene should have been drenched in massive amounts of DNA evidence. Here's Brendan's summary of the assault on Teresa:

Wiegert: Tell us what exactly happened to her, what order it happened in. You said there were basically three things prior to you guys shooting her. Explain those in… the order that it happened.
    Brendan: Starting with when we got in the room?
    Fassbender: OK.
    Wiegert: Yeah. What you guys did to her.
    Brendan: We had sex with her.
    Wiegert: OK.
    Brendan: Then he stabbed her.
    Wiegert: Then who stabbed her?
    Brendan: He did.
    Wiegert: Who's he?
    Brendan: Steven.
    Wiegert: OK. And then what?
    Brendan: Then I cut her throat.
    Wiegert: OK.
    Brendan: And then he choked her and I cut off her hair.
    Wiegert: OK. So, he choked her after you cut her throat?
    Brendan: *(nods)* Mm-huh.

Wiegert: OK. Kind of show me like on your throat where you cut her.

Brendan: Like right here.

Wiegert: How deep?

Brendan: Just as long as the knife went through.

Wiegert: OK.

Fassbender: With your finger, show me how deep you went into her throat.

Brendan: About that much.

Fassbender: I mean like, like this, like that, like that, like that.

Brendan: Like that.

Fassbender: About that far?

Brendan: *(nods)*

Wiegert: When Steven stabbed her, tell me again where he stabbed her.

Brendan: Like right here.

Wiegert: How far in did the knife go?

Fassbender: Again, with your hands, if you can.

Brendan: About like that.

Wiegert: OK.

Brendan: *(nods)*

Wiegert: And then he, tell me how he choked her. Where was he when he choked her?

Brendan: On the side of the bed.

Wiegert: On the side of the bed.

Brendan: *(nods)*

Fassbender: With your hands, show me what, pretend that her neck is there, whatever, show me how he did it.

Brendan: Like this.

Fassbender: How long?

Brendan: 'Bout two, three minutes.

Wiegert: He must have had a lot of blood on his hands then, huh?

Brendan: *(nods)*

Wiegert: How did he get that off his hands?

Brendan: Washing it off.
Wiegert: Where?
Brendan: In the sink.
Wiegert: Which sink?
Brendan: In the bathroom.
Wiegert: Did he wipe any blood up with anything?
Brendan: *(shakes head)* Just that paper towel that he dried his hands with.
Fassbender: After you cut her throat, was she still alive?
Brendan: Barely.
Fassbender: And how do you know that?
Brendan: 'Cause she was breathing like a little bit.
Wiegert: When do you think she quit breathing?
Brendan: When we were bringing her outside.
Wiegert: Outside, what do you mean outside, where?
Brendan: Out in the garage.
Wiegert: How do you know she quit breathing then?
Brendan: 'Cause her belly wasn't moving.
Wiegert: 'Cause her belly wasn't moving?
Brendan: *(nods)*

Teams of police combed the Avery property for Teresa's DNA. Violent torture and rape produces bodily fluids that splatter everywhere. It's impossible for amateurs to clean up the biological material, yet after eight days, all that the teams found was deer blood. If Teresa had been raped, the sheets and mattress would have been contaminated with bodily fluids, none of which were present. Teresa had supposedly been chained to Steven's bed. One end of the bed had no means to accommodate chains and there were no scratch marks on the other end to indicate that chains had been used to hold someone down who had been violently assaulted.

Kratz's claim that Steven and Brendan used bleach to clean the scene is ludicrous. It was based on bleach allegedly found on Brendan's jeans. If they had cleaned the scene so perfectly with bleach, then there would have been no traces left of deer blood. Steven's home was such a mess that it appeared on *Making a Murderer* never to have been cleaned.

The lack of DNA evidence would have caused any rational-minded police department to start looking elsewhere for a crime scene, but in Manitowoc, when the evidence doesn't fit their agenda, they plant it, especially when $36 million are at stake.

At the trial, Steven's lawyers alleged that he was framed in five ways:

1: Teresa's car was planted on Avery's Auto Salvage.
2: Steven's blood was planted in Teresa's car.
3: A bullet with Teresa's DNA on it was planted in Steven's garage.
4: Teresa's key was planted in Steven's bedroom and his DNA was planted on it.
5: Teresa's bones were planted by Steven's home.

1. Teresa's car was planted on Avery's Auto Salvage.

The prosecution blamed the absence of DNA evidence at the crime scene – the blood and bodily fluids associated with torture, sexual assault and stabbing – on Steven Avery's genius at getting rid of DNA with a bottle of bleach. But when it came to the largest piece of evidence – the RAV4 – the prosecutor would have us believe that Steven drove it past his own car crusher and kept it on his property, where it could easily be found.

The defence alleged that Teresa's RAV4 could have been driven onto the lot by a back route, unnoticed by the people living on the property.

Pamela Sturm found the RAV4. She is a second cousin to Teresa and formerly a private investigator. According to Pamela's testimony, on November 4, 2005, she saw the news that Teresa was missing. She sought confirmation from relatives. On November 5 at 9 am, she attempted to join a search party, which had already set off. She and her daughter headed for the last place they believed that Teresa had been seen alive: the Avery property.

On a mission to locate Teresa's car, Pamela Sturm drove to the main office building on the Avery property, arriving around 9:50 am. The two women approached two men chatting outside. Pamela asked Steven's brother Earl if she could search the property. He consented.

They decided to do a search from left to right, walking north to south along the side of the yard, checking the vehicles. Pamela noticed a ridge on one side of the property and headed towards it. On a forty-acre lot hosting almost 4,000 cars, they discovered the RAV4 after searching for less than forty minutes. The RAV4 was camouflaged by branches, a door frame and the hood of another car. Its licence plates had been removed. They took photos with a camera given to them by Teresa's roommate, Scott Bluedorn. She also testified that they tried to open some of the doors, but they were locked.

Around 10:30 am, they called Sheriff Pagel and left a message. His direct number had been given to them by Teresa's ex-boy-friend Ryan Hillegas. Investigator Wiegert told them to not touch anything and that the deputies would find her. They waited for the deputies to arrive to confirm formally that the RAV4 was Teresa's.

The RAV4 had been tucked away by a patch of trees, approximately 1,000 feet from the main entrance where Pamela and her daughter had commenced searching on foot. When asked how she had possibly found the vehicle so quickly, Pamela claimed that God had shown her the way.

Pamela testified: "My heart started going... oh my goodness, maybe this is it. I became very very worried for our safety because, 90%, this is probably Teresa's car, and we're in danger."

Residing only 1,400 feet from where the RAV4 was found, old Wilmer Siebert would be a great person to interview for future seasons of *Making a Murderer*. According to an article by the free-lance photojournalist and writer Jeff Klassen, Wilmer has lived there since the 1970s. His home is by the entrance to the quarry road that runs behind the Avery property. Several back entrances were accessible in 2005, but have since been closed.

Wilmer came across to Klassen as an independent observer of events. His relationship with the Averys was a casual one. Having watched *Making a Murderer*, Wilmer wasn't interested in the attention from the case, but it had made him recall what he'd witnessed around the time of the search for Teresa.

Wilmer told Klassen about two incidents he had seen in early November 2005. Before the RAV4 was found, Wilmer was sitting in his backyard, when he saw a RAV4 – followed by a white Jeep – driving down the quarry road. While acknowledging that he could never be absolutely certain that it was her car, he remembered its colour was the same blue-green as Teresa's. He made a mental note of the RAV4 because he hadn't seen many others like it. Both vehicles were speeding at about 40 mph. The distance was such that the drivers were indiscernible. Both vehicles continued up the road until they went out of sight. Approximately half an hour later, only the Jeep made the return journey out of the Avery property. He said that the RAV4 was located by Pamela shortly thereafter.

Considering the speed in which Pamela had located the RAV4, Wilmer recalled that he'd once obtained a gas tank for a truck from the Averys. To locate the truck, he'd been given the row that it was in and what kind of truck it was. Armed with that information, he still took much longer to find the vehicle than Pamela had.

On the afternoon of November 4, members of the Calumet County Sheriff's Office flew over and filmed the vehicles on the Avery property. They did not see the RAV4, which strengthens Wilmer's claim that the RAV4 entered the property on a back road later that day.

2. Steven's blood was planted in Teresa's car.

Steven's blood was found in six places in the RAV4: front driver's side portion, floor by the console, right of the ignition area, front passenger seat, CD case on front passenger seat and a metal panel between the backseat and cargo area. The prosecution alleged that these bloodstains could only have been left by the murderer. It was suggested that a cut on Steven's finger was the source of the blood, and that the cut had arisen during his assault on Teresa.

If Steven was meticulous about getting rid of blood and DNA evidence, why would he leave his own bloodstains in Teresa's car?

Photos show Steven's finger with a cut towards the top below a nail. For his blood to have dripped onto the RAV4, his hands must have been uncovered. If he wasn't wearing gloves, then his fingerprints should also have ended up on the RAV4. His fingerprints were absent because it's far easier to plant blood than fingerprints, which would have required a prosthetic-type device crafted to match Steven's fingers.

After the prosecution announced the discovery of the blood in Teresa's RAV4, Steven stated publicly that it wasn't his, and that it must have been planted by the same corrupt Manitowoc County Sheriff's Office that had set him up before.

Believing that the police had planted Teresa's key in Steven's trailer, Jerry Buting – Steven's defence counsel – assumed that they must have gone a little bit further by planting Steven's blood in the RAV4. The defence team pondered the source of Steven's blood.

Initially, Special Prosecutor Ken Kratz mocked the defence allegation of the police accessing Steven's blood. He made a sarcastic remark about the police carrying around vials of Steven's perspiration.

There were several sources for Steven's blood. Working on metal in the scrapyard, Steven and his brothers often cut their hands. There were blood drops in his bathroom. Photos showed that the middle of one blood stain had been removed. Buting said that it looked as if someone had taken a Q-Tip to the stain, swabbed the bulk of it up and left the outer ring.

Steven told his lawyers that during his first wrongful conviction he had given blood and saliva samples. His lawyers contacted the lab, which said they had only used a fraction of the sample: 1

millilitre. More research led them to discover that the remaining blood had been shipped back to the Manitowoc County Clerk's Office.

With an investigator, Buting went to the clerk's office and asked to see Steven's file. They were taken beyond a partition to a large cardboard box, which was out in the open and unsecured. In the box, under the pleadings, court decisions and transcripts, they found a white box, which, on the outside, had information pertaining to Steven Avery's blood such as the date the sample had been collected. On one side, it was sealed, but the seal was loose. Buting filed a court order for permission to open it.

Making a Murderer showed the opening of the white box.

Upon inspecting the container of the purple-topped vial, they noticed that the evidence tape on the box had been cut through. After they opened the box, they saw a pinhole in the cap of the vial. Buting assumed that the existence of the hole meant that a needle had been inserted into the vial to extract blood to plant it in the RAV4. Steven's lawyers spoke to an employee at Labtech, who confirmed that they did not make pinholes in vial caps to test blood samples.

Although it is correct that Labtech hadn't inserted a needle through the cap to withdraw a sample, the hole in a blood vial is considered a normal finding as that is how blood is deposited into the vial. Having pointed this out, some Steven Avery detractors have claimed that this debunks the theory of the planted blood. However, even if the hole in the cap is normal, the same hole could have been used to extract his blood.

Detractors have pointed out that the vial did not appear to have any blood missing. In the FBI examination of the 10-ml vial, 5.5 millilitres were present, leaving room for 4.5 millilitres to have been extracted – sufficient to plant six bloodstains.

As proof that the blood had not been extracted from the vial, Kratz seized on the absence of EDTA detected in the blood in the RAV4. EDTA is a preservative added to the blood in purple-topped vials to prevent it from coagulating. In the chapter

– Strategy 5: Pay Expert Witnesses to Lie – I put to rest this assertion by Kratz.

By focusing on one specific vial, other sources of Steven's blood were ignored. Steven said that they took multiple samples of his blood over the years. The other vials may have contained preservatives other than EDTA.

In August 2006, Kathleen Zellner, Steven's lawyer, put in a request for post-conviction scientific testing of evidence used to convict him. She stated that Steven's blood was planted in the RAV4 prior to it being moved from a quarry adjacent to Avery's Auto Salvage on Friday night, November 4, 2005 – which is when Wilmer saw the RAV4 arrive with the white Jeep. A scientist who contacted Zellner offered to perform a radiocarbon test on the bloodstains, which could definitively establish the age of Steven's blood and determine, based on the age, whether it was planted.

Making a Murderer YouTuber Erekose emailed me documents suggesting that Kratz had made a false statement to the court in relation to the vial. In a motion, Kratz had written, "The prosecution had no knowledge of the blood vial, prior to Dec. 6, 2006." Yet in an email dated February 7, 2006, Kratz told Sherry Culhane that "Mark Wiegert is checking the 1985 Manitowoc blood sample taken, to make sure what it was."

3. A bullet with Teresa's DNA on it was planted in Steven's garage.

On November 5, 2005, investigators looking for Teresa performed an eight-minute sweep of Steven's garage. On November 6 – one day after Teresa's vehicle was found – Steven's garage was searched for approximately two hours. Law enforcement brought Luminol, a chemical that emits a blue glow in the presence of blood or certain other activators, including copper and bleach. Several areas reacted to the Luminol, including a large stain approximately 3' x 3'. They removed a snowmobile, but left all the other equipment and vehicles in place. Calumet County sheriff's deputy Daniel

Kucharski testified that he found no bullet fragments when he and three Manitowoc County deputies searched the garage on November 6. On November 8, they returned looking for tools.

On March 1, 2006, a confession coerced out of Brendan turned the garage into a crime scene. Dissatisfied with Brendan telling the truth about doing odd jobs for Steven, Fassbender and Wiegert twisted the details Brendan provided into a grotesque narrative:

Brendan: Well then, then he [Steven] called and said that he wanted help on his car.

Wiegert: OK. Did he call you or did he come over?

Brendan: He called me.

Wiegert: On your cell phone or on the house phone?

Brendan: The house phone.

Wiegert: He calls your house phone?

Brendan: *(nods)* Yeah.

Fassbender: And this is about what time now?

Brendan: 'Bout six, six-thirty.

Fassbender: OK. And what does he say to you?

Brendan: He says do you wanna help me with the – to fix the car because he said that if I would help him on his cars, he would like, help me find a car.

Fassbender: OK.

Brendan: And so I did and then that's when he like cut something and then it was leaking on the floor.

Wiegert: Let's stop right there. So, he called you and asked you to help fix a car?

Brendan: *(nods)* Mm-huh.

Wiegert: And you go over to this house?

Brendan: *(nods)* Mm-huh.

Wiegert: And where do you go?

Brendan: Into the garage.

Wiegert: And what's in the garage?

Brendan: His Monte.

Wiegert: His Monte.

Brendan: *(nods)*

Wiegert: Where's that Suzuki?

Brendan: On the side.

Fassbender: Is the big garage door open?

Brendan: *(nods)* Mm-huh.

Fassbender: So, you walk in there… This is Halloween.

Brendan: *(nods)*

Fassbender: OK. And what's he doing?

Brendan: He's working on his Monte.

Fassbender: What about the fire?

Brendan: Do you mean if it was started or something? No, it wasn't. *(shakes head)*

Fassbender: OK. We're not gonna go any further in this 'cause we need to get the truth out now. We know the fire was going. We know that he had already had his altercation with Teresa. We don't believe there's a Monte in there. I talked to you the other night and you said nothing about the Monte. You said nothing about something getting punctured and leaking out. We talked about cleaning something up in that garage. You told me that you thought thinking back now there was blood. It was red in colour, plus you're at your house. You said six, six-thirty. I'll go that far with you. It might even [have] been earlier. What's going on? Let's talk it through honestly now.

Brendan: *(nods)*

Wiegert: Come on, Brendan, be honest. I told you before that's the only thing that's gonna help you here. We already know what happened. OK.

Brendan: *(nods)*

Fassbender: We don't get honesty here. I'm your friend right now, but I gotta believe in you, and if I don't believe in you, I can't go to bat for you. OK. You're nodding. Tell us what happened.

Brendan: *(nods)*

Wiegert: Your mom said you'd be honest with us.

Brendan: *(nods)*

Fassbender: And she's behind you 100% no matter what happens here.

Wiegert: Yep, that's what she said 'cause she thinks you know more, too.

Fassbender: We're in your comer.

Brendan: *(nods)*

Wiegert: We already know what happened. Now, tell us exactly. Don't lie.

Fassbender: We can't say it for you, Brendan. OK.

Brendan: Well, that morning he said that if he wanted me to come over like at six-thirty, and he had the fire started 'cause he wanted to... burn some tires.

Fassbender: Uh-huh.

Brendan: So, he had it started and the jeep was still in there.

Wiegert: Who's jeep?

Brendan: The Suzuki.

Wiegert: It was still in where?

Brendan: In the garage.

Fassbender: So, the Monte's not in there?

Brendan: *(shakes head)*

Fassbender: Whose car was in the garage? Tell me the truth.

Wiegert: We already know. Just tell us. It's OK.

Fassbender: The truth, that's, it's so easy to tell the truth. It's hard to make things up.

Brendan: Her jeep.

Fassbender: That's right.

Wiegert: Her jeep was in the garage, wasn't it?

Brendan: *(nods)*

Fassbender: And you, you tell me if I'm wrong, but when you were at the house, you just went over there 'cause you had talked about it in the morning. Is that correct?

Brendan: *(nods)* Mm-huh.

Fassbender: There was no call from Steven asking you to come over was there? And you went over. Was the big door closed?

Brendan: *(shakes head)* Mm-uh.

Fassbender: You sure about that?

Brendan: *(nods)* Yeah.

Wiegert: So, the big door is open and her truck is in there when you get over there?

Brendan: *(nods)* Yeah.

Fassbender: By her truck. Who are we talking about?

Brendan: Well, if I wanted to come over later.

Fassbender: No, whose truck?

Wiegert: Whose truck?

Fassbender: Is in there?

Brendan: Oh, the truck?

Fassbender: Yeah.

Brendan: Her jeep.

Fassbender: Who's her?

Brendan: Teresa's.

Fassbender: OK. And that jeep is a what? Do you remember?

Brendan: Like what colour?

Fassbender: Colour or make?

Brendan: Green like a greenish blue.

Fassbender: OK.

Wiegert: Is it drove in or is it backed into the garage?

Brendan: It's backed in.

Wiegert: OK. Now, let's be honest. What did he tell you? What did he show you?

Fassbender: What did you see and what did he tell you?

Brendan: He showed me the knife and the rope.

Wiegert: Where was she? Come on we know this already. Be honest.

Brendan: In the back of the jeep.

Wiegert: Dead at that time? She was in the back of the jeep?

Brendan: *(nods)*

Wiegert: Was she alive or?

Brendan: Dead.

Fassbender: Are you sure?

Brendan: *(nods)*

Fassbender: OK. What did you see in the back? Now this is hard, but what did you see in the back of the jeep?

Brendan: That she was laying there with like a small blanket over her.

Fassbender: Do you remember where her head was?

Brendan: *(shakes head)* Not really.

Fassbender: Did she have clothes on?

Brendan: Yeah. *(nods)*

Fassbender: She was clothed.

Brendan: *(nods)* Yeah.

Wiegert: Was she tied up already? Or did you help him do that?

Brendan: *(shakes head)* She was tied up already.

Fassbender: Where? Tell me how she was tied up.

Brendan: Like the rope was right here around her body.

Fassbender: Are you sure?

Brendan: *(nods)*

Wiegert: Did Steve have any blood on him at that time?

Brendan: On his finger.

Wiegert: What about on his body and his clothes?

Brendan: No. Not that I know of.

Wiegert: Where did you see blood?

Brendan: Like, like right here.

Wiegert: Where else in the garage?

Brendan: On the floor.

Wiegert: A lot?

Brendan: Like drips.

Wiegert: Where was it dripping from?

Brendan: I don't know.

Wiegert: What did he tell you he did to her?

Brendan: That he stabbed her.

There is a pattern of DNA evidence magically materialising in places that Brendan Dassey described such as the garage – after he had been coerced into saying these things. After his March

1, 2006, interrogation, deputies returned to the garage to search it again. They removed a vehicle and the equipment and sifted through a large amount of debris. On this search, they found two bullet fragments. One was a small, partially destroyed fragment in a crack in the cement. The other was under an air compressor in the back of the garage.

There are methods to detect whether a bullet or a shell casing has been fired by a certain gun. Each gun that is manufactured has slight differences in the barrel and the bore that can mark a bullet in a unique way. Experts can examine bullets and shell casings and opine as to which gun they were fired from.

The bullet found in the crack was too destroyed to match to a gun. The prosecution claimed that testing proved that the second bullet had come from the .22 calibre rifle found in Steven's home. Others in the neighbourhood possessed .22 calibre rifles, including Bobby Dassey. The rifle found in Steven's room was a common model.

According to Buting, the method of determining the source of a bullet is subjective. In Steven's case, it was never proven beyond a reasonable doubt that the second fragment had come from the .22 found in Steven's home. The markings were similar, but other rifles of the same model could not be ruled out.

The bullet fragments and casings found in Steven's garage were hardly suspicious either. Shell casings were found all over the junkyard because it was inhabited by hunting-shooting folk. They shot rabbits. They sighted their rifles for deer hunting. They even target-practised on old cars. Nevertheless, the prosecution seized on the bullet fragments in the garage because they suited the narrative coerced from Brendan Dassey.

For testing, bullets were sent to DNA Analyst Sherry Culhane, whose lab notes showed direction from Special Agent Tom Fassbender directing her to "try to put [Teresa] in [Steven's] house or garage." She went on to testify that the expectation "had no bearing on my analysis at all," which was her attempt to cover her tracks after the conspiracy had been exposed. As part of a team effort to frame Steven, Sherry violated critical aspects of scientific protocol.

Sherry had also played a role in Steven's first wrongful conviction. After comparing a hair from Steven's T-shirt with a hair found on Penny Beerntsen, Sherry had concluded that the hairs were a possible match. When prosecutor Vogel's role in Steven's first wrongful conviction was on the verge of being exposed, Vogel blamed the conviction on Sherry's hair analysis. It also took Sherry over a year to carry out the DNA test that exonerated Steven in the Beerntsen case.

Sherry found traces of Teresa's DNA on the bullet from Steven's garage, while also finding traces of her own DNA on the control samples. The test was contaminated. She should have performed the test again, but that option wasn't available because she had used up the entire sample. To put Teresa in Steven's garage, Sherry ignored the protocol and glossed over problems because the test results gave Kratz exactly what he was looking for.

The bullet supposedly had Teresa's DNA on it, but no presumptive blood test was done. The test only takes a moment in the field and does not destroy DNA. It involves applying a drop of a chemical compound called phenolphthalein to the item, and if human haemoglobin is present, the sample will turn a specific colour. Since no test was done, it leaves open the possibility that a bullet from Steven's yard could have been rubbed on Teresa's clothing, or any other items collected by law enforcement for DNA samples. Did someone on the day the bullet was recovered in Steven's garage purposely skip that test knowing beforehand no blood was present?

The .22 found in Steven's home wasn't even his. It was Roland Johnson's. He owned the trailer that Steven had lived in. A retired tool and die-maker, Roland Johnson had bought an acre of land from the Averys decades ago. He'd allowed Jodi to live there, and eventually Steven had moved in. In court, Roland was shown the alleged murder weapon:

Roland: That looks like the Marlin .22 that I had up there.

Buting: Let me actually show you that exhibit for a moment. This is Exhibit 247.

Roland: That is my gun. I can remember it by the scratch back here.

Buting: OK. You're sure of that?

Roland: I am sure of that now.

Buting: And when did you purchase this gun?

Roland: Prior to 1977 or '76, I know for sure. I don't know exactly when, but I'm positive I bought it at Fleet Farm.

Buting: OK. And where did you keep it when you lived there?

Roland: On the gun rack that was on the wall in the bedroom. That – with the black powder rifle – were the two guns that were sitting up there.

Buting: OK. And did you ever use that gun on the property?

Roland: Many times. Many, many times.

Buting: Have you ever fired that gun?

Roland: I fired that gun at chipmunks, and I fired that gun at targets all over the lot. I mean, I could have been standing [at the] back end of the lot, down by [the] far end of the lot. I fired it all over the yard. I fired it off the deck.

Buting: All right. What would you be shooting at?

Roland: Depending on – more often than not, targets. But targets of opportunity were gophers.

Buting: Gophers? … Let me direct your attention to the garage area… Did you ever fire that gun in the area of the garage?

Roland: I fired it all around the garage. I fired it all around the lot. There, again, mostly for gophers. It was fired many times.

Buting: Was there a gopher somewhere near the garage or–

Roland: Several of them. The whole yard was full of them.

Buting: That's – Um, well, what would happen to the shells?

Roland: Basically, they'd be ejected. No matter where I was, that's where they were ejected and that's where they stayed.

Buting: So, they would just fall on the ground?

Roland: Yes, they would.

Buting: Did you pick them up?

Roland: No, I did not.

Buting: Why not?

Roland: Why? They're only a little .22 shell. There's no value in them. They are not worth picking up. They're small enough that they don't hurt anything. I just left them. In fact, if you take a metal detector and go over the yard, you'll probably find many of them out there.

Buting: All right. Would that be true near the garage as well?

Roland: Any place on that lot, on that acre, it would be true.

Buting: All right. Did you ever fire the gun in the garage?

Roland: Not that I recall. I, basically, don't believe in guns in a building.

Buting: Sure. I understand. But how close do you think you ever were to the garage when you'd be shooting it?

Roland: Right at the garage door opening.

Buting: Why?

Roland: The main door. Here, again, gophers. I had a hole under that door about that big, and I don't know how far the tunnel went in, but I fired… into that hole many times.

Buting: And that hole is where in relation to the garage?

Roland: Right. Basically, on the left-hand side of the main garage door…

Buting: All right. I just want to verify that. I'll show you Exhibit 101. Show me, approximately, where these – this gopher hole was?

Roland: Approximately right in front of that truck. Right by the edge of the door.

Buting: All right. Can you give me any kind of estimate of how many times you would have – well – would have fired that gun in front of you on that one-acre parcel?

Roland: Maybe five or six bricks – which are 500 in a brick – 3,000 times.

Buting: Speaking of bricks: what kind of ammunition did that gun use?

Roland: Used .22 long rifle.

Buting: Did you buy that kind of ammunition while you were there?

Roland: While I was there. Lots of it.

Buting: OK. Now, you left the gun there while you rented it out to–

Roland: Yes, I did. Most of the furnishings and stuff were mine, and I kind of figured if I'd come up on a weekend and wanted to use it for any reason or come up there, it was there.

Not only was the alleged murder weapon Roland's gun, but he'd shot it thousands of times, leaving bullet fragments and casings all over the property. When it came to framing Steven, the investigators could have claimed that Teresa had been murdered anywhere on the salvage yard and found bullet pieces in that location to back up their claims.

4. Teresa's key was planted in Steven's bedroom and his DNA was planted on it.

In plain view on the floor, a key alleged to be Teresa's was found in Steven's bedroom on November 8. It was the sixth time that his home had been accessed by the police. It was attached to a lanyard fob that Teresa's sister claimed she had obtained during an event where it was given away as a promotional item: "I was at the EAA [Experimental Aircraft Association] convention two summers ago, and I was at an exhibition building. And it was the Air National Guard had like a little stand, and they had free lanyards, and I picked it up."

Steven's DNA was found on the key, but not Teresa's. Tests were never performed to ascertain whether his DNA on the key originated from blood or another source, such as skin cells. The lanyard was never tested for DNA.

The first police entry into Steven's home was a ten-minute sweep on November 5 after the RAV4 was found. At this stage, the deputies were hoping to locate Teresa alive. Another search on November 5 that commenced at 7:30 pm lasted for almost three hours. Deputies seized approximately fifty pieces of evidence. On November 6, they returned for over twenty minutes to collect items, including weapons, a vacuum cleaner and bedding from the spare bedroom. On the same day, members of the State Crime Lab used special lighting to search for DNA evidence. They collected swabs from a few spots of blood. On November 8, deputies entered Steven's home for seven minutes to collect the serial number from his computer. They did not enter the bedroom. On the same day, they searched for almost four hours and located the key.

Deputies claimed they were collecting pornographic material from a bookcase, which they bumped and shook. When they were finished with the bookcase, Lieutenant James Lenk spotted the key on the floor. The deputies claimed it must have been on or in the bookcase, and had fallen out when they had moved the bookcase. The back panel of the bookcase was separated from the body, so it was proposed that the key might have fallen through the back as it was turned and searched.

Deputies Lenk and Colborn were searching under the supervision of Deputy Kucharski from the Calumet County Sheriff's Office. His job was to monitor their activity. Kucharski testified that he wasn't watching the deputies the whole time. Even though he did not believe that the key was planted, he testified that the opportunity was there to plant it while he was distracted.

Even if Lenk and Colborn hadn't planted the key, maybe someone else from law enforcement had. The neighbour who claimed to have seen the arrival of the RAV4, Wilmer Siebert, also witnessed something that suggests that the key may have arrived shortly before it was found. Early in the investigation, deputies barricaded the entrance and blocked off the section of the quarry road that went towards Avery's Auto Salvage. The deputies asked Wilmer to report anyone trying to get past the barricades.

Late at night on November 7, Wilmer saw two Manitowoc

County Sheriff's Office vehicles enter the Avery property by circumventing a barricade. Their unsupervised arrival was in violation of the judge's orders for Manitowoc to have handed off the case to Calumet County. Wilmer's daughter notified the police, who told her she had nothing to worry about. The call was recorded. The next day, the key was found.

The manifestation of the key on the sixth entry raises many questions. Why would Steven clean up the blood and yet leave a key in his house? Where was Teresa's original keyring with her keys on it, including her key for the RAV4? Why would Steven's DNA be on the key and not Teresa's? Had a replacement key been planted with only Steven's DNA on it?

Kathleen Zellner tweeted on February 4, 2016: "That special RAV4 key only absorbs DNA of Plaintiff in civil rights suit against MC not owner's. Magic"

One scenario is that the key had been wiped clean to avoid leaving DNA evidence that could link back to whoever had planted it. On Steven Avery's floor, the key would have picked up his DNA, probably from skin cells which are scattered around everywhere like dust.

Throughout the investigation, evidence often conveniently popped up, sometimes in places that Brendan had been manipulated into describing. But in the case of the magical key, the method worked in reverse. Months after the key had been found, Fassbender and Wiegert coerced Brendan into simply stating that Steven had dropped it in his home:

Brendan: Well, at first, he had it in his room in his dresser.

Wiegert: OK.

Brendan: And he took it out 'cause he was going to get rid of it, but he, he had to hurry up and get the phone because he had to answer it, so he left the key there.

Wiegert: He left the key where?

Brendan: On the floor. He dropped it.

Wiegert: How do you know that? How do you know that,

Brendan?

Brendan: 'Cause I was there that day.

Wiegert: You were there the day he dropped it? And what day was that?

Brendan: November 2nd.

Wiegert: Did he show you the key that day?

Brendan: No.

Wiegert: Well, then how do you know he dropped it?

Brendan: 'Cause I seen him pulling his dresser drawer and I seen it in his hands.

Wiegert: OK. And what else did you see? So, you were in the bedroom with him?

Brendan: No, I'm sitting on the couch.

Wiegert: You can't see the dresser from the couch, can you?

Brendan: Well, before he had, he had his room different.

Wiegert: You're starting to lie again, aren't you?

Brendan: 'Cause he had the bed where the window is.

Wiegert: He had the bed where the window was when Teresa was there?

Brendan: Yeah.

Wiegert: Why did he move stuff around?

Brendan: I don't know.

Brendan: That he had the key in his hand and he dropped it to answer the phone.

Wiegert: And then what?

Brendan: And then he walked into the living room and sat down by the computer and talked to whoever was on the phone.

Wiegert: Where did he drop the key?

Brendan: By the dresser.

Wiegert: And you saw that happen?

Brendan: Yeah.

Wiegert: Did he ever pick it up?

Brendan: No.

Wiegert: Who was he talking to on the phone?

Brendan: I don't know.

Wiegert: On November 2nd, you were at his house. What were you guys talking about that day?

Brendan: Well, he was asking me what my future plan was.

Wiegert: Did you guys talk about Teresa at all?

Brendan: No.

Wiegert: Come on, you just… killed a girl and you didn't talk about it at all? I don't believe that. You told me he was going to get rid of that key. What was he gonna do with the key? Why did he go get the key that day?

Brendan: 'Cause he was gonna get rid of it.

Wiegert: Get rid of what?

Brendan: The key.

5. Teresa's bones were planted by Steven's home.

Bones were found in three locations: Steven Avery's burn pit, Bobby Dassey's burn barrel and in a burn pit along the property line of the Avery compound in an adjacent quarry, just over a quarter of a mile away.

Despite the bizarre distribution of the bones, the prosecution procured several witnesses to implicate Steven Avery. Under Strategy 5: Pay Expert Witnesses to Lie, I show how the prosecution obtained experts and why their testimonies were meaningless and harmful.

One of the state's witnesses was Leslie Eisenberg, a forensic anthropologist. She claimed that Steven's burn pit was the primary burn site because a fragment of almost every bone in the human body was there. She suspected that two bone fragments found in the quarry were derived from human pelvic bone. She added that bone breakage would have occurred if the bones had been transported from another location. She said that it was highly unlikely that the bones were not burned in Steven's burn pit.

Another witness for the state was Rodney Pevytoe, an employee of the Arson Bureau at the Wisconsin Department of Justice. In Steven's burn pit, he said he found wiring from more than five steel-belted radial tires, with bone fragments "inside the wire, deeply inside of it in some cases… to the point where I actually had to physically pull apart the wire in order to get in there." He believed that the bones could not have been thrown on top of the wire after having been burned. They had been burned with the tires found in the burn pit. He stated that the average tire can generate twice the amount of British Thermal Units than an average home furnace does, and that the polyurethane foam found in the van seat also burned in the fire is referred to as "solid gasoline" by fire investigators.

Steven Avery detractors have jumped on this testimony to claim that Steven burned Teresa's body in his fire pit with the help of tires and polyurethane foam; however, this would have taken several hours and caused a noxious stink in the neighbourhood. The findings by Pevytoe are not suspicious because Steven did burn tires in his pit. It's suspicious that the bones were never tested for the presence of accelerants that would have left a residue or chemical trace such as that left by a burning tire and that, as of this writing, Zellner has been denied access to the bones for testing.

Also held against Steven were implements found near the fire with evidence of charring and oxidation. A rake supposedly had wires from steel-belted tires in its teeth. A spade and screwdriver could have been used to splinter bones. Even the soil was described as consistent with what soil looks like after being exposed to the oils from burning tires.

Detractors have theorised that Steven burned Teresa in the fire pit. He chopped up some of the bones, and moved larger pieces into a burn barrel hoping to burn them further. After breaking down the bones in the burn barrel, he ended up with two larger pelvis bones that he disposed of in the quarry, where he mixed them with animal bones as camouflage.

Common sense debunks these theories and the expert witness statements. If Steven had burned Teresa and moved her bones, why would he have left most of the bones in his own burn pit? The expert witnesses insisted that Teresa had been burned right outside Steven's home, yet the prosecution in Steven's and Brendan's trials could offer no explanation as to why some of the bones were moved to other locations.

Netflix omitted that a Canadian expert on cremains testified at Steven's trial about the difficulty of burning a body in an open fire. With the high heat used at a crematorium, a body takes several hours to burn. To get the desired result from an open fire would have taken up to sixteen hours and required constant vigilance and stoking. There was no evidence of any such prolonged fire, only a bonfire.

As the fragments in Steven's barrel had come from all over Teresa's body, and there was no evidence of him creating a fire hot enough to cause such bone damage, Buting has stated that he believes the bones were burned at another location, scooped into a barrel and dumped on Steven's property.

Some researchers have challenged the validity of the testing of the bones. I received an email from a fellow *Making a Murderer* sleuth Kilauea:

Facts Concerning the Bones:

Only 60% of Teresa's bones were recovered. Most were found in Steven's burn pit. A few larger bones were found in the burn barrel along with a burned-up cell phone. Only a couple of pieces of bone were found in the quarry pit, which were identified as female pelvic bones.

There was enough muscle material left on the bones taken from Steven's burn pit and the burn barrel for Sherry Culhane to DNA test. Due to the degraded nature of the tissue, only 7 of 16 genetic markers could be matched. Culhane testified that this is 1 in a billion. Prosecution claimed this absolutely proved it to be Teresa.

Some studies back this up, but real world tests show 12 to 13 out of 16 only gives 1 in 65,000. The FBI only enters DNA info into CODIS (the system that helped track Gregory

Allen in the Beerntsen case) if 9 or more markers out of 16 can be determined. YouTube sleuth Casey Martinez remarked that 7 out of 16 only proves that the donor is a 4-legged animal, but I've heard real life stats that 7 out of 16 is about 1 out of 100 at best. Calumet County also sent samples of the tissue to the FBI. The only conclusion the FBI could make was that Teresa could not be excluded. This did not keep Calumet County Sheriff Jerry Pagel from stating that the FBI had definitively matched the bones to Teresa.

No DNA was found on the bones from the quarry pit, and they were only tied to the other bones because of consistent burn patterns and discoloration of the bones found in the other two locations. No test was ever done for accelerants, such as gas, diesel or rubber from burned tires. If this had been done, it might have pointed to the method and possibly another location of cremation.

When Teresa's car was found on Nov 5, Earl Avery was the only family member still at the Salvage Yard as the rest of the Averys were at a family cabin ninety miles away in Crivitz. Law enforcement secured the scene with lighting and armed guards. The bones in the barrel were discovered first, then the burn pit second. This was about Nov 9 or 10, and soon after the pelvic bones were discovered at the quarry pit.

Standard operating procedure is to immediately call a medical examiner or a coroner. The Manitowoc coroner was not called. She learned of the discovery of the bones from the TV news. She immediately grabbed supplies and went to the Averys. Manitowoc County Sheriff's Department would not allow her on the scene, citing that they were not allowing any Manitowoc officials to take part in the investigation due to the conflict of interest concerning the ongoing civil suit brought about by Steven.

Speculation is that law enforcement was up to no good,

and knew the coroner would not play ball because of a prior incident. Months before, it's alleged that Manitowoc County Sheriff's Department had been despatched to a late-night party, where someone was either dead or passed out in the street. When the Manitowoc County Sheriff's Department arrived, they accidentally ran over the victim. They wanted the coroner to claim that the death had happened prior to their arrival, but the coroner put the time of death as undetermined.

Reports say no professionals were called for the exhumation of the pit. Arson investigator Agent Pevytoe was called. Calumet County had taken over. When Pevytoe showed up, he checked in with Calumet Sheriff Rick Reimer. Pevytoe testified that he, Reimer, and one other man preliminarily sifted through the burn pit on their hands and knees.

Reimer's own account in Calumet County's written report stated that the recovery was accomplished using two skid loaders, like mini-bulldozers. He never mentioned being on his hands and knees. There is a local long distance helicopter shot shown on TV showing one of the skid loaders pouring out dirt and rubble from the pit onto a level piece of lawn, and a sheriff going through it with a steel rake. This of course would potentially destroy evidence.

Agent Pevytoe testified that five steel-belted radials were found in the pit and could have been used to accelerate the fire. I watched YouTube video of someone burning a steel-belted radial. Yes, it burned furiously, but only for about fifteen minutes. Keep in mind, you would need enough fuel to evaporate about twenty gallons of water, and more fuel to incinerate 40% of the bones. And even more fuel taking into consideration the inefficiency of an outdoor pit. It's estimated that if burned in an open pit, it would take at least ten hours of constantly adding fuel and stirring the remains.

The Calumet County coroner was eventually called, but

he claimed he was only called to provide sifting equipment and gloves. He said he normally takes pictures of the site, but didn't in this case because the site had been altered.

No photos were taken to document the bones in the pit, either before, during or after. The exhumation was not done with a string grid system, whereby strings are placed like an XY graph over the site. Small hand trowels and paint brushes are then used to recover and clean evidence without damaging it. Where each fragment is found is documented, possibly proving by the placement of the bones whether they were burned there, or placed there randomly after the fact. None of these procedures were followed.

Fact vs Fiction:

Forty percent of the bones were not found. This indicates that either the fire was hot enough to consume 40% or the body was cremated elsewhere and only 60% was moved. Can we consider the body was cremated elsewhere to the point that only 60% was left and all the bones were moved?

At the very least, this indicates that it would be unlikely the initial burn site was Steven's pit due to the extreme heat and time needed to reduce Teresa's body to this state. It's speculated that a fire that size in Steven's pit would have scorched the garage, at least leaving a residue.

Scott Tadych claimed he saw a fire at Steven's that night, but he gave multiple accounts of how large the fire was ranging from three feet to ten. Scott nor anyone else ever stated they smelled anything out of the ordinary. Holocaust survivors claim you can smell the nasty and distinct odour of a burning body from a great distance.

Small animal bones were found at both pits. This is important because when Teresa was incinerated to that state, animal bones would have burned to nothing first. Reddit users surmise that the quarry pit was not the initial site, as too many small animal bones were there. This though is inconclusive.

I had believed the original site was the quarry pit, but after reading what it really takes to reduce a body to that state, I am not so convinced. It would have required a crematorium, a smelter or a cow incinerator. Some farms in the area had cow incinerators to get rid of diseased cow carcasses.

Only one tooth was found in Steven's pit. Actually, two fragments. Teresa's dentist took the two fragments and managed to fit them back to one tooth. He claimed the tooth was consistent with one of Teresa's, but wouldn't testify that it was conclusive.

The teeth are the hardest to burn to nothing. The absence of the rest of Teresa's teeth suggests that she was cremated elsewhere.

Prosecution surmised that Steven pulled all but one of her teeth out, or he went through the pit afterward and removed her teeth to avoid identification. It's one thing to burn a body, but it takes a special kind of monster to pull the teeth out of the head of a corpse.

At least in Brendan's case, they claimed that Steven shot Teresa twice in the head, eight or nine times in the torso, in the garage. If this were true, there would be up to ten more bullets at the original burn site. Even if melted, they still would have been in the pit and would have been difficult if not impossible to have been removed from the pit, but easily detected later with a metal detector.

Since Brendan recanted his confession, the prosecution in Steven's case decided not to pursue the story of the shooting in the garage. However, they did state that Steven cremated her in his pit, but only after assaulting her and putting her body in the back of her RAV4 for some unknown reason. This would have been difficult for Steven to do, as the key found was a valet key and only worked in the driver's door and ignition. It didn't open the rear hatch door. I believe that Mike Halbach had gone through his sister's room and took the key, eventually getting the key to Colborn and eventually to Lenk, who did the drop behind the small bookcase. Lenk probably checked that the key fit the door, but was unaware it was a valet key.

I believe that the bones are Teresa's. Even if you discount the theory that she was burned at the quarry, I still believe she was cremated elsewhere and moved to Steven's pit via the barrel. This was all done to incriminate Steven, the obvious patsy. Law enforcement had the place on lock-down from Nov 5. It would have been difficult to plant the bones after that due to the constant attention at the site. It's possible, but there's a greater chance of being seen, or more people being complicit if not a conspiracy.

It's more likely that the bones were placed there between Nov 1 and 5, before the discovery of Teresa's car. I know everyone but Earl left for the cabin sometime between the evening of Nov 4 and the morning of Nov 5. Whoever placed the bones in Steven's pit would have to be comfortable with the scene, and not be out of place if seen. Given the time line and opportunity, I believe someone local planted the bones shortly after Steven left for the cabin, and before the discovery of Teresa's car – a window of perhaps twelve hours. It would only take a few minutes to spread the bones and mix them in a bit with the tires and such.

Amanda Knox's case has similarities, including bogus DNA evidence. An overzealous prosecutor who fancied himself as Sherlock Holmes triggered an emotional reaction with a narrative of wild sex parties turning violent. Amanda claimed to be at her boyfriend's house on the evening of the murder. A knife in her boyfriend's house had Amanda's DNA on its handle, and traces of her roommate's DNA on its blade. Amanda could not explain this. The highest court to review her case determined that the lab responsible for the DNA testing was simultaneously testing other items with her roommate's DNA on it while testing the knife. Cross contamination could not be ruled out. She was exonerated.

The strategy of planting evidence was successful in helping to convict two innocent people, but thanks to scientific advancements, the tainted evidence may ultimately get Steven freed. This was explained in detail by Kathleen Zellner during an August 2016 press conference:

"I filed a motion for new scientific testing on the Steven Avery case. We're requesting to test dozens of items from the crime scene. The testing spans all the way from radio carbon-14 testing, DNA methylation, body identification testing, new DNA testing: testing of items that were previously tested with new DNA methods. Micro-trace testing different items to detect whether there were contaminates on those items so we can determine whether or not the items in evidence were planted.

"I think this will be the most comprehensive testing motion ever filed in the State of Wisconsin. Probably one of the most comprehensive motions ever filed in the United States. We're using scientists from Stockholm, Sweden, Vienna, Austria, California, Illinois. So, we got a large number of scientists that will be doing the testing. We have completed testing on items that we don't need to request from Calumet County... So, procedurally, what's going on is the motion that's filed today will stay the appeal that's pending in Wisconsin appellate court. That appeal was filed pro se by Mr Avery and does not involve the... new issues we want to raise with the court.

"So, we're going to file a post-conviction petition as soon as we get these test results... Most wrongful conviction cases, I would say almost all of them, are not overturned on direct appeal. They're overturned at the post-conviction stage. So, that's our plan. That's how we will proceed. I know there was confusion about the appeal on Monday, but we have to have these test results combined with the investigation we've already done. So, that's where we're at. This is the motion. We have copies of it. It's got exhibits attached."

"Can you talk about the procedural aspect of this?" a journalist asked. "This isn't a done deal. You have to get a judge to [approve it]?"

"Oh, we already have a court order from 2007. Judge Willis very wisely entered a DNA order saying that any future DNA testing that was done, that the defendant wanted to have done, could be done. So, that's step one. Step two is under the Wisconsin statute. Typically, the state would have to pay for the testing. That's not going to happen here. The defence – we're paying for the testing. So, that's already done.

"We foresee absolutely no problems getting this testing done. Because, if you think about it, no one who's guilty would ever allow this extensive testing to be done. From fibres to contaminates to DNA to blood agents: all of those things are going to be done in this. I think the thing you most want to take away with this is to read the motion. No one who's guilty would ever allow this to happen. Because these tests are going to establish definitively the age of the blood in the victim's vehicle. So, we are going to know through radio carbon or DNA methylation whether the blood in the RAV was planted from the '96 vial.

"In addition to that, there were many, many items that should had been DNA tested that weren't. There was presumptive DNA testing done. There was not confirmatory DNA testing done. So, for us, the case is amazing how much forensic evidence there is that can be tested. For the public, I think that it also will be very encouraging because we're going to find out one way or the other was the evidence planted. And we're also going to be able to get test results that we believe will completely exonerate Mr Avery.

"The other thing we're going to do, and the petition is, we're going to lay out all of our investigation that we have done that will point to a third party. So, that was not successfully done at the trial level. So, I think the most reassuring thing is that we are going to get to the bottom of who killed Teresa Halbach. And we currently believe that we will establish it was not Steven Avery."

"What have you learned from the testing you've done already?"

"Yeah, we're not going to disclose that until we do the post-conviction petition. But, I can tell you that the testing we've already done will establish Mr Avery's innocence. But we are going to do the whole thing. We're going to do every conceivable test. We've been contacted by scientists all over the world, volunteering, offering us ideas. And now we've got it pinned down to the testing we need to do to determine once and for all was the evidence in the vehicle planted. Was the DNA on the bullet planted? Was the car key planted? Was the DNA on the car key planted? We're going to be able to answer all of those questions because it's been almost ten years since the verdict and there have been really huge developments in forensic science."

"How long do you think this will take?"

"Probably about three months. Maybe less. Some of it's going to be done really rapidly..."

"Is the blood in the car the key for you? Is there one bit of evidence that's key to you?"

"Well you know what the contention is. The planted evidence is the blood in the car. It's Mr Avery's DNA that shows up on the magically appearing car key. It was also her DNA on the bullet. We're requesting these ballistic tests that will establish whether the bullet, the fragment, even came from the shells Mr Avery had. So, what's great about this case is all the testing is out there. It's all developed. It's all validated. So, we can take the mystery out of this mystery, and we think we know what the answer will be."

"What are you doing next? You said you're going to see Mrs Avery?"

"Yeah, I am..."

"Do you just have one suspect in mind or are you looking at multiple suspects?"

"In fairness, yeah, we are looking at multiple people, but we are narrowing it down, so..."

"Would you like to say something to the Avery family group [on Facebook]?"

"Oh, yeah. Just that we're excited. This is going to answer everything. It's testing that wasn't done, testing that didn't exist at the time. But we are going to exhaust it when we go back through. Many of the swabs weren't tested. Presumptive testing was done.

Presumptive blood testing wasn't done. Now we can do confirmatory tests with the Carbon-14 we are going to be able to – within a year – date this blood. So, we can answer that."

"If the tests come back and shows the blood is from 2005?"

"Gee, that will be the risk that we're taking. Every client I represent I tell them, 'You want to be innocent when you hire me because I'll get to the bottom of it with the testing.' And so, Mr Avery has encouraged us to do all of these tests. He is just like every other innocent client I've represented, where he has no hesitation about it. But remember there are a lot of things planted in this. So, we're not just talking blood. We're talking buccal swabs. There's a lot of different variations on this. So, that's the problem – if you do something or if you did plant the evidence – that science is going to catch up to you. That's what we're going to see in this."

"Does Brendan Dassey's case have any impact on this?"

"It does, yes. Particularly on the hood latch. Because the court really zeroed in on Dassey's testimony about the hood latch. Because remember that the hood-latch swab was not taken until March, not tested until April. After the confession on March 1, then they go back and they get the swab and then they test that swab. We're going to be able to, I think, show that that's saliva on the hood latch. So now the test exists so you can tell if it's saliva or blood or just epithelial cells. There's no such thing as sweat DNA. So, we've got, I think, the best scientists in the country and they are going to answer all of those questions."

"Any idea how long these tests are going to take?"

"I think they should take about three months. One of the tests is going to be done in Vienna, Austria. But we're thinking on that, the actual test, the Carbon-14 test phase – [they] have to use a mass spectrometry machine – will probably take about two months to take the data and results from it."

"So, you're going to have to wait until everything gets back before Steve can even be considered to be released?"

"The procedure on post-conviction: OK, so Steve's been in

ten years from this conviction. Almost ten years. So, to undo a conviction like this, there's 27,000 pages of records. There's many, many swabs that were never tested. So, we've had to go back through everything, and we've had to find the scientists who can go through this very carefully because you don't get repeated chances to do this. So, we've been working about seven months on it.

"Some post-convictions last a few years. We don't anticipate that because we have so much forensic evidence with us. So, this one I think will go – I haven't had one that has lasted over three years, so I don't imagine it will take this long once I get the tests. Because, he never made any incriminating statements, all right? The [Dassey] confession has been invalidated. So, you're down to the evidence at the crime scene. You're down to the key, the hood latch, the blood in the RAV and the bullet."

"Have you talked to Steve today?"

"Yes. Today, no. Yesterday, yes."

"What did he have to say?"

"He was thrilled. He's absolutely thrilled. He can't wait for the results…"

"Why did you decide to take this case?"

"I decided to take it because I knew that he's innocent. I thought when I watched the documentary, which I did – Steven Avery had contacted me in 2011 when I was on trial in Washington in a civil rights case. But I decided to take it because I think that the crime scene doesn't make sense. A couple other things that make absolutely no sense. There's no mixture of blood in the car. We've never seen that before. None of my forensic scientists have. You have all of Steven Avery's blood in the front, all of the victim's blood in the back. He's supposedly cut and he throws her in the car. So, my scientists were saying they've never seen that where there isn't a mixture of the victim's blood along with the alleged perpetrator.

"The bones were moved. That was admitted. There was a human pelvis found over in the quarry. The bones were in different spots. The body was not burned whole. It's not possible to do that. So, you've got the same bone in three different places. You've got only 30% of the bones recovered. You have twenty-nine of the teeth never recovered. The bones look like they were planted. The property was closed down. The coroner from Manitowoc was not allowed on the property and actually was not notified it was a murder. That violates the Wisconsin statute.

"So, when I looked at the case, I could see all kinds of problems, but I could also see a lot of evidence that could be tested. Evidence that could be retested. And that we could determine if the evidence was planted. So, I thought, *Great cause.* You know, *I want to be involved in it.* I met with him eighteen times. I'm positive that he's innocent. I won't have to prove he's innocent, but I would like to because I absolutely believe that he's innocent."

"What can you tell us about the suspect?"

"Nothing. Nothing. Not until I file."

"Procedurally, does this federal hearing, do you know where [it stands]?"

"It depends on whether the attorney general agrees to the testing. As I said, there's already an order in place, so there's nothing to talk about on the DNA testing. Judge Willis entered that in 2007. So, that's done. The rest of the testing, I would think, they would want that done. Because it gives them the opportunity to [find out] whether the evidence is planted or not and we're paying for it..."

On January 15, 2017, journalist John Ferak summed up several significant issues with the evidence in a *USA Today Network* article titled "Avery case in lull, but things will heat up."

Ferak pointed out:

Cell phone records obtained by Zellner have shown the time of Teresa's departure from Steven Avery's home. "Her last call-forwarded message at 2:41 pm occurred," Zellner stated in a court document, "when her cell phone was still powered on and registered. That call pinged off the Whitelaw Tower, which was approximately 13.1 miles from the Avery Salvage Yard."

The videotape of the flyover of the salvage yard appears to have been heavily edited. It purposefully pans away from the area where Teresa's RAV4 was found the next day. This strengthens Wilmer Siebert's claim that the RAV4 was absent during the flyover, and subsequently planted.

Zellner has homed in on the amount of time that investigators spent searching for Teresa's remains in various quarries, including one owned by Joshua Radandt, who told the police that he saw a large fire on Steven Avery's property at approximately 4:30 pm on Halloween.

According to the Redditor MsMinxster, "Josh's younger brother, who helps run the family business, is married to the only granddaughter of a 27-year veteran of the Manitowoc County Sheriff's Department (a former captain of the detective unit and deputy inspector). This retired detective was around for Steven Avery's 1985 frame-up, and though he didn't participate in the shenanigans, the whole corruption crew owed him for keeping his mouth shut at the time."

Journalist John Ferak speculated that Teresa's body may have been found buried, and then dug up and dismembered in one of the quarries. He pointed out that cadaver and tracking dogs were more active on Kuss Road and the quarries than at Steven's home. One bloodhound traced Teresa's scent to a concrete stoop at the south-entry door of a red house trailer on the Radandt deer camp property. Of course, Ken Kratz either omitted or downplayed this evidence.

STRATEGY 5: PAY EXPERT WITNESSES TO LIE

When court is theatre, the state needs to hire the most talented actors to put on the best show in town. Expert witnesses fall into this category. These miscreants get paid large sums of taxpayers' money – sometimes tens of thousands per court appearance – to say whatever the state desires. There is even a word for it: testi-lying. Expert witnesses usually dazzle the jury with academic credentials and scientific jargon. Of course, they are available to the defence, too. Masters of persuasive speaking, they will certify the view of whoever is bidding the most – prosecution or defence – even though the views are opposing.

The best expert witnesses lack any conscience. For the love of money, they are willing to lie on the stand even if it means an innocent person could get the death penalty. If that sounds far-fetched, then consider the case of Ray Krone, a death-row exoneree whose life my lawyer, Alan Simpson, fought to save.

On December 29, 1991, in Phoenix, Arizona, the body of a 36-year-old waitress was found stabbed to death in the men's restroom at the bar where she worked. There were bite marks on her neck and breast. Saliva was found on her body that had come from someone with the most common blood type, but no DNA tests were performed.

The victim had told a friend that a regular at the bar – a postman called Ray Krone – had helped her to close the bar the previous night, so the police asked Ray to make a Styrofoam impression of his teeth. His teeth didn't match the bite marks on the victim, but on December 31, 1991, Ray was arrested and charged with murder, kidnapping and sexual assault.

Ray maintained his innocence. The footprints, fingerprints,

palm prints and hair found at the crime scene didn't match his. He'd been asleep at home at the time of the murder. Trusting in the justice system, he figured that the truth would prevail at his trial and the terrible mistake of his arrest would be rectified.

The authorities didn't need Ray's teeth to match. All they needed was an expert witness to say that they matched. A bite-mark expert received over $50,000 to testi-lie – over ten times the $5,000 Ray received to defend himself. The expert swore under oath that the wounds on the victim could only have been made by Ray's teeth.

The trial lasted for three and a half days. In 1992, Ray was found guilty and sentenced to death. In the courtroom, his mother sobbed and screamed in anguish. The jury stated that the guilty verdict was entirely based on the testimony of the expert witness.

Ray was on death row for ten years. My lawyer, Alan Simpson, obtained a court order that forced the authorities to release evidence found at the scene for a DNA test. The test proved that the saliva on the victim's tank top had not come from Ray. It had come from a sex offender who had lived near the bar, and had ended up in prison for sexually assaulting and choking a 7-year-old. Ray was finally released.

The testimony of the same bite-mark expert put another innocent man away for longer than Ray. Robert Lee Stinson was accused of raping and murdering an elderly woman in Wisconsin. The expert claimed that marks on the victim matched Stinson's teeth "to a reasonable degree of scientific certainty." Robert Lee Stinson served 23 years before DNA testing exonerated him in 2009.

The expert was never held accountable for testi-lying. As usual, the Wisconsin justice system refused to take any responsibility. In the end, the Wisconsin Supreme Court concluded "that the evidence presented was sufficient to convince the jury, to a moral certainty, that there was no reasonable hypothesis of Stinson's innocence." The law prevented Robert Lee Stinson from suing the expert, setting a precedent for other experts to lie without risking any punishment.

At the time of Steven Avery's second case, the authorities still had in their possession a vial of his blood from his first wrongful conviction in '1985. *Making a Murderer* showed that the vial had been tampered with. Whoever had accessed the blood had done so surreptitiously. The prosecution didn't want the jury to know about the vial. On January 3, 2007, the prosecution filed a "Motion to Exclude Blood Vial; or in the Alternative to Analyze the Vial of Blood." This motion was filed on the basis that there was no evidence of foul play by the police, only speculation.

If the vial were to be admitted by the judge, then the prosecution wanted the blood to be tested for EDTA. To preserve the blood, a chemical had been added called EDTA. If the bloodstains found in Teresa Halbach's car were Steven's, as alleged by Ken Kratz, then a test showing the absence of EDTA would surely prove that the bloodstains had not been planted.

"Too many allegations," said Milwaukee County assistant district attorney Norm Gahn, "have been made against people who are public servants or law enforcement officers, and we must have the opportunity to have the vial and do the testing that is suitable to meet the defence. There will have to be assumptions by the jury that some law enforcement officer had access to this vial somehow. This isn't a case of negligence we're talking about here. It's an intentional crime committed by LEOs [law enforcement officers] and possibly along with the clerk of courts. There are so many collateral issues that this evidence lacks probative value and would be a waste of time and confusion for the jury. The state is asking the court to not allow the evidence to come in."

"The blood evidence," Dean Strang said, "goes directly to the integrity of some of the most damning evidence against Avery that the state intends to offer: the small amounts of blood that the state will say were found in Teresa's vehicle. Mr Avery has been saying from the beginning to anybody with a microphone and TV camera, initially in early November 2005, that if his blood is in the Toyota RAV4, somebody planted it."

On February 2, 2007, the judge allowed the vial as evidence.

Norm Gahn defended deputies Colborn and Lenk: "We have

a responsibility to be able to restore their good names. They've protected this community and put their lives on the line. They are both good decent family men. They deserve to have their reputations protected. The best we can do is to allow us the opportunity to test the vial of blood."

With the trial only weeks away, Gahn stated why the prosecution had only just requested EDTA testing. "While the defence knew about the blood vial at the very latest in July, they waited until December sixth to put this on us."

"Mr Gahn is being disingenuous," Buting said, "if he is comparing this in any way to DNA, where you can look at one, look at the other and say, 'Yes, there is a match.' There is no such test."

"If there is probative evidence," Judge Willis said, "that can be derived from testing the blood in the vial, I think it's important to both parties that such evidence be presented to the jury regardless of which party the evidence supports."

With no such test considered reliable anywhere in the world, all Gahn had to do now was to get an expert witness to manufacture, in record time, the test and the results desired by the prosecution. Anything is possible with taxpayers' money.

The expert witness the state procured, Dr LeBeau, commenced by mesmerising the jury with his credentials: Unit Chief of the Chemistry Unit at the FBI Laboratory in Quantico, Virginia; a Ph.D. in toxicology from the University of Maryland, four years of postdoctoral work at St Louis University, a directorship at the Society of Forensic Toxicologists, member of the International Association of Forensic Toxicologists, member of the American Academy of Forensic Sciences, publication of numerous peer-reviewed professional and scientific articles…

Having developed the test himself for the presence of EDTA in the blood found on Teresa Halbach's RAV4, LeBeau stated, "I took the results and compiled them, formed an opinion as to what they meant, wrote the report myself, issued the report after it had been reviewed by an independent scientist that works within my unit, and, of course, came here today to testify."

LeBeau's definition of an independent review was to have one of his underlings stamp approval upon his report.

"Have you ever testified as an expert before?"

"Yes, I have."

"And how many times?"

"I don't keep track of the numbers, but it's roughly forty or fifty times I have testified."

"Have you ever been rejected as an expert in your field?"

"No, I have not."

Asked how he got involved in the case, LeBeau said, "I received a phone call from the District Attorney's Office asking if we had a method that would allow us to determine if EDTA was present in a bloodstain or not. Through the course of the conversation, we were asked if we would be willing to work this case for the state. And we agreed to do the work on this case."

"And why would the FBI be concerned about a case that involves allegations of planting evidence by law enforcement officials?"

"Well, one of the many type of cases that the FBI investigates are corruption by public officials. So, it's one of the areas we consider to be a very serious accusation for two reasons. If there's a crooked public official out there, we want to make sure they get off the streets. And, likewise, if an innocent public official is being wrongly accused of something, we want to at least try to set the record straight to ensure the public's trust in that organisation or that individual."

"OK," Buting said, "can you show me anywhere in that request [from the State of Wisconsin] where it says our purpose is also to find out if there might be any evidence that there's a corrupt cop in Manitowoc County?"

"No. I don't see anything of that nature, but I can elaborate if you like."

Heading off any elaboration, Buting posed that the FBI had got involved to "eliminate the allegation that this file was used to plant evidence. Isn't that true?"

"No, sir. If I can elaborate, I will be happy to explain."

"You can elaborate later, sir... Could you tell the court what it was that was sent to you?"

"We received a number of different items. They were swabs collected from a vehicle, a... Toyota RAV4, as well as control swabs and a tube of blood from Steven Avery."

"And what type of instrument did you use in testing these items?"

"We used the LC/MS/MS instrument."

He then proceeded at length to blind the jury with the scientific details of mass spectrometers, analytical chemistry and LC/MS/MS technology.

"Did you find EDTA in the tube of blood of Steve Avery?"

"Yes, we did."

"Did you find EDTA in any of the three bloodstain swabs from Teresa Halbach's RAV4?"

"No, we did not."

"Based upon your training and experience, and based upon your test results using the LC/MS/MS technique, and based upon all of the data and compilations that you reviewed, and basically the entire case file that you have: do you have an opinion, to a reasonable degree of scientific certainty, whether the bloodstains from Teresa Halbach's RAV4 that you tested came from the vial of blood from Steven Avery, which was in the Manitowoc County Clerk of Court's Office?"

"I do have an opinion on it."

"What is that opinion?"

"My opinion is that the bloodstains did not come from that tube of blood."

In the cross-examination, Buting started by poking holes in LeBeau's EDTA credentials. "You said you authored or co-authored fifteen to twenty articles."

"That's correct."

"How many of those articles did not involve drug-facilitated rape?"

"Seventeen."

"And how many of those involved post-mortem fluids, analysis of post-mortem fluids? Do you know what I'm talking about, from deceased bodies?"

"Yes, I know what you are talking about."

Buting pointed out that LeBeau's speciality, as indicated by his publications and presentations, was drug-facilitated sexual assaults and post-mortem fluids.

"Have you ever in your life been asked to give a presentation on EDTA interpretation in bloodstains?"

"No, I have not."

"You are not a sought-after presenter on that particular topic, are you?"

"No, sir. I'm not."

"Have you ever before testified in a court of law as an expert who is giving opinions about the interpretation of EDTA and bloodstains?"

"No."

Buting made the case that EDTA testing was considered so unreliable that it was rarely used. The last time it had been used by the FBI was in the case of OJ Simpson, twenty years earlier. In that case, EDTA was detected, which hurt the prosecution as it fit the narrative of the police framing OJ. The FBI was criticised.

"As a matter of fact, you mentioned, so the FBI is not embarrassed, the FBI was embarrassed by the EDTA stain test in the OJ Simpson case, weren't they?"

"I would disagree."

"Well, they never did it again, did you?"

"We were never asked to do it again. We don't control the cases that come into our laboratory. Law enforcement agencies ask us for their assistance and if we are able to provide that assistance, we will... but if we were not asked to do a test, we don't have control over that."

"And, of course, defendants can't ask you to do tests, can they?"

"That's correct. We are a law enforcement agency. And the

funding that we get from the US Congress is to support law enforcement investigations."

"OK."

"You are aware, though, that, over the course of the year, the last decade, there have been some cases where defendants have sought to do some sort of EDTA test on bloodstains, right?"

"Yes, I am."

"Most often post-conviction cases, right?

"Yes."

"Like the Kevin Cooper case?"

"Yes."

"And would you agree with me that in every one of those cases that you have heard of, the government has been opposing the use or the protocols or the methods that a defendant has used to try and get EDTA stain evidence in, bloodstain evidence in?"

"I don't believe they were opposing the idea of testing a bloodstain for EDTA. My understanding – and I'm only aware of two cases – my understanding is they were opposing the approach that was taken by the scientist, that he didn't use good science. The techniques that he employed, the instrumental techniques, as we talked about in direct, these are techniques to identify chemicals. So, a chemical is a chemical."

"Sure."

"But if you don't apply good science to getting to that answer, that's what becomes in question. They weren't his... My understanding is, his approach was not a well validated approach."

"And his approach, when you say his, we're talking about Dr Kevin Ballard, right?" Buting said.

"That's correct."

"At the National, NMS, what's it called?"

"National Medical Services Lab?"

"That's correct."

"You disagreed with his protocol?"

"I didn't see his protocol. I disagreed with the approach–"

"OK."

"–that he testified to in the Cooper case, I believe it was."

"OK. Can you tell us of any lab anywhere in the world that has ever used the protocol that your colleagues published in Exhibit 436?"

"There would be no way to know that. We don't… There's not a data base that people have to report to us if they are choosing to take a journal in a public – an article out of a public journal and use it in their own laboratory."

"Well."

"We would never know if they used it or not."

"Well, let me just give you an example. Oftentimes, people publish, in fact, there are some articles you cited, on the use of LS/MS/MS for a particular technique, right?"

"Yes."

"And oftentimes in academia, what researchers will do is, they will take one test that's published and they will test it, report back whether they get the same results, right?"

"That's common when you are dealing with, like, a breakthrough in a new area of science."

"Sure."

"You might have multiple researchers from different research teams working independently, yet together, to prove that a new scientific hypothesis is actually working as they expect."

"Sure. That's what science is, right, the whole idea that you can replicate someone else's study?" Buting said.

"That is part of it, yes."

"And can you tell me of any article anywhere of anybody who ever studied and replicated or tried to replicate the test that's – or the study that's reported in Exhibit 436?"

"Yes."

"Who?"

"Me."

"Oh. OK. Anybody besides you?"

"Not that I know of."

LeBeau tried to regain some credibility for the test he had

developed in record time at the urgent request of the State of Wisconsin by claiming that "an independent group of scientists looks through all of the validation data and signs their name that they agree with the work that was done and the findings of the validation study."

But Buting was having none of it. "Let me stop you there for one second. A group of independent scientists: you are talking about FBI people?"

"That's right."

"Not outside independent labs, right?"

"That's correct."

"Not other academic researchers, right?"

"Yes, that's right."

"And this protocol, for instance, has not been peer reviewed like it would be if it's published like our Exhibit 436, right?"

"Well, the changes were very minor from off the published–"

"Sir."

"–protocol."

"This protocol, Exhibit 434, was – has not been peer reviewed by anybody outside of the FBI Lab. Is that right?"

"Sir, very few of our protocols are reviewed by anybody–"

"Judge–"

"–outside the FBI Laboratory."

"He's entitled to an answer to his question," the judge said.

"No, this was not peer reviewed by anyone outside of the FBI–"

"Thank you."

"–as it's written here."

"That's right. And that protocol did not arise out of any kind of ongoing research independent of this litigation, right?"

"I'm not sure I understand your question."

"The development of this protocol was not something that just came out of independent research your lab was doing on determining whether or not you could find EDTA in bloodstains."

"That is correct. This was generated specifically by the request to do the analysis of evidence in this case."

One of the things Buting enjoys about being a lawyer is that it forces him to become an expert in certain fields. Studying OJ's case, he discovered that the FBI had learned that EDTA wasn't used exclusively in blood tubes. Lots of common household products contain EDTA. The car cleaner Armorall contains a high concentration of EDTA. One of Armorall's uses is to keep dashboards shiny. When it comes to detecting EDTA, there is a limit of detection for the instrument and a limit of detection for the method. Government labs sometimes blur that distinction, and talk about them as if they are the same. In the OJ case, the FBI's level of detection in the method was so low that they picked up background EDTA from household products such as detergents and Armorall.

As Buting progressed with the frame-up defence, the prosecution demanded postponing the trial, so they could contact the FBI about EDTA testing. The FBI agreed to do the test, but as they hadn't done it in ten years, they said it needed a new protocol to validate it, which Buting translated to mean that they were going to come up with a new test with such a high limit of detection that no EDTA would be detected at all, including background EDTA like that detected during the OJ case.

After the judge had refused to postpone the trial, the prosecution suddenly announced that the FBI had agreed to develop and validate the test in approximately four to six weeks. They had agreed to stop everything, retool their machines and come up with a protocol before the trial was over.

When Buting objected that the defence didn't have any time to come up with their own tests or to test whether the protocol was valid, the prosecution responded that it would be validated and not to worry.

Buting anticipated that LeBeau wouldn't find any EDTA. On a Friday before the cross-examination of LeBeau – which had been scheduled for Monday – the prosecution had given Buting a stack of information about the FBI's EDTA testing and protocols. The defence scrambled around to try to find an expert to study the information to determine whether the test was valid.

On a Monday, they shipped the information to Janine Arvizu, who worked in Albuquerque, New Mexico, as a laboratory quality auditor. She dropped all her other work, and by Thursday she was testifying.

Out of the six stains sent to the FBI, only three had been tested. The FBI had opined that the three untested stains contained no EDTA based on the first three stains containing no EDTA. The FBI's official final report claimed that they had a low limit of detection. Janine determined that their claim was false and misleading. In theory, the FBI's instruments could go that low. They reached that limit by injecting pure EDTA into the machine. They then kept reducing the EDTA by half and re-injecting it. Finally, they reached a point where they could no longer detect it.

Janine saw that their calibration was problematic because in Steven Avery's case the EDTA was nine years old. No one knew whether EDTA would still be present in a vial of blood after nine years. Environmentalists debate over how rapidly it deteriorates.

LeBeau had claimed that the limit of detection was so low that if there had been EDTA in Steven's blood samples it would have been detected.

Even more suspicious was that LeBeau had swabs of the stains and control swabs from areas that didn't have blood on them, so that the two could be compared. Some control swabs were taken from the dashboard. Teresa kept her RAV4 clean, yet no EDTA was detected in the control swabs – it should have arisen from cleaning products like in the OJ case.

Janine determined that the method's limit of detection was highly different from the instrument limit. The FBI never recorded their method limit. They didn't know their own limit because they had never tested it.

The samples they tested were extremely diluted. They extracted some of the dashboard stain by taking a swap with distilled water. The sample was dried. To extract it from the swab, they added more solution. It was centrifugally separated. Every step of the way, the sample got smaller and more diluted. Janine estimated that any EDTA in such a sample was 1/200 of what was in pure EDTA.

Some viewers of *Making a Murderer* found the parts about EDTA confusing. On the stand, Janine tried to simplify things:

"I do independent contracting for people who use analytical data and want to understand how reliable and how valid the data are." Her job involved going into labs to discern the validity of the data the labs were reporting.

"The people who use lab results," she said, "it's not like buying a pound of sugar or buying a pound of flour. Different laboratories produce different quality data. And so, if the data that are being used by a data user are real important and they make real important decisions based on those results, then they can hire an auditor to come in and look at the lab's operations and see whether or not the lab was operating in accordance with good scientific principles and had good quality control practices at the time the laboratory work was done.

"And so, over the course of my career, the majority of my work assessing data quality and looking at labs has been done for the federal government, because they are probably the biggest consumer of laboratory results. They use a lot of analytical results… and they make very important decisions based on those results, so it's real important to them to understand how reliable and how valid their data are…

"Experience has shown in the measurement-in-science business that the best way to ensure the reliability and validity of the results is to have a very rigorous quality assurance program in place." She added that, "It's really essential to understand exactly the scope of what you are trying to use the results for.

"So, on-site, I'm looking at everything from how they actually perform the manipulations; whether they use good laboratory practices; whether they seem to understand the principles of contamination control, which are so important in a laboratory; to looking at the heating, ventilating and air-conditioning system. I'm looking to see where the make-up vents provide air, to see whether that could be a potential contamination problem. I'm looking at how they set up instrumentation. I'm looking at the documentation maintained by the lab. I look at everything."

"You look at the, specifically, protocols. Is that something that you examine, consider and evaluate in the process of doing these lab audits you refer to?"

"Absolutely. Always read the protocols before going on-site to understand how they say they do their method, and then watch them and look at the written work that they generate to see whether they, in fact, followed their method. The nature of chemistry is such that it's so very important to follow protocols. For anytime that you deviate from a protocol, then you have got to make a note of it.

"It's a lot like a recipe. Again, if you don't follow the recipe exactly, then that chocolate cake isn't going to be as good as the one that grandma makes. But if grandma doesn't want to share her recipe, and she leaves out ingredients, or doesn't really follow hers exactly, you're not going to be able to reproduce her work.

"The same thing applies in the laboratory. As scientists, we want to be able to reproduce somebody else's work. That means they have to have a completely documented protocol and they have to follow it…"

Asked to identify a document, Janine stated, "That's a copy of the FBI Laboratory's report in this case."

"By?"

"Authored by Marc LeBeau."

"OK. And have you reviewed that report?"

"Yes."

"All right. And I'm going to show you what's Exhibit 434. And tell us what that is."

"This is a nine-page standard operating procedure by the FBI Laboratory that describes their procedure, their recipe for analysis of EDTA in dried bloodstains."

"OK. And the date of–"

"This particular procedure is dated 2/15/2007."

"OK. And then, also, Exhibit 446, can you identify that?"

"Well, without looking at every page, this looks like the package that I received for review in this case that consists of a letter from your office as well as all the materials received from the FBI Laboratory in this case."

"OK."

"It's about the right size."

"OK. Going to the report, do you have an opinion whether this protocol, as reported in the report… can determine, with scientific validity, whether – if a stain is tested for EDTA under this protocol, and not found, whether that – a conclusion can be given that it was not present in the stain?"

"I do have such a conclusion, and it's based on more than just the procedure, but the fact that a stain – EDTA is not detected in a stain, does not mean that EDTA was not present in the stain."

"OK. Do you have an opinion about whether if one tests three stains and gets some results, or lack of results, whatever, whether one can express an opinion about what may or may not be in three untested stains?"

"Well, I'm in the business of analytical chemistry, and we're not in the business of just making guesses about what might be in samples. We have instrumentation to test samples and that's how we determine results. There's no way for an analytical chemist to know what's in a sample unless we test it."

"All right. Going more particularly to the materials that you reviewed, let's talk about the protocol for a moment. It's 434, I believe. There's a section called scope. Does the protocol appear to be adequate for the scope as it's defined?"

"Yeah. It's a very short description of scope and it's an accurate description of the applicability of this method. It states that this procedure allows for the screening and confirmation of EDTA in suspected bloodstains. So, that's exactly what it does, it allows you to screen for EDTA in a bloodstain and to detect EDTA in a bloodstain. I will mention that that's probably the shortest description of method scope I have ever read."

"OK."

"They are generally much more – there's a little more scientific meat in it in terms of describing under what conditions and so forth."

"Does this protocol, as its designed, or reportedly designed here, you say that it – if one follows this recipe and there is EDTA present, that this protocol would allow one to detect it. Is that right?"

"To detect and identify it."

"OK. Is it also possible, from this protocol, to draw any conclusions, though, if one runs the tests and does not detect EDTA?"

"That's really the problem. The issue with this procedure is not whether or not it's a valid result. If you were actually detecting EDTA, this is a good method. If the results end up that you detect EDTA and you identify EDTA, that's a good indication that EDTA was present in that sample. The problem really occurs when EDTA is not detected in a bloodstain. And the problem in that regard is, from this method, I don't know whether that's simply because they didn't detect it or because it wasn't there. I can't tell the difference between those two for this method. I don't know, really, what their method detection limit is. So, I don't know whether they didn't see it or it wasn't there."

"OK. You mentioned method detection limit. Is there also something called instrument detection limit?"

"Yes."

"And as you look at this protocol – or I'm sorry – look at the report for a moment, on Page 2, where Mr LeBeau indicates that using the procedure employed in this case, EDTA is readily identified at a concentration of thirteen micrograms?"

"Milligrams per litre. The common term is parts per million."

"OK. As you go through his – the stack of data there that was provided to you, is that an instrumentation limit or is that a method limit?"

"From reviewing the data that appears to be an instrument detection limit. That is, they figure that out by starting out with a 100 PPM sample and they would inject that right into the instrument and see if they could see EDTA, and they did. So, they cut it in half, diluted it in half, and ran it again. When they ran 50, they still detected EDTA. And each time they cut it in half. When they ran 25, they detected EDTA. When they cut 25 in half, at 12.5, or 13, they still detected it. But when they cut that sample in half and cut it down to about six parts per million, they were not able to detect and identify EDTA. So, based on that, they drew the conclusion that their detection limit… was 13 parts per million. That, however, represents sort of the theoretical best case of injecting a sample directly into the instrument. It does not reflect the detection limit for going out and swabbing a stain and extracting the sample from that stain and diluting it before you get it into the instrument. Those are two different things. Instrument detection limits are usually very small. Method detection limits are larger. That's just sort of the natural order of things."

"OK. Well, focusing specifically on this type of a method detection limit, why would it be different? Why would you be able to detect a smaller amount if you just inject the sample directly into the machine versus if you have to go through the process of taking a dried stain, swabbing it, extracting that, diluting it, all of that? Why is there a difference?"

"The difference is really because there are so many other complicating factors associated with taking a real-world sample and getting it to the point where it's clean and pristine enough to be able to inject it into an instrument. In the case of a bloodstain, that sample is on a surface. It has to be removed from that surface, so it's swabbed. There may be interferences from the swab. They may not completely recover the stain. Then they try to extract the blood sample off of the swab. Extractions, generally, are not completely efficient. In some of the reference material in this case, some work done some years ago, extraction efficiencies were typically 90% or so, on a first run. It was quite common, if you do multiple extractions, to extract more DNA so – or more EDTA. So, in each step of the process, you will lose a little bit. There's issues that arise. And so, by the time you get to the instrument, your effective method detection limit is much higher."

"Is it possible to determine what the effective method limitation is, in this case, from the materials you reviewed?"

"No, it is not."

"Do you have an opinion whether it is the actual effective method limit of this – this test, to be able to detect EDTA in a bloodstain, is higher than 13 parts per million?"

"Yes, I do, and I believe that it is."

"Can you quantitate how much higher?"

"Unfortunately, that's a study that's best done empirically, by actually doing analytical work. Method detection limits are best determined using actual analytical work. I can infer some information from the data that were obtained in this case, but I can't just compute one from the data that are available."

"And looking at the data that is available in this stack, the validation tests that were done and those sorts of things, is there any indication that the FBI ever found out what the actual detection limit or method detection limit would be for this kind of a test?"

"No. There's no such indication in these data."

"OK. Well, what does that tell you about the use of this kind of a protocol?"

"This kind of protocol, there's basically two things that can happen when you run this kind of a method: either you detect EDTA or you don't. From an analytical perspective, the results either say, yes, we detected EDTA, or, no, we did not. This report makes it seem like those two outcomes only can arise from two conditions. And it makes it seem like if the answer is, yes, we detected EDTA in a bloodstain sample, then it kind of makes it seem like then that means it must have come from a tube of EDTA preserved blood. There was reference to the fact that the control samples that they took from the car were blank, so that's probably the more likely interpretation. The problems really come if the results from testing are, no, there is no EDTA present in those samples. Nothing there. We didn't see anything. The problem is, you just don't know whether EDTA – you didn't detect EDTA because there was none there or because your detection limit wasn't low enough to see it, even if it had been there. That's really the problem. So just because EDTA is not detected by the laboratory, doesn't mean that that blood sample came from somebody actively bleeding onto that spot. It still means that if your detection limit is out of sync with the samples in question, there could be EDTA in those samples from that blood tube. You just didn't see it."

"All right. Now, the next sentence in… Dr LeBeau's report talks about, that EDTA is also detectable when a 1-microliter drop of EDTA preserved blood is analysed. As you reviewed the data in that four- or five-inch package there, would you agree or disagree with that statement?"

"I disagree with that statement."

"And why is that?"

"Because in the results reported by the laboratory, if this statement says, I tested a 1-microliter drop of blood from a purple-topped tube, from an EDTA tube, and I detected it, the problem is – and that was done in this case – the problem is, they ran a 2-microliter drop of EDTA preserved blood on a spot, a more real-world kind of application, and they did not detect EDTA in this lab. Now, gosh, that might sound a little bit counterintuitive – what do you mean they could detect 1 microliter? – but they couldn't detect – they detected EDTA in a 1-microliter sample, but they didn't detect EDTA in a 2-microliter sample. If, in fact, the detection limit used by this laboratory was down around that level, that's – I just have to tell you, that's not an unexpected result. Sometimes you see it and sometimes you don't, if an element – if a compound is present near its detection limit. In fact, that's, essentially, the definition of a detection limit. It means that if it's present at that concentration, sometimes you'll see it and sometimes you won't. So, to state that he – that the lab is – that EDTA is detectable when a 1-microliter drop of preserved blood is analysed, is really not a true statement, even as evidenced by his own results, because he didn't detect it in a 2-microliter sample of blood."

Janine's testimony challenged the authenticity of the EDTA test results manufactured by LeBeau. One of her most important points was that just because EDTA is not detected in a stain does not mean that EDTA was not present in the stain. Under cross-examination, Janine was just as strong and convincing:

"What is the difference between a qualitative assay and a quantitative assay?" the prosecution asked.

"That's a very good question. A qualitative assay or qualitative measurement doesn't tell you how much of something is present. It simply detects it and identifies it. So, qualitatively, I can say that EDTA is present, but it says nothing about how much EDTA is present. In contrast, a quantitative assay tells you how much of something is present. There is an entirely different calibration protocol to get to how much of a given compound is present."

"And both are scientifically sound procedures?"

"Absolutely."

"And how would you characterize the FBI's protocol or testing methodology in this case?"

"This is a purely qualitative method."

"And that, again, is a valid scientific method of developing an analysis methodology?"

"Absolutely."

"Now, if you would please pick up the – their protocol, please. Do you have that?"

"The FBI's protocol?"

"Yes, please."

"Yeah. Yes. OK."

"And on Page 7, under Paragraph 14, Limitations, No. 8, the Limit of Detection, is it – it was your testimony that this was under a valid method for determining their limits of detection?"

"It's not a universally used method, but it's an appropriate means of getting to an instrument detection limit."

"And one that could be used in detecting the levels of EDTA, whether in a purple-topped tube or in a dried bloodstain?"

"No, the method that they used, that they referred to in this paragraph, is simply a means of determining an instrument detection limit. So, it's – it detects how much – it gives you an indication of how much EDTA you can detect from a solution that you actually take a syringe and inject into the instrument. It doesn't tell you anything about how much EDTA you can detect from a stain sample."

"But the limitations in their protocol clearly state, and the data shows, that they are able to detect – 1-microliter drop is readily detectable in this protocol?"

"I don't believe that that's true."

"So, when they state that the 1-microliter drop was readily detectable using this technique, are you saying that's not true?"

"That particular statement is in reference to this paragraph about a separate LOD study where some EDTA was placed into a lavender-topped tube. That's not what I'm referring to when I say they had problems detecting it in a 2-microliter spot. I'm referring to the actual case samples in this case, where they – where they were not able to detect it from a 2-microliter set of blood of Mr Avery's blood, as opposed to this one, which is a more sort of theoretical pristine case."

"I think we're talking about the same thing, but maybe my question was not very good."

"OK."

"The system that they developed, the methodology that they developed, allows them to detect levels of EDTA to the 1-microliter level?"

"OK. The reason that's not a true statement, generally, is because we don't know how – the concentration of EDTA that's present in that microliter. I don't know if there's 100 micrograms or 1 microgram present in that 1-microliter sample. So, saying it's possible to detect EDTA in 1 microliter of blood really, scientifically, doesn't mean much unless you also know the concentration of EDTA. In this case, they state that the 1-microliter drop that they prepared from a whole blood sample and known EDTA, they knew the concentration of EDTA in that sample. I was unable to find the data related to this particular experiment that they described. It wasn't in this package, as far as I could tell."

"And that would be important in a quantitative aspect?"

"It is absolutely important in a quantitative assay, but it's – the reason it's important qualitatively is because when you say not detected, it's not detected at what level. Is it not detected at a very, very concentrated level, or is it not detected at a very, very weak level? If I have my glass of water here and I drop in two… crystals of sugar, there is sugar in my water. But I may or may not be able to detect it. If I run it by some techniques, I may say not detected. It doesn't mean it's not there. It just means I can't detect it… If I run it by a method with a very high detection limit, I won't be able to… find the sugar. It doesn't mean it's not there. It just means that I can't find it. If I put a lot of sugar in there, that method might be able to detect it. And I would say, yes, I saw sugar in that water. So, it really depends on how much sugar is in my water sample, or how much EDTA is in the blood sample."

Throughout her testimony, Janine remained impenetrable.

The strategy of paying expert witnesses to lie is so effective because usually only the prosecution can afford expert witnesses. There are innocent people in prison across America because they didn't have the resources to counter the state's highly-paid experts. In Ray Krone's case, the $5,000 the state gave him to defend himself rendered him unable to buy an expert witness. If Steven Avery only had $5,000 to defend himself, he would have found himself in the same situation as Ray Krone. But Steven had money from his settlement and his expert witness neutralised the testimony of the state's expert witness.

STRATEGY 6: ENSURE PUBLIC DEFENDERS WORK FOR THE PROSECUTION

Public defenders are assigned to people who cannot afford a lawyer. The state pays them a fraction of the prosecutor's budget to ensure that their performance in the courtroom is substandard – which guarantees the prosecution's monopoly on putting on the best show in town and achieving endless guilty verdicts. Even well-intentioned public defenders cannot compete against the state's ability to lavish taxpayers' money on actors such as expert witnesses. Wisconsin is renowned for its stinginess in paying public defenders.

Public defenders operating on a shoestring budget want to do as little work as possible. They avoid going to trial because of the extra effort involved. Even when defendants insist on going to trial, public defenders will try to talk them out of it. That's why over 90% of state and federal cases conclude as plea bargains. Defendants who go to trial and lose receive aggravated sentences as a deterrent to others foolish enough to want to exercise their constitutional right to a trial. Trials cost the state money, and the justice system is a business model.

A plea-bargain is a deal brokered between the defence and the prosecution. Reduced sentences are offered to those willing to acknowledge their guilt without going to trial. Negotiating plea-bargains, prosecutors employ the tactics of used car sales people. In my Ecstasy trafficking case, I had over twenty charges. I was told that each charge carried anywhere from 5 to 10 years. If I didn't sign a plea-bargain, and I lost at trial, the judge would give me the aggravated sentence – 10 years – on twenty charges, which

I would have to serve consecutively, so I was facing a maximum sentence of 10 years x 20 charges = 200 years. With the help of a private lawyer who cost almost $100,000, I fought my case for 26 months. Over time, I got my plea bargain down to 9½ years. If I had been assigned a public defender instead of hiring a private lawyer, I'd probably still be in prison.

The worst kind of public defenders work against the interests of their clients, and for the benefit of their paymaster: the state. They want their clients to sign plea bargains admitting guilt, so that they can move on to the next clients/victims. Prisoners call these lawyers "public pretenders."

I was guilty as charged, but several of my co-defendants, who had allegedly worked for me, had never even met me. They had been falsely accused. When they told their public defenders this fact, they were instructed to plead guilty and to sign an exhibit that stated that they knew me and had worked for me. If they refused, they would get much bigger sentences.

Brendan Dassey was assigned the worst kind of public defender. Len Kachinsky wasn't the slightest bit interested in proving Brendan's innocence. He wanted Brendan to immediately sign a plea bargain admitting guilt and implicating Steven Avery, so that he could move on to his next client/victim, which would keep the money flowing to him. Perhaps lacking the time and courage to manipulate Brendan face-to-face, he hired a private investigator, Michael O'Kelly, to do the dirty work.

Fassbender and Wiegert took their time feigning rapport with Brendan Dassey because their salaries were guaranteed by the taxpayers of Wisconsin. Kachinsky and O'Kelly, on the other hand, were operating on a limited budget. Over five months, Kachinsky and O'Kelly received $15,268 from Wisconsin taxpayers:

Kachinsky:
- 8.8 courtroom billable hours, at $40 per hour
- 174.6 non-courtroom billable hours, at $40 per hour
- 51 billable hours of travel, at $25 per hour

- 2,520 miles of travel (38.5 cents per mile)
- $167.87 other expenses
- Total compensation $9,749

O'Kelly:
- Total compensation: $5,519

The State of Wisconsin spent millions prosecuting Steven and Brendan. Steven fought back with his compensation money, but Brendan had no resources to put on his own theatre show.

Due to financial limitations, Kachinsky and O'Kelly were motivated to extract a false confession from Brendan in record time. Effectively, they were working for the prosecution. In the face of Brendan telling the truth, O'Kelly wasted no time in procuring a written confession. Excerpt from the May 12, 2006 meeting between Michael O'Kelly and Brendan Dassey:

Brendan: They were trying to do my bail today.

O'Kelly: What do you understand is going to happen with your bail?

Brendan: I don't know.

O'Kelly: Give me an idea what you think.

Brendan: That they might raise it or something.

O'Kelly: Might what?

Brendan: Raise the price.

O'Kelly: That's a possibility. Let's do this here that I've laid out for you. This is your polygraph. Can you read up here?

Brendan: *(shakes head)*

O'Kelly: You can't see that far? Can you see what colour it is?

Brendan: Red.

O'Kelly: OK. Well, I'll read it for you. It says deception indicated. Probability of deception is point nine eight. That's 98%.

Brendan: So, what does that mean?

O'Kelly: What do you think that means?

Brendan: That I passed it?

O'Kelly: It says deception indicated.

Brendan: That I failed it.

O'Kelly: Yes. That doesn't surprise you. Let me show you some things. This is the original poster for Teresa Halbach. OK. This is Teresa's website. This is her family. You see them in court, right? OK. This is the last thing that Teresa saw. She saw this sign right here. Do you recognise this sign? What does this sign say?

Brendan: Dead end.

O'Kelly: OK. It's pretty prophetic, isn't it?

Brendan: *(nods)*

O'Kelly: And this right here: what is that picture right there?

Brendan: Our driveway.

O'Kelly: Where is it going to?

Brendan: My mom's house. Steve's house.

O'Kelly: OK. Teresa sees this sign right here that says dead end, and she goes down that road, right, and she ends up here at this red house, right? Whose red house is that?

Brendan: Steven's.

O'Kelly: OK. She ends up in the bedroom. Top picture – like that? Before there, she has to go down the hallway, right? *(shows pictures)* OK. Do you recognize this? It's inside Steven's. Can you think where that might be in his house?

Brendan: *(shakes head)*

O'Kelly: OK. Do you recognise this right here?

Brendan: *(inaudible)*

O'Kelly: OK. What do you think it is?

Brendan: The stuff that they found on the... *(inaudible)*

O'Kelly: Whose car is that?

Brendan: I don't know.

O'Kelly: Whose do you think it is?

Brendan: Teresa's.

O'Kelly: Why do you think it's hers?

Brendan: They said that it was a Toyota, and on the back it says Toyota.

O'Kelly: Recognise this photograph here?

Brendan: I seen it on TV.

O'Kelly: OK. Maybe looks something like this here? You know what building that is right there? That's Teresa's church. *(pauses)* Now let me tell you this: I know everything I need to know at this stage except for two things. There are two things I don't know. What do you think they might be?

Brendan: I don't know.

O'Kelly: Think about it. *(pauses)* You have to put your hands down. I can't hear you.

Brendan: Maybe if I helped him.

O'Kelly: Continue.

Brendan: If I helped him with any of this.

O'Kelly: Continue.

Brendan: *(inaudible)*

O'Kelly: The two things I don't know is: are you sorry for what you did and will you promise not to do it again? Those are the two things I don't know. I know everything else that I need to about this case except for those two things. What I want you to do is make a decision. I want you to read this form, and then we're going to fill it out. You mark the boxes where you think the boxes should be marked.

Brendan: *(reads form silently)*

O'Kelly: Are you sorry?

Brendan: I don't know because I didn't do anything.

O'Kelly: Brendan, look at me. If you're not sorry, I can't help you. What I don't want you to do is spend the rest of your life in prison. Can you look at me? Do you want to spend the rest of your life in prison? You did a very bad thing.

Brendan: Yeah, but I was only there for the fire though.

O'Kelly: Brendan, you haven't told me the truth yet. Listen to me carefully. Why don't you look at me? Brendan? Brendan, look at me please. This is your choice. Listen very carefully. Somebody is going to cooperate and tell the truth. I'd prefer it's going to be you. If it's not, because your confession has been admitted, you heard that today. Right now, they're asking for life plus 72 years. That's your greatest exposure right now. If you tell the complete truth, the complete truth, not just part of the truth, there's a door open for you. You will still have to serve some time in prison. You don't get to go home now. Somebody died. But this is your chance to tell the truth. If Steve Avery decides to get up and lie and testifies against you, then he may get an offer and a deal with the prosecutor's office and that's my concern. Right now, only the two of you know what happened inside that crime scene. You know what happened. You know why it happened. You know what time it happened. But like I said, I don't know if you're sorry. I don't know if you're going to do this again. Those are the two things I don't know. Steve right now is saying that you're to blame for part of this and so is Bobby. Are you aware of that?

Brendan: *(shakes head)*

O'Kelly: Is Bobby to blame for any of this?

Brendan: No.

O'Kelly: Did he see the girl?

Brendan: He seen her when he left to go bow hunting.

O'Kelly: OK. Steve says that she and Bobby were together. Is that the truth?

Brendan: No.

O'Kelly: How do you know it's not the truth?

Brendan: Because I'm friends with, ah, the guy, the friend's brother, and they said that they go hunting together.

O'Kelly: Remember how you told Detective Wiegert. His name is Mark, right? He's a pretty good guy, right?

Brendan: I don't know.

O'Kelly: He was nice to you?

Brendan: *(shrugs)*

O'Kelly: Do you remember telling Mark about a bullet? Remember that?

Brendan: I never seen the gun that day.

O'Kelly: Well, guess what? What you described to Mark and to Special Agent Fassbender turned out to be completely true, because the DNA is from Teresa that's on one of the bullets that's in the garage on the floor. *(shows picture)* That's the bullet. *(pauses)*

Brendan: *(eventually starts writing on form)*

O'Kelly: What'd you decide to do?

Brendan: Check I am very sorry for what I did.

O'Kelly: That's a good beginning. Continue.

Brendan: *(writes)*

O'Kelly: Brendan, stop for a second. The last time you and I were here, what you wrote was not the truth. Do we agree with that?

Brendan: *(pauses)* Maybe some of it.

O'Kelly: Part of the truth was that you got up that day and went to school, so, yes, there was some truth. But everything else you said wasn't the truth. And what I don't want you to do now... Can you look at me for a second? What I don't want you to do right now is tell me any more lies. If you lie to me, guess what I have to do? I have to stand up, put everything away and leave because that means that you're going to go to prison for the rest of your life. If you want to go to prison for the rest of your life because you're going to hang onto some lies, then I can't help you. When you're all through telling the truth tonight, then you and I can have a talk about something else. Will you help me with that? It's a good thing. You get to tell me all about your family history and what got you to this point last October 31 that caused all these problems to happen. I have to unravel all of that and ask the court to consider leniency based upon your family history and what's happened to you. I can only do all these things if you tell the truth. If you say even one single lie, I cannot help you at all. You've got to make a decision before you start writing anything. You're going to write the complete truth, no matter what the truth is, because then Mike can help you. If you write a lie, then Mike can't help you at all. First question you have to ask yourself is: do you want to spend the rest of your life in prison?

Brendan: *(inaudible)*

O'Kelly: So, is that a yes or a no? I can't hear you.

Brendan: No.

O'Kelly: Want me to try and help you? *(pauses)* I specialise in working with folks like yourself. To make sure that you don't go to prison for the rest of your life. Do you want to get out and have a family some day? That means you have to cooperate with me and have me work with you. And how much you cooperate, how much you help me, will depend on what happens with you.

Brendan: *(writes)*

O'Kelly: Need more room? Need more paper?

Brendan: *(shakes head)*

O'Kelly: Is there anything missing from this statement here?

Brendan: No.

O'Kelly: Is Teresa in that statement?

Brendan: No.

O'Kelly: Then it's missing. Then it's not a truthful statement. *(silence)* I want you to read this right here. Out loud.

Brendan: I am very sorry for what I did.

O'Kelly: OK. What does it say down here?

Brendan: I promise I will never do this again.

O'Kelly: Are those the truth?

Brendan: *(silence)*

O'Kelly: Are you really sorry? That's a question. *(pauses)* If you're not sorry for what you did, I can understand that, too. I just need to know which one it is. *(pauses)* If you are sorry: that's one kind of person. If you're not sorry: that's a different kind of person. And of course, I can't help the people who aren't sorry. So, are you sorry? Is that a yes or no?

Brendan: Don't know.

O'Kelly: You don't know if you're sorry or not? *(silence)* Would you do this again?

Brendan: *(shakes head)*

O'Kelly: Why not?

Brendan: *(shrugs)* I didn't do nothing.

O'Kelly: That's not true.

Brendan: I was only there for the fire.

O'Kelly: I wish that was true.

Brendan: It is.

O'Kelly: You were also in the mobile home.

Brendan: Not that day, though.

O'Kelly: And you were in the garage.

Brendan: Only for a little bit, though.

O'Kelly: That's because she was in the garage, too.

Brendan: *(shakes head)*

O'Kelly: Brendan, I want you to understand something. Want you to look at me, so I know you can hear me. *(grabs Brendan's arm)* Come on, look at me.

Brendan: The only thing that was in the garage was a lawnmower and a, ah, snowmobile.

O'Kelly: Brendan, you have the details. You gave the details to the police department.

Brendan: Yeah. They were false.

O'Kelly: Well, they turned out to be true.

Brendan: It's 'cause I had too much stuff on my mind. That's why I agreed [with] whatever they said.

O'Kelly: Well, you gave them details.

Brendan: Yeah, but they told me that they knew it all what had happened already.

O'Kelly: And you gave them information that they didn't already have.

Brendan: That's 'cause I was guessing.

O'Kelly: Well, you guessed pretty accurately about a whole bunch of details. And you couldn't guess with all those details. That's why the bleach is on your pants. That's why the bullet has Teresa's DNA. Right here in the garage. This is what you can do. You can try and help yourself – you can do what's right – and I'll help you through this process and you will not be doing life in prison. *(pauses)* And just so you know, just so you're perfectly clear, I want you to testify against Steven Avery and tell the truth. And this is how I can help you. If you decide not to, I want you to understand that your confession is coming in. When your confession is in, no matter what it is, truth or not truth or anything else, when your confession is in, there's nothing I can do to help you then. So right now, we're at the stage that I can help you. But I can't help you with those words that you wrote down. Those words, I can't help you at all. *(pauses)* If you want to stay in prison the rest of your life, then let's just take those words and say that's it. Is that what you want to do: prison for the rest of your life?

Brendan: *(shakes head)*

O'Kelly: Well, now's the chance to help yourself. But you can't help yourself with those words. You and I both know that that is not the truth. It's missing information.

Brendan: *(writes)*

Kachinsky and O'Kelly were so desperate to frame Brendan and Steven that a written confession from Brendan wasn't quite enough. Knowing that drawings of the crime scene by one of the alleged murderers – waved in the faces of the jurors – would surely earn guilty verdicts, O'Kelly continued to apply pressure on Brendan, using methods lifted from the Reid Technique:

Brendan: What'd happen if that's the only four pictures that I can draw?

O'Kelly: OK. What's this right here?

Brendan: Where he's got the gun.

O'Kelly: He's shooting her there? And where is he stabbing her?

Brendan: He does it before that.

O'Kelly: Where?

Brendan: In the garage.

O'Kelly: OK. Why don't you draw another picture over here about him stabbing her?

Brendan: *(draws)*

O'Kelly: OK. And now, where did you have sex with her at?

Brendan: In the house.

O'Kelly: OK. Why don't you draw a picture down here of you having sex with her there?

Brendan: *(draws)*

O'Kelly: And what do you have right there?

Brendan: Two people on the bed.

O'Kelly: And what's that? What's next to it?

Brendan: Steven.

O'Kelly: Was he watching?

Brendan: *(nods)*

O'Kelly: OK. And where'd you stab her at? And cut her hair? In the house or in the garage?

Brendan: I cut her hair in the house and stabbed her outside.

O'Kelly: OK. Was she alive when you stabbed her?

Brendan: No.

O'Kelly: Why'd you stab her then?

Brendan: Steve told me to.

O'Kelly: Where did she actually die at?

Brendan: In the garage.

O'Kelly: So, she was alive in the garage when you took her out there?

Brendan: *(nods)*

O'Kelly: Was she screaming?

Brendan: Yeah.

O'Kelly: What was she saying?

Brendan: *(long silence)* Like not to do what Steve tells me to do.

O'Kelly: What were her exact words?

Brendan: Don't listen to him.

O'Kelly: OK. Draw a picture down here of you cutting her hair.

Brendan: *(draws)*

O'Kelly: And where's this at?

Brendan: *(writes)*

O'Kelly: Is she in the bedroom – I mean – in the bed or where?

Brendan: Lying on the bed.

O'Kelly: OK.

Brendan: *(writes)*

O'Kelly: And how come she didn't get up from... the bed?
Brendan: Because she was tied down.
O'Kelly: What was she tied down with?
Brendan: Like, rope.
O'Kelly: And what else?
Brendan: Cuffs.
O'Kelly: What kind of cuffs?
Brendan: Leg cuffs.
O'Kelly: I'm sorry?
Brendan: Leg cuffs.
O'Kelly: I don't know what you mean.
Brendan: Like the ones that they put on their legs.
O'Kelly: So, they had chains?
Brendan: *(nods)*
O'Kelly: OK. OK. Why don't you do this? Why don't you draw a picture of the bed and how she was tied down? But draw... a big size so we can see it.
Brendan: *(draws)* So how should I draw the chains?
O'Kelly: I don't know. I didn't see it, so I can't help you.
Brendan: So, circles?
O'Kelly: OK.
Brendan: *(draws)*
O'Kelly: What about her hands? Are they chained also?
Brendan: *(inaudible)*
O'Kelly: What do you think was there?
Brendan: Rope.
O'Kelly: OK. Go ahead and put the rope then.
Brendan: *(draws)*
O'Kelly: Was she wearing clothes at this time?
Brendan: No.
O'Kelly: Where were her clothes at?
Brendan: On the floor.
O'Kelly: Can you put them where they were?
Brendan: *(draws)* Should I draw like a T-shirt in there?
O'Kelly: Whatever you want to do.

Brendan: *(draws)*
O'Kelly: And what is that?
Brendan: Pants and a shirt.
O'Kelly: OK. What about shoes?
Brendan: *(draws shoes)*
O'Kelly: OK. Anything else?
Brendan: No.
O'Kelly: OK. Is this the bed that she was tied to? *(shows Brendan photo of headboard)* Where did the rope go to? Can you show me here?
Brendan: Right here. *(points to photo of headboard)*
O'Kelly: OK. Why don't you put an X right there then?
Brendan: *(draws X on photo)*
O'Kelly: And what about the other side?
Brendan: *(draws X on photo)*
O'Kelly: OK. What was she saying when she was tied up like this?
Brendan: Telling Steven to let her go.
O'Kelly: And what did Steven say?
Brendan: That he wasn't gonna.
O'Kelly: What did he tell her?
Brendan: That he wouldn't let her go 'cause she was gonna go to the police.
O'Kelly: What else did he say?
Brendan: *(inaudible)*
O'Kelly: How long was he planning this?
Brendan: I don't know.
O'Kelly: What's your idea?
Brendan: *(long silence)* I could have a reason why he could have done it.
O'Kelly: Go ahead.
Brendan: That I think he wanted to do it because like maybe he wanted to go back to jail.
O'Kelly: Why do you think that?
Brendan: Because some days he couldn't control his temper, so

the whole family told him to go see the people that you go talk to about your feelings and that. And he, he got pissed off and he went for a ride.

O'Kelly: What time did you go to the trailer that day? The real time.

Brendan: Eight.

O'Kelly: So, you were cutting her hair and having sex with her after eight. So, she was alive until then? How did you know she was in the trailer?

Brendan: He told me to follow him to help.

O'Kelly: And what happened next?

Brendan: He showed me her and then told me to have sex with her.

O'Kelly: Continue.

Brendan: And I looked at him and then I was thinking of going home, but then I seen that he – I thought he was too strong for me, so I did it.

O'Kelly: Continue.

Brendan: Then after I was done, I cut off her – he told me to cut some hair off, and then when we were done, we took her off and we brung her outside into the garage and then he stabbed her and then shot her.

O'Kelly: How did she get from the bed to the garage?

Brendan: He carried her.

O'Kelly: How?

Brendan: In his hands.

O'Kelly: Describe it.

Brendan: *(long silence)* Like he had her in his hands, like … her legs were right here and her back was right there.

O'Kelly: OK.

Brendan: And when he had his hands like this, he had the gun in his hands.

O'Kelly: And where'd he get the gun from?

Brendan: In the bedroom.

O'Kelly: What kind of a gun was it?

Brendan: Twenty-two.

O'Kelly: OK. And what was she saying while this was happening?

Brendan: Saying not to do it and to let her go.

O'Kelly: And how come she didn't run away?

Brendan: She was trying to.

O'Kelly: What was she doing?

Brendan: Like, squirming, trying to get away from him.

O'Kelly: What stopped her from getting away?

Brendan: He was holding her too tight.

O'Kelly: And what else?

Brendan: She was tied up.

O'Kelly: How was she tied up?

Brendan: Her feet were tied and her hands.

O'Kelly: Why don't you draw a picture right here of how she was tied up.

Brendan: *(draws)*

O'Kelly: OK. Was she wearing any clothes?

Brendan: No.

O'Kelly: What happens next?

Brendan: He stabbed her and then he shoots her and then we put her into the fire.

O'Kelly: And she was still alive when you put her in the fire?

Brendan: No.

O'Kelly: How do you know?

Brendan: She wasn't moving.

O'Kelly: When did she stop moving?

Brendan: When he shot her.

O'Kelly: Where did he shoot her at?

Brendan: In the stomach.

O'Kelly: And where else?

Brendan: In the heart.

O'Kelly: In where?

Brendan: In the heart.

O'Kelly: The heart? And how do you know he shot her in the heart?

Brendan: I don't know. Just guessing because I wasn't even looking.

O'Kelly: Did you see him shoot her?

Brendan: No, because I can't look at that stuff.

O'Kelly: How do you know he shot her then?

Brendan: Because I heard the gunshot.

O'Kelly: Maybe he was shooting at you. *(pauses)* What was she saying while he was shooting her?

Brendan: To stop.

O'Kelly: What did she sound like exactly?

Brendan: *(long silence)* She was crying and saying to stop what he was doing.

O'Kelly: Was there blood in the garage?

Brendan: Yeah.

O'Kelly: Whose blood was it?

Brendan: Hers.

O'Kelly: And how do you know it was her blood?

Brendan: Because when I cleaned it up, that's where the spot that he shot her was.

O'Kelly: How many times do you think he shot her?

Brendan: Five times.

O'Kelly: And why do you think five?

Brendan: That's how much shots I heard.

O'Kelly: Was the fire already going in the... pit?

Brendan: You mean behind the garage?

O'Kelly: Yes.

Brendan: Yeah.

O'Kelly: Was it a small fire?

Brendan: Not really.

O'Kelly: How did she get in the fire?

Brendan: He carried her.

O'Kelly: And where's the knife that he used to stab her?

Brendan: I don't know what he did with it.

O'Kelly: Where'd you last see it?

Brendan: In the garage.

O'Kelly: Where in the garage?

Brendan: Right behind the lawnmower.

O'Kelly: Behind the lawnmower. Was it hidden?

Brendan: No, it was just lying on the floor.

O'Kelly: Describe the knife to me. Let's draw a picture of the knife. How's that? *(hands paper to Brendan)*

Brendan: How big?

O'Kelly: The bigger the better, so you can have details.

Brendan: *(draws)* I don't know how to draw the details.

O'Kelly: Just draw it how you think it should be.

Brendan: Something like that.

O'Kelly: And describe these parts, what they look like.

Brendan: Like the colour and that?

O'Kelly: Everything. Sure.

Brendan: *(draws/writes)*

O'Kelly: And how long is it?

Brendan: *(draws/writes)*

O'Kelly: Is the whole thing eight inches?

Brendan: *(nods)*

O'Kelly: And where'd it come from?

Brendan: In the house.

O'Kelly: Where in the house?

Brendan: In the kitchen.

O'Kelly: Did you see it?

Brendan: No.

O'Kelly: How do you know it came from the kitchen?

Brendan: She was still tied up on the bed. He went in the kitchen and got it.

O'Kelly: OK. Go ahead and put from the kitchen in.

Brendan: *(writes)*

O'Kelly: Where's the first place that she was stabbed at?

Brendan: In the garage.

O'Kelly: OK. When did you know he was going to kill her?

Brendan: *(long pause)* I don't know.

O'Kelly: When did he tell you he was going to burn her?

Brendan: That night.

O'Kelly: Did she know that he was going to burn her?

Brendan: What do you mean?

O'Kelly: Did he tell her? Did she hear him say that he was going to burn her?

Brendan: No.

O'Kelly: How many times did he have sex with her?

Brendan: I don't know.

O'Kelly: What did he tell you about him having sex with her?

Brendan: He didn't tell me nothing.

O'Kelly: And did he have sex with her then?

Brendan: *(inaudible)* I don't know where though.

O'Kelly: Did he use any... sex toys on her?

Brendan: I don't know.

O'Kelly: Do you know what a sex toy is?

Brendan: No.

O'Kelly: It's something that you put in the girl's vagina. And it vibrates sometimes. Was that used on her that day?

Brendan: Not that I know of.

O'Kelly: Was anything used on her at all?

Brendan: No.

O'Kelly: OK. Did you see him touch her at all?

Brendan: Just to pick her up off the bed and that.

O'Kelly: When she was in the garage, where was her car?

Brendan: I don't know. I never seen it.

O'Kelly: It wasn't in the garage?

Brendan: No.

Brendan saying that the RAV4 wasn't in the garage was problematic because Wiegert and Fassbender had already coerced Brendan to say that it was. The details of the story Brendan fabricated to satisfy his tormentors changed over time. Just like Fassbender and Wiegert, O'Kelly wanted Brendan to say that Teresa had been shot in the head to match the bullet hole found in Teresa's skull. Anyone with common sense could have seen that

Brendan was making things up – such as taking time out in the middle of a murder, torture and rape to cut Teresa's hair – but Kratz wasn't searching for the truth. Kratz cherry-picked details from Brendan's statements to spoon-feed to the jury – backed up by the pictures procured by O'Kelly and evidence planted by the police.

O'Kelly: What was in the garage besides Teresa, Steve and you?

   Brendan: Just the snowmobile and the lawnmower.

   O'Kelly: The snowmobile. Was it… on the trailer?

   Brendan: No.

   O'Kelly: OK. And the lawnmower: is it a riding lawnmower?

   Brendan: Mm-hmm.

   O'Kelly: Let's do this. *(hands paper to Brendan)* I want you to draw a picture of the garage, where you were, where Teresa was, where Steve was and where the lawnmower and the snowmobile was. Please.

   Brendan: Should I just draw a square?

   O'Kelly: Sure. But draw a big picture so we can see.

   Brendan: Yeah, I mean for the lawnmower.

   O'Kelly: OK. Sure.

   Brendan: *(draws)* Should I say that this door was open?

   O'Kelly: Whatever the truth is.

   Brendan: *(inaudible)*

   O'Kelly: That's you? OK. The door's open?

   Brendan: *(nods)*

   O'Kelly: Everybody can see you? *(O'Kelly's cell phone or pager beeps, he gets up and goes off camera, returns on camera and changes tapes in audio cassette player that is on the table)* So the garage door is open? How about this door right here, is that open?

   Brendan: Just a little bit.

   O'Kelly: OK. And what's happening over here?

   Brendan: That's where he set her on the floor and then stabbed her and shot her.

   O'Kelly: OK. And you stabbed her over there, too?

Brendan: *(nods)*
O'Kelly: How many times?
Brendan: Once.
O'Kelly: Where at?
Brendan: In the stomach.
O'Kelly: And where did he stab her at?
Brendan: In the stomach.
O'Kelly: You think she was in a lot of pain?
Brendan: Yeah.
O'Kelly: Why do you think she was in a lot of pain?
Brendan: She was telling him that it hurts.
O'Kelly: What was she saying?
Brendan: She was crying.
O'Kelly: How much?
Brendan: A lot.
O'Kelly: What do you call a lot?
Brendan: Her tears were always running down her, one after another.
O'Kelly: How long was she crying?
Brendan: Until he shot her.
O'Kelly: Continue.
Brendan: Then after that he took her outside and put her on the fire.
O'Kelly: Continue.
Brendan: Then we were just standing, like, probably fifteen feet away from the fire and, and, my mom came home. She went in the house and called Steven on her cell phone and told him that I would have to be home at 10 o'clock. And she asked if I had a sweater on.
O'Kelly: Continue.
Brendan: That was at 9 o'clock about. And so, we waited for a little bit and then the fire went down and, so, actually we threw some stuff on there and we waited for the fire to go down. When it did, it was about like 10 o'clock, so Steve told me that I should go home and go to bed. So, I did and I, when I got home, I talked

to my mom a little bit, like how her day was and that. And I went to sleep.

According to Brendan's story, he and Steven had managed to torture, rape, murder, mutilate and incinerate Teresa in between 8 o'clock and 10 o'clock. If the fire was already diminishing by 10 o'clock, they had incinerated a corpse in approximately an hour without stinking the neighbourhood up. To create such damage to Teresa's bones would have required at least half a day in a bonfire or a source of extremely high heat such as a crematorium. After committing such heinous crimes, a teenager would have been in shock, and incapable of going home and asking his mother how her day had been.

O'Kelly: What was Steve saying while she was in the fire burning?
    Brendan: Not much.
    O'Kelly: What were his words?
    Brendan: That I should keep my mouth shut.
    O'Kelly: Continue.
    Brendan: That's it.
    O'Kelly: OK. Where was the Suzuki all the while this was happening?
    Brendan: The grey Suzuki?
    O'Kelly: Yes.
    Brendan: On the side of the garage, like right here.
    O'Kelly: OK. How did he get her car down to… the pit?
    Brendan: I don't know.
    O'Kelly: I heard that Chuck and Earl knew it was down there.
    Brendan: I don't know.
    O'Kelly: Did you hear anything like that?
    Brendan: No.

If Brendan had said yes, O'Kelly and Kachinsky would have earned extra brownie points from the prosecution by implicating

Chuck and Earl in the murder conspiracy. Four convictions would have meant double the accolades, prizes and promotions for everyone involved in the framing. Fortunately for Steven's brothers, Brendan's storytelling didn't cross that line.

O'Kelly: Let me show you. Do you know where the car was found?

Brendan: I seen a picture.

O'Kelly: Why don't you walk over here. I'll show you.

Brendan: *(gets out of seat, moves off camera)*

O'Kelly: *(off camera)* You see right there? The car was in the middle of the road facing that direction. This is the car. This is his house. How'd he get it over there? Did you see the car any place there at all? You never did?

Brendan: But I know there's a back road that goes *(inaudible)*

O'Kelly: Show me how.

Brendan: *(inaudible)*

O'Kelly: And then how?

Brendan: *(inaudible)*

O'Kelly: OK. And drive back here? OK. *(O'Kelly and Brendan return to seats on camera)* Let's do this. I want you to take the red pen and this is the garage. *(pointing to Brendan's drawing)* OK. Put the word garage there so you know it's the garage. OK. At what time is she over here?

Brendan: Should I write it down?

O'Kelly: Oh, yes, please.

Brendan: *(writes)*

O'Kelly: And then put the name of the person here and the name of each one of these people here, please.

Brendan: How do you spell Teresa?

O'Kelly: However you think it should be spelled.

Brendan: *(writes/draws)*

O'Kelly: OK. Good. And then this was the knife that was used to stab her?

Brendan: *(nods)*

O'Kelly: Go ahead and write that then so we know what it is.
Brendan: *(writes)*
O'Kelly: And put her name there.
Brendan: *(writes)*
O'Kelly: OK. And then describe what these things are please.
Brendan: *(writes)*
O'Kelly: OK. What does that say?
Brendan: Bed where Teresa was roped and chained.
O'Kelly: OK. And who's this person here?
Brendan: Teresa.
O'Kelly: Go ahead and put, write what everything is, please.
Brendan: *(writes)*
O'Kelly: OK. And what's this down here?
Brendan: *(writes)*
O'Kelly: And what's happening with her?
Brendan *(writes)*
O'Kelly: And where'd the rope come from?
Brendan: The rope that he used right there?
O'Kelly: Yes. Where'd this rope come from?
Brendan: In the garage.
O'Kelly: OK. Can you describe the rope? You can start with what colour it is.
Brendan: Yellowish.
O'Kelly: OK. Go ahead and write it down here.
Brendan: *(writes)*
O'Kelly: And how do you know it came from the garage?
Brendan: Because he had quite a few ropes in the garage that I see sometimes when I go over there.
O'Kelly: And describe what these things over here are, please.
Brendan: *(writes)*
O'Kelly: And whose are these?
Brendan: *(writes)*
O'Kelly: OK. Teresa's clothes?
Brendan: *(writes)*
O'Kelly: And what happened to them?

Brendan: They ended up in the fire.

O'Kelly: And how do you know that?

Brendan: Because that's what we used to clean up the reddish-black stuff.

O'Kelly: Explain.

Brendan: Like he would throw that, the bleach in there on the spots where the blood was and we'd use the clothes to try to get it cleaned up.

O'Kelly: Whose clothes were they using?

Brendan: Hers.

O'Kelly: OK. How do you know it was her clothes?

Brendan: He told me to grab them.

O'Kelly: And did you?

Brendan: *(nods)*

O'Kelly: And where'd you get them from?

Brendan: From right there on the floor.

O'Kelly: Where was he when he told you to grab the clothes?

Brendan: He was right here getting, grabbing her.

O'Kelly: And what was she doing while he was grabbing her?

Brendan: Trying to get away.

O'Kelly: How was she trying to get away?

Brendan: Trying to squirm out of his, his grip.

O'Kelly: Were you holding her also?

Brendan: No.

O'Kelly: Not even for a minute?

Brendan: *(shakes head)*

O'Kelly: Why not?

Brendan: I was grabbing the clothes and the shoes.

O'Kelly: And what was she saying?

Brendan: To let her go.

O'Kelly: Was she begging for mercy?

Brendan: Yeah.

O'Kelly: What was she saying?

Brendan: To please stop to do and… I don't know. *(inaudible)*

O'Kelly: Was she crying there also?

Brendan: Yeah.

O'Kelly: How much?

Brendan: Like, a little bit.

O'Kelly: Did she mention God?

Brendan: Huh?

O'Kelly: Did she ever mention God?

Brendan: No.

O'Kelly: Before she died? Did she mention anybody's names before she died?

Brendan: *(shakes head)*

O'Kelly: Do you think she knew she was dying?

Brendan: Not that I know of.

O'Kelly: OK. And what time is this when you first saw her?

Brendan: *(writes)*

O'Kelly: Now over here you wrote eight.

Brendan: *(inaudible)*

O'Kelly: OK. What's the first time that you knew that she was in there?

Brendan: When I went in there.

O'Kelly: And that's what that time was? What'd you do from five?

Brendan: Well, when I came home from school, I do what I always do: play PlayStation 2. And, I played that until five, and I called my friend to see if, what he was doing that following weekend. And so, after that, I watched TV and I got a phone call like six from Blaine's boss. And at seven I got a phone call from Steven, but I didn't go over there right away. And he called again to see where I was, and I told him I was getting ready.

O'Kelly: OK. Why don't you go ahead and put the times for what these things are – what each picture is?

Brendan: What do you mean, like what time this is?

O'Kelly: Sure, and also what it is.

Brendan: *(writes)*

O'Kelly: And put also that Steve was watching you if that's true.

Brendan: *(writes)*

O'Kelly: And what was she saying when you were doing that?

Brendan: Should I write it down here?

O'Kelly: Um, here, why don't you write it – and use this – right there.

Brendan: *(writes)*

O'Kelly: OK. Describe where she was while you were doing that – while that was happening.

Brendan: *(writes)*

O'Kelly: What did Steve say to you during that week after this happened?

Brendan: About this?

O'Kelly: Mm-hmm.

Brendan: I don't know.

O'Kelly: Why didn't you tell anybody?

Brendan: I was afraid to.

O'Kelly: Afraid of what?

Brendan: Afraid that the family wouldn't like me anymore.

O'Kelly: Which family?

Brendan: My family.

O'Kelly: And why wouldn't they like you anymore?

Brendan: For listening to Steven.

O'Kelly: What was Steven wearing when you, when you first went... in his house?

Brendan: Shorts.

O'Kelly: What colour?

Brendan: Red.

O'Kelly: What colour top?

Brendan: Grey.

O'Kelly: And what happened to those clothes?

Brendan: I don't remember.

O'Kelly: Did he burn anything else in the... pit besides Teresa and her clothes?

Brendan: Just tires, a cabinet, wood and a van seat.

O'Kelly: OK. I just asked you what else you think's important that we should know, and what'd you come up with?

Brendan: Nothing else.

O'Kelly: Well, I thought you were going to start to tell me something.

Brendan: Huh?

O'Kelly: I thought you were going to start to tell me something.

Brendan: No, I said I didn't know anything else.

O'Kelly: Oh. *(flips through form)* Let's see. Here's a page there for you to read, please.

Brendan: Should I do it in blue?

O'Kelly: Yes please. Take your time.

Brendan: *(writes)*

O'Kelly: *(off camera)* Hi, Len [Kachinsky]. Hi Len, this is Mike O'Kelly. Hi. I'm with Brendan right now, and we're in the GED room of the facility. Um, and he's given a detailed statement. Um, my next question to you would be that, would you like me to call Special Agent Fassbender and have him interview Brendan at this time? *(pauses)* Oh, quite well. Quite well. Quite well. Very well. *(pauses)* Let me get clearance from the jailer otherwise I can't give him the phone. *(pauses)* Yes, officer, this is Mike O'Kelly. I've got the attorney on my cell phone, and he'd like to talk to Brendan Dassey. Is that possible? OK. Want to walk down? *(inaudible)* That sounds fine. It's Brendan Dassey's attorney. I'd also pass the phone to you folks to verify. I will. That's fine. *(hangs up)* OK. They're going to check with their supervisor and then they're gonna walk down… This is a nice jail facility. Oh, sure, definitely. Brendan's doing quite well… Brendan, Len wants to talk to you.

Brendan: *(takes phone)* Hello? *(long pause) (inaudible)* …think about it. OK. OK. OK. *(hands phone to O'Kelly)*

O'Kelly: *(off camera)* Hi, Len. Does he understand how valuable it can be for him? Ah, no, and that's my concern. At this point in time, we can do so much to save him. That won't do any good, though. That won't do any good, just so you know. Would you mind if I visited with him a little bit more and explained to him the value? And if there's a change I'll call you back then. That sound fine? Thanks very much. Thanks, Len. Bye… OK. Let me explain this to you. You're writing a truthful story, am I correct?

Brendan: Mm-hmm.

O'Kelly: You're writing a truthful story to help yourself?

Brendan: *(nods)*

O'Kelly: You realise that you're not going to go home by writing the truth, right?

Brendan: *(shakes head)*

O'Kelly: OK. You realise that what you did was wrong and you're sorry for it, right?

Brendan: *(nods)*

O'Kelly: OK. You realise that you're going to have to go to prison for some period of time, right?

Brendan: *(nods)*

O'Kelly: OK. I would also like you to testify against Steve Avery.

Brendan: *(long pause)*

O'Kelly: That's the right thing to do. Do you agree?

Brendan: Yeah.

O'Kelly: OK. You've pretty much told me the same story as you told the police, and I'd like you to work with the police and tell them the truth… My concern is for you and I'd like you to cooperate with the police department. They want to interview you also, if you'll let them, and if you work with them, I feel comfortable that the Halbach family will also support you for doing the right thing. This is the time in your life that you can turn around and do as much as you can to right as much as you have wronged. You can't bring Teresa back, but you can certainly do the right thing in her memory. Do you agree?

Brendan: Yes.

O'Kelly: And if Teresa were alive right now, she'd want you to testify against Avery, right?

Brendan: *(nods)*

O'Kelly: And she'd want you to tell the truth to the police department. And would you like me to be there when you talk to the police?

Brendan: I don't know.

O'Kelly: I'm more than willing to be with you when you tell the police the story.

Brendan: When am I going to be doing this?

O'Kelly: They might want to come over tonight, if you'll let them.

Brendan: I don't know. But I wanted to watch a show today though.

O'Kelly: This is pretty important for Teresa.

Brendan: If I don't pick today, when will they come up here?

O'Kelly: I don't know. How would you feel if we came over in the morning?

Brendan: *(shrugs)*

O'Kelly: Would that be OK with you? After you had breakfast?

Brendan: How long will it take though?

O'Kelly: I don't know. About as long as you and I took because now that you got the truth out, now it's easy.

Brendan: Tomorrow would be OK.

O'Kelly: OK. Let me call Len and tell him. Would you like Len to be here, too?

Brendan: *(shrugs)* Don't matter to me.

O'Kelly: OK. *(dials cell phone)* Hi Len, this is Mike. Brendan would like to watch a TV show tonight. He has something that he'd like to see on TV, so, he'd like to forego tonight and he said after breakfast tomorrow morning would be fine. Ah, the interview by law enforcement can occur after breakfast tomorrow morning. Yes, I will. OK. Perfect. Of course, yes. You know, I don't know. I'd presume that they would, and I'd presume that they'd like to see what he gave me this evening. I think it'd be easier for Brendan to visit with them using this statement here. It'd be easier on Brendan than it would be to start all over again. OK. OK *(laughing)*. OK. Sounds great, Len. Thank you very much. Take care. Bye. *(hangs up, dials another number)* Yes, this is Michael O'Kelly calling for Special Agent Fassbender. Hi there. Hi there. I'm inside the Sheboygan County jail facility, and I'm sitting here with Brendan, and we've had several conversations with the attorney, and Brendan would like to visit with you folks. He'd like to watch a movie tonight, so he said you can come by tomorrow morning after breakfast. And he's also prepared a document for me, and it'll be up to you if you want to copy it or not. Len mentioned that – discovery issues and let you make that decision. Let you make that decision if you want it or not. OK. And this is what he suggested. He suggested you send him an e-mail and he'll confirm everything in writing for you. That way you'll have the authorisation in writing. OK. I'll call him right back now. I understand, I understand. That sounds fine. Take care. Bye. *(dials cell phone)* Hi Len, this is Mike again. Would you call Special Agent Fassbender at his cell phone? It's 427-4671-920. And just let him know – ask him to give me a call if he decides to come over in the morning, and I'll meet him at Sheboygan County facility. All right? Thanks so much. Take care. *(hangs up)* What else do you think? Who moved the Suzuki down there into the pit? Who moved your mom's van down into the pit?

Brendan: I didn't even know it was down in the pit.

O'Kelly: Yeah, they were both down there.

Brendan: I don't know.

O'Kelly: Did Teresa ever come near the Suzuki?

Brendan: I don't know.

O'Kelly: OK. Who else knows that he killed her?

Brendan: *(shrugs)* I don't know.

O'Kelly: Your grandmother?

Brendan: *(shakes head)*

O'Kelly: What does she think?

Brendan: That he didn't do it.

O'Kelly: And Earl and Chuck: what do they think?

Brendan: I don't know.

O'Kelly: Does Blaine know what you did?

Brendan: Not right away, before – after the first interview.

O'Kelly: How much did you tell him?

Brendan: Before the interview?

O'Kelly: So far.

Brendan: Well, when we went to Fox Hills after the first interview, we were telling him why he had to come up to Fox Hills and that. That's pretty much it.

O'Kelly: Is that in November?

Brendan: No, it was February.

O'Kelly: So, you didn't tell Blaine until February? Did you tell him you had sex with her too?

Brendan: No.

O'Kelly: What'd you tell him?

Brendan: I just told him that I was by the fire.

O'Kelly: With the body in the fire.

Brendan: Well, I didn't tell him that her body was in there.

O'Kelly: He knows that you were there when she died, right?

Brendan: I think he knows.

O'Kelly: Why do you think that?

Brendan: I think he knows because he's all hearing it on TV and from family members.

O'Kelly: Did you also tell them things?

Brendan: What do you mean?

O'Kelly: Did you tell him things about Teresa that day?

Brendan: No.

O'Kelly: Who else did you tell besides me?

Brendan: No one.

O'Kelly: You haven't told anybody else at all?

Brendan: *(shakes head)* But on May 4 when they questioned my mom, you know, and they asked her if she knew why I was losing weight and depressed, and she said she didn't know, it wasn't because of this.

O'Kelly: What was it?

Brendan: It was because I was trying to impress my girlfriend. But then when I met her, she broke up with me. So, after that I was feeling sad and then two weeks after that I went by my friend's house, and he said that he knew another girl and he'd like to go over. And the Wednesday when they arrested me, that's when – that day I was going to go see her.

O'Kelly had no time to waste entertaining the truth. Anything that didn't fit the narrative of Fassbender and Wiegert was redundant. Working for the prosecution, O'Kelly couldn't wait to hand over Brendan's written confession and the drawings that he had coerced. Cognisant that Brendan might have reverted to telling the truth, O'Kelly was insisting on being present at the interview, so that he could steer Brendan back into storytelling mode. His insistence on Brendan getting interviewed right away was because he had manipulated Brendan into that mode. He knew that the longer it took to interview Brendan, the more likely Brendan would have returned to telling the truth, and then O'Kelly and the investigators would have had to restart the manipulation.

O'Kelly: How many times have you thought about committing suicide?

Brendan: Never.

O'Kelly: What about hanging in the garage? One of your friends told me that you... were thinking about committing suicide. What did you tell them?

Brendan: *(shakes head)* Maybe I was talking to my friend about his future job. Because he wanted to be a suicide bomber.

O'Kelly: And who's that?

Brendan: Travis.

O'Kelly: And who is he going to suicide bomb?

Brendan: I don't know. He said that was one of his careers that he wanted to do.

O'Kelly: Was he thinking about suicide bombing the school?

Brendan: No.

O'Kelly: He's been having some difficulty at school, you know.

Brendan: Mostly everybody at school has a problem with school.

O'Kelly: Do you feel better right now?

Brendan: *(pauses)* A little.

O'Kelly: Good. You did the right thing. You still have my card?

Brendan: Mm-hmm.

O'Kelly: OK.

Brendan: It kind of sucks up here, though, because if I wanted to call my friend and talk to him, I couldn't unless I ordered a phone card. At first I could have, but then after this one day, I couldn't. It says it's restricted or something.

O'Kelly: *(long silence)* What are you going to watch tonight on TV?

Brendan: I don't know. What time is it now?

O'Kelly: *(shows watch)*

Brendan: Well, if I go right now there's only fifteen minutes.

O'Kelly: Of what?

Brendan: Wrestling.

O'Kelly: What do you think should happen to Steve?

Brendan: I don't know.

O'Kelly: How come you knew about her plates being taken off her car?

Brendan: I didn't know about that.

O'Kelly: You didn't? You told the police that.

Brendan: I didn't know though.

O'Kelly: What do you think should happen to you?

Brendan: Probably get, like, I don't know, probably, quite a few years.

O'Kelly: What do you call quite a few years?

Brendan: Like 10, 15.

O'Kelly: What if they gave you 20 years?

Brendan: I don't know.

O'Kelly: Would that be fair for what you've done?

Brendan: I guess so.

O'Kelly: It's better than life without parole, isn't it? Do you think you can keep this between you and I and Len right now, and not tell your family at all or your mom or anybody? Keep this real quiet? Anything you want to ask me? You know you can always call me collect, right? *(hands ribbon to Brendan)* Take this with you, something of Teresa's.

Brendan: I don't want it.

O'Kelly: Let's do this. Let's go ahead and stop for this evening, unless you have questions you want to ask me, anything you want to say. Then we'll probably come back in the morning and we'll just go from there. Thanks for doing the right thing. You made a good choice. I think you'll feel better, too. It'll be hard facing Steve, but if you want I'll be there when we face him in court.

Brendan: *(nods)*

O'Kelly: And you don't have to worry. He can't get to you. He can't hurt you. *(pats Brendan on back)* OK? *(gets up)* Yes, officer, this is Mike O'Kelly. We're ready to come back.

Not only was the defence working for the prosecution, but O'Kelly had attempted to brainwash Brendan into not even telling his mother what was going on. O'Kelly was desperately trying to get Brendan to agree to a 20-year sentence as opposed to life, in exchange for Brendan testifying against Steven.

Hardly anyone knew a video existed of O'Kelly interviewing Brendan until the post-conviction hearing. Attorney Robert Dvorak tracked O'Kelly across the country and slapped him with a subpoena. That's when the interrogation was exposed.

At Brendan's post-conviction hearing, O'Kelly was grilled on the stand about his unethical conduct. Suddenly, O'Kelly started sobbing in a fake and theatrical way over Teresa's memorial blue ribbon, the same ribbon he had tried to give to Brendan.

Asked to read an email that he had sent to Len Kachinsky, O'Kelly responded in court: "I am learning the Avery family history and about each member of the Avery family. These are criminals. There are members engaged in sexual activities with nieces, nephews, cousins, in-laws. Customers or their relatives unwittingly become victims of their sexual fantasies. This is truly where the devil resides in comfort." O'Kelly sobbed and sniffled. "I just keep thinking about that blue ribbon. I'm sorry. I can find no good in any member. These people are pure evil. A friend of mine suggested, 'This is a one-branch family tree. Cut this tree down. We need to end the gene pool here.'"

When asked about her thoughts on O'Kelly's gene-pool remark, *Making a Murderer* producer Moira Demos grew immediately angry and replied, "That statement is incredibly offensive. This family has deep bonds, an incredibly sound moral system, and has been vilified by people who don't know them."

O'Kelly was held accountable for an email that he sent to Kachinsky, which detailed the efforts he was making on behalf of the prosecution: "This possible linking evidence and Brendan's truthful testimony may be the break-through that will put [the state's] case more firmly on all fours... I am not concerned with finding connecting evidence placing Brendan inside the crime scene as Brendan will be the state's primary witness... This will only serve to bolster the prosecution. It will actually benefit the state if there's evidence attributed to Brendan. It will corroborate his testimony and colour him truthful..."

As well as coercing Brendan, O'Kelly tried to obtain additional evidence for the prosecution. He claimed to have developed inside information about the knife used to stab Teresa. He had Barb collect Brendan's medical, educational and family history specifically for sentencing and penal placement. He wanted to collect a wooden spoon that he alleged Barb had beat Brendan with.

Without Brendan's authorisation, Len Kachinsky emailed Wiegert and copied in Kratz to advise them that O'Kelly had "developed some information in the course of talking to Brendan's relatives that might shed some light on the whereabouts of the Suzuki and Barb's van, which may contain some evidence useful in the case. You are authorized to talk to [O'Kelly] directly... We would prefer to stay unnamed in any affidavit for search warrant if at all possible."

In another email, O'Kelly told Kachinsky to hold off on giving Brendan a "general pep talk," so that O'Kelly could manipulate Brendan with maximum effect. O'Kelly emailed that such a visit by Kachinsky "would be counterproductive to our goals for Brendan. It could have Brendan digging his heels in further. He could become more entrenched in his illogical position [protesting his innocence] and further distort the facts. He has been relying on a story that his family has told him to say about October 31... Brendan needs to be alone. When he sees me this Friday, I will be a source of relief. He and I can begin to bond. He needs to trust the direction that I steer him into. Brendan needs to provide an explanation that coincides with the facts/evidence."

Working for the prosecution, Len Kachinsky was only interested in helping to convict Brendan. He was also out to capitalise on the media interest in the case. Over three weeks, Kachinsky spent one hour with Brendan and at least ten hours communicating with the press. He appeared on the *Nancy Grace Show* to discuss Brendan's case before he had heard Brendan's confession or reviewed any discovery other than the original criminal complaint. He unleashed O'Kelly on Brendan, who set about trying to bolster the prosecution's case with unnatural zeal.

In Judge Duffin's habeas decision his disdain for Kachinsky was evident in this statement: "Although it probably does not need to be stated, it will be: Kachinsky's conduct was inexcusable both tactically and ethically. It is one thing for an attorney to point out to a client how deep of a hole the client is in. But to assist the prosecution in digging that hole deeper is an affront to the principles of justice that underlie a defence attorney's vital role in the adversarial system."

STRATEGY 7: NEUTRALISE HONEST WITNESSES

Honest witnesses can be neutralised in various ways. They can be ignored, so that their testimony never makes it into the courtroom, or, if they take the stand, they can be discredited and made to seem unreliable.

Dave Begotka was ignored. Dave was at the beach when Penny was assaulted and he joined the search party. Years later, he saw Steven Avery on Halloween 2005, the day of the alleged murder of Teresa Halbach.

While Gregory Allen stalked Penny on the beach, Dave was jet-skiing with a friend. When Penny didn't return to her family from jogging, her husband asked Dave and his friend to help search for her.

After receiving a description of Penny, Dave jet-skied approximately seven miles. Upon spotting a group of people, he stopped and asked if they'd seen Penny. They said she had gone the other way, so Dave turned around. He saw Penny sprint over a sand dune "as if she was on fire." He took his jet ski onto the shore and ran up to her at the exact time as her husband and the police were walking up the beach. In a bloody and battered state, Penny ran past Dave to her husband.

Having grown up in the area and knowing every trail, Dave ran across the dunes to see if any suspects were around.

"No, no! Come back!" the police started yelling at Dave. "Get down from there!"

Dave stopped at the top of the dunes, from where he saw approximately six people on the other side. Stooped over picking something up, a man with sandy blonde hair saw Dave and expressed surprise. The man was wearing street clothes and a dark jacket. Since learning about Gregory Allen and seeing his photo, Dave is convinced that the man he saw was Allen.

With the police still yelling at him to come back, Dave returned. He was told by Manitowoc County deputies that the people on the other side of the dunes were police, and not to go over there, otherwise he would disturb the crime scene. Dave found the claim odd because none of the people he saw on the other side of the dunes had on police uniforms or appeared to be police. He also wondered what they were doing at the crime scene so soon as Penny had only just run over the dunes.

The deputies knew Dave, but he was never asked to give a statement or to appear in court.

Years later, Dave heard Penny on a radio show, describing her ordeal. "In her account," Dave said, "she said that she was passed-out on the dunes and somebody found her. That isn't what I saw. She came running over the dunes as fast as she could."

A year later, Dave invested in a bar. Some of the patrons attempted to pressurise him into joining a secret society whose members included local officials, business owners and Manitowoc County law enforcement. One showed Dave some naked pictures of men whom Dave knew from around town. Dave said he wasn't interested in joining.

His bar manager owed money to members of the society. She told Dave that she was afraid of the sheriff. Months later, she died under strange circumstances while Dave was out of the county. Although she was covered in blood with a gun next to her, her death was ruled a heart attack. "Who knows what they [Manitowoc County] did to her [Dave's bar manager's] crime scene."

With his insider knowledge, Dave believes that the bigger picture of Teresa's death revolves around the financial interests of some powerful people. "The Manitowoc County Sheriff is the strong arm of the big guys. It's all about money. When I heard of Kratz's deviant sexual activity, I thought it matched the modus operandi of this secret society and he would fit right in."

On Halloween 2005, Dave and his wife, Sandra, packed their bicycles into a pickup truck and drove into the town of Two Rivers. After parking, they got on their bicycles and rode around, checking out the Halloween decorations. Just after dark, they were returning to the pickup truck by cycling past a gas station called Patsy's Mobil. Unable to recall the exact time, Dave estimated it was around 6 pm. Sunset was at 4:41 pm.

"I noticed Steven Avery at this gas station," Dave said. "He was filling up a gas can. He had a nice dark F-250 pickup truck. I told Sandra, 'There's that Steven Avery guy.' I knew what he looked like because he'd been on the news quite a bit, saying he was living in his ice fishing shanty and things like that. We watched him get in his truck and turn and drive away."

"I recognised him, too," Sandra said. "I had seen him on the news a lot. I was familiar with him because, when I met Dave in 1999, it was one of the things that he told me almost immediately: his story about his involvement in the search for Penny Beerntsen. We even walked along the beach where it had happened. When Dave pointed him out to me, there was no question it was him. He was wearing a red and white jacket, which looked like the jacket you see in the documentary. With the nice truck and all, I told Dave, 'It looks like he's doing pretty good.' He was also with a young blonde woman."

"We really didn't think any more of it until a few days later," Dave said, "when all of the news came out. I couldn't believe it. My gut turned. I was kind of involved again. I didn't want to say anything, but I figured I had to. We sent a letter to the Manitowoc County Sheriff's Office, and I called once."

"We didn't understand that the Manitowoc County Sheriff's Department," Sandra said, "might not have been the best people to contact because that didn't come to light until after Steven's trial was done."

"The news had convinced everybody that Steven had killed Teresa," Dave said. "That he had gone crazy in prison. They made it sound like an open and shut case."

Dave's offer of alibi witness testimony was ignored by the Manitowoc County Sheriff's Office. It didn't fit their narrative: Steven was supposed to have been busy raping, torturing, murdering and burning Teresa at that time.

During Steven's 1985 trial, an honest expert witness for the defence, Dr Penrod, testified about how Penny's memory of her assailant could have been altered. Prosecutor Vogel went beyond neutralising the witness. He used Penrod's testimony to make the jurors question whether the memories of Steven's alibi witnesses had been altered.

"How are you employed?" Steven's lawyer asked Dr Penrod.

"I'm a professor of psychology at the University of Wisconsin in Madison."

"What's your educational background?"

"I have a bachelor's degree from Yale in 1969 and I have a law degree from Harvard Law School in 1974 and a Ph.D. in psychology from Harvard University in 1979."

"Where were you employed prior to the University of Wisconsin, Dr Penrod?"

"I was a graduate student at Harvard University where I was employed as a teaching and research assistant. Prior to that time, I was in the Navy. I worked as a legal officer in the Navy, and I had various other and sundry jobs before that."

"What are your duties at the University of Wisconsin?"

"First would be teaching, second would be research and third would be administrative responsibilities. Most of my research is conducted in areas where psychology and law interact... At the moment, my primary research activities are focused on issues concerning eyewitness reliability, problems of eyewitness identification and methods that might be used to assess the reliability of eyewitness identification. A couple of years ago, I conducted a series of seminars for the Madison Police Department on methods of investigation, interrogation of witnesses, and construction of line-ups, problems of eyewitness identification."

The judge asked the prosecutor if he had any objections to Penrod testifying further.

"I believe he's stated his qualifications in terms of his background," Vogel said, "but I'm not sure if he specifically qualified himself as an expert on—"

"Well, I can do with a yes or no," the judge said.

"Yes," Vogel said.

"Thank you," the judge said. "The court will receive further testimony from Mr Penrod."

"Would you please tell the jury how human memory operates, Dr Penrod?" Steven's lawyer said.

"Most psychologists break human memory down into four stages. The first stage is perception, which just refers to the stage at which whatever sensor system we're using – I'll concentrate on our visual system – actually receives stimulation. In the case of the eye, it receives light. Stimulated by light, we pick up visual images. That's the perception stage. A second stage commonly discussed is the encoding stage. It really refers to the active processing in terms of thinking about the information that's perceived. The third stage is commonly referred to as the storage, or sometimes, the retention interval. It refers to the period of time between the perception and encoding of information and then the later effort to pull that information out of memory. And finally, the retrieval stage, which is that stage of trying to retrieve information out of memory. Now, the reason that we break them down into those stages is because in fact different things are happening at those stages in terms of forming the memory, and the eyewitness is prone to a variety of errors or problems at each of those different stages.

"We also know that things can happen even while information is being stored. So even if the person starts out with a good rich solid memory for an event, that doesn't mean that at some later point in time they're going to be able to retrieve that information from memory in its original and pure pristine form. The reason is that events that take place after, let's say a crime, events that take place after viewing a crime can change or distort the original memory, and what happens is that if people pick up information after the crime, that information can literally become part of their original memory. While information is sitting in the storage stage, it can undergo changes or transformations that in essence can destroy the original memory. We know, for example, there have been several studies on the effects of overhearing another person talk about the characteristics of the perpetrator. Let's say witnesses had seen a staged crime or a videotape of a crime, and later they hear somebody say, 'I think he has a moustache,' or, 'I think he has curly hair,' those characteristics, those pieces of information – and they're false information and they've been sort of set up by the researcher to see what effect it will have on the witnesses' memories – those pieces of false information can find their way into any individual witness' memories, and at a later point in time they are significantly more likely to misidentify an individual who has the moustache as the perpetrator when the original perpetrator didn't, or an individual who has curly hair when the original perpetrator didn't have curly hair. These effects can be produced in very subtle ways."

"I was going to ask: is that a conscious process?" Steven's lawyer said.

"Absolutely not. This is not something where people sort of intentionally take that information and now put it into their memory. It's something that happens unintentionally, and indeed the witnesses who display these kinds of effects are trying the best they can to make a totally accurate report, but these influences are very, very subtle, but can nonetheless have a very profound effect on the witness' memory, and in some sense, the most disturbing aspect of this is that it proves to be virtually impossible for a witness to somehow go back and restore or retrieve their original memory."

"You said the viewing of a photo line-up could change the original memory. How is that?"

"Well, because the information that is picked up after an event

– but it's relevant to the event – in a sense now becomes intermingled with the original information. We don't know exactly what goes on in the brain that produces this effect, but what we do know is that post- event information seems to become mingled, intermingled with the information from the original event. It can in some instances literally displace it, so that it's impossible to retrieve memory about the face of the original perpetrator because it's been supplanted, replaced by, pushed out by or intermingled with information that's picked up from these photographs."

"This change in original memory, is that a conscious process?"

"No. Again, it's not a conscious process and it's something that proves to be fairly difficult to prevent. Indeed, it's a common problem."

"We're specifically interested, Dr Penrod, in what effect expectation might have on a photo-identification."

"If a person has an expectation that the perpetrator is going to be there, it seems to change the identification task for them. Instead of having the sole responsibility for saying, well, out of these six possible suspects, this is the person, and then the case proceeds solely on the basis of that identification, the task now seems to be one of confirming or disconfirming police suspicions and the thought is that if a misidentification occurs – if the wrong person is picked – there won't be any harm done. On the other hand, if I pick the same person that the police have picked, we'll have some corroborating identification, if you will, so it seems to change the task and simply make people more willing to make identifications. They're just as conservative about making their identification."

Steven's lawyer asked whether there was a correlation between the confidence of the person making the identification and the accuracy of the selection.

"Unfortunately not. And despite the fact that it defies common sense, there have been a large number of studies which show that if there is a relationship between confidence and accuracy, it's only a weak relationship. We just are not very good at sort of crawling inside our memory and trying to determine whether it's good solid memory or not so good a memory."

Vogel chose to counter Penrod's two hours of honest testimony by tapping into local prejudices. Without attempting to rebut anything Penrod had said, Vogel launched an ad hominem attack against Penrod whom he characterised as being insulated by academia and out of touch with the real world. His next strategy was to use Penrod's expert testimony to discredit Steven's alibi witnesses. If memories were malleable, as Penrod had stated, then surely the memories of the Avery family members would have changed in a way that would have made them more predisposed to say things in Steven's favour – especially if they had colluded.

"Is there a term called 'feedback factor,' Mr Penrod? Do you know what that means?" Vogel said.

"I'm not sure what you're referring to," Penrod said.

"Alright, when witnesses have a chance to get together and talk to each other about what they've seen. Is there a psychological term for that?"

"Well, people may have a psychological term, but it's not one that's in widespread use."

"Have you done research in that area?"

"No, sir."

Vogel went on to discredit Steven and his family. On the stand, Steven told the jurors exactly where he'd been on the day of Penny's assault. Under cross-examination, he remained calm and came across as honest. His wife, Lori, testified the same. A receipt was presented that proved they were in Green Bay at 5:13 pm.

Steven's lawyer asked Lori if she had had any contact with Steven prior to her giving the police a written statement describing where she and Steven had been on the day of Penny's assault.

"No. I didn't hear from Steve until a week later, on August 7, when he was allowed to make his first phone call."

"Did Steven ever tell you what to put in your statement?"

"No, he didn't even know I wrote them up."

"Did anybody tell you what to put in your statements, Lori?"

"No, they didn't. I was there by myself when I wrote them."

Penny had described her attacker as wearing white underwear, so Steven's lawyer asked Lori, "Does Steve wear clothes when he sleeps?"

"No, he doesn't. Just socks sometimes if his feet are cold."

"Was he wearing underwear when he was arrested?"

"No, he wasn't. He doesn't wear underwear."

"Does he own any underwear?"

"No, he doesn't."

Numerous witnesses testified that Steven had been at the salvage yard at the time of Penny's assault. Chuck Avery had watched Steven take his sister, Barb, to the gravel pit in-between 3 pm and 3:30 pm. When *Divorce Court* had almost finished, Rose Scherer had gazed through a window at the cement truck and Steven outside. After helping Steven pour concrete, Lloyd Scherer had watched Steven and his family leave the salvage yard at approximately 3:50 pm, when the assault was commencing.

Long after the trial, a deputy revealed that he had seen cement dust on Steven Avery's shirt on the day of the crime, which backed up Steven's alibi of having worked with concrete. Penny had said that her attacker had smelled clean, and had on clean clothes. Told he would lose his job if his honest testimony ever made it into the courtroom, the deputy had been neutralised. At the trial, the crime lab testified that Steven's clothes that day had contained no trace of cement dust.

Judy Blanke testified that Steven had come into the house at the end of *Divorce Court* – 3:30 pm – and had turned off the TV as a prank. She and her husband had left the salvage yard at the same time as Steven and his family. They had watched Steven drive away, and had waited for the dust to settle before leaving because their car had just been washed.

Vogel neutralised these alibi witnesses by questioning each in a way that provoked answers that damaged their credibility. He asked if they had discussed the case amongst themselves. Those who said yes were cast as collaborators. Those who said no were cast as liars. Steven's mother had answered no.

"You mean you didn't talk to your husband about the time when all the women got together, you didn't discuss that with anybody?" Vogel said.

"No," Dolores said.

"You didn't get together and try to remember what time it was you got together at your house?"

"No, uh-uh, because I know we watched *Divorce Court*, us women and all, so–"

"You didn't sit down and discuss what time it was when he may have left the house that day?"

"No."

"So, you and Allan haven't talked about this case at all?"

"Uh-uh, no."

"You talked about what happened on the day of the twenty-ninth amongst yourselves to try to figure out where everybody was and what everybody did, right?"

"I told you exactly what I remember."

"I know that. I'm just asking you. You have talked about it with the other people, trying to figure out what happened that day?"

"No, not about, no, I haven't."

"You haven't stood around, and I'm not talking about the last couple of days, I'm talking about before the last couple of days when you've been to court – you stood around talking with the other people that have been here to just try to figure out what happened on the twenty-ninth?"

"I don't have to figure out what happened on the twenty-ninth. I know what happened on the twenty-ninth."

"Right, but you've asked other people if they remember what happened on the twenty-ninth."

"No. I haven't."

"I'm not accusing you that because of talking to people there was any harm. I don't want you to get that impression. I'm just asking if you talked amongst your family members about what happened on the twenty-ninth, and you said before that there were some statements that you heard, and I'm just trying to find out from you what those statements might have been, or who might have made those statements. Do you understand?"

"Oh, I don't remember nothing like that."

"That's all."

"Has all your testimony today been the truth?" Steven's lawyer said.

"Yes, it has," Dolores said.

"That's all I have."

Vogel attempted the same technique on Steven's sister, Barb, and suggested that Steven's lawyer had coached her on what to say. "Did anyone tell you what to say, Barb?"

"No."

"Did I?"

"You just told me to be honest and tell the truth."

"Ms Avery, did you sit down and discuss where Steve was that day and where he might have been, what he was doing?"

"No 'cause I already knew."

"Did someone tell you to say you went down in the pit with Steve and his jeep?"

"No."

Barb managed to resist Vogel's technique, but most of Steven's honest witnesses were neutralised.

STRATEGY 8: PROCURE DISHONEST WITNESSES

When it comes to courtroom theatre, dishonest witnesses can have a more corrosive effect on the jury than expert witnesses. Dishonest witnesses come in a variety of forms. The most effective ones are crime victims who are manipulated into dishonesty by corrupt police and prosecutors. When the police take the stand to deliver their own lies, jury members are more likely to be sceptical. But put a crime victim on the stand, and jury members will usually side with the victim, especially if the victim is a woman and the culprit is a man with criminal history. This strategy is so potent because a victim tricked into delivering lies believes he or she is telling the truth. Lies delivered with conviction from a victim will permeate the minds of jury members.

In Steven's first case, the police immediately set about converting the victim into an instrument to obtain a wrongful conviction without her even knowing it. Within hours of the assault on Penny, the Manitowoc County Sheriff's deputies were discussing Steven as a suspect.

While still at the hospital consoling Penny and her family, whom he knew personally, Sheriff Kocourek called the jail for a mugshot of Steven to be delivered to the hospital, with an assortment of other mugshots of bearded men fitting the same description. Steven's photo was rushed to the hospital in record time as the Sheriff's deputies had never seen the Sheriff take the lead in an investigation and express such urgency.

After the mugshots arrived, Kocourek requested the presence of Chief Deputy Gene Kusche to draw a sketch of the culprit. His task was simplified by Kocourek, who allowed Kusche to see Steven Avery's mugshot.

In shock, severely wounded, with her face swollen up, Penny had been moved to the second floor of the hospital. Kusche was sitting on a chair next to her bed. His manipulation of Penny commenced with small talk.

Penny's description of the assailant did not match Steven Avery, right down to the brown eyes. That was irrelevant to Kusche, who drew a sketch of Steven from the mugshot he'd just seen. Kusche later testified that his drawing had been completed when Penny was "satisfied in her mind that it was a reasonable representation of what her memory was." Even the trial judge noted an "uncanny resemblance" between the sketch and Steven's mugshot.

Working on the sketch with Kusche had imprinted Steven's face onto Penny's mind. To test whether this brainwashing technique had succeeded, Sheriff Kocourek subjected Penny to a photo array. With Kusche still present, Kocourek placed nine mugshots on a table and asked Penny to identify the assailant. She immediately picked Steven. After looking at the other mugshots for a second time, she stated that it was Steven who had attacked her.

With Penny successfully converted into a dishonest witness, Kocourek got a warrant issued for Steven's arrest.

When Penny had first arrived in the emergency room, she had been interviewed about the assault by Deputy Dvorak, who had requested a description of the assailant. Penny's statement had taken almost four hours, during which time she had suffered an intrusive rape-protocol kit, stitches to her face, x-rays of her skull and other medical procedures. Due to everything going on, Penny had given a statement in a disjointed fashion. It had not been recorded. The female deputy had taken notes.

While Penny was still on the emergency room table, Dvorak handed the statement to her. "Read each page and initial the bottom."

"I can't read this," Penny said as her vision was too blurred.

"It's OK. Sign it anyway."

A few days later, problems in the framing of Steven Avery occurred. Penny had received phone calls from someone who knew details of the assault. Upon being interviewed again by Deputy Dvorak, Penny insisted that her assailant's hands had been clean. Working in a scrap yard had layered Steven's hands with grease and grime. Even a witness who had seen Steven an hour after the assault on Penny had described his hands as greasy.

Dvorak took Penny over to the Sheriff's Department to view a line-up. She was handed a paper with the numbers one to eight.

"If you see your assailant among the eight men, check the appropriate number and fold the paper in half."

"What if I don't see him in here?"

"Don't mark anything. Just fold the paper in half."

In a dark hallway, with the Sheriff, her husband and prosecutor Vogel present, Penny gazed through a one-way glass window at eight men. It took her a long time to pick the only one who she had seen in the original photo array and who resembled Kusche's composite drawing: Steven Avery.

An assistant public defender who had been present later testified that it took Penny close to ten minutes to select Steven. She added that one of the participants stared at Steven during most of the line-up, and that Steven stuck out like a sore thumb. The assistant public defender was denied access to the line-up form that Penny had signed because it had been immediately handed to the Sheriff, who exited the room.

A few days later, prosecutor Dennis Vogel went to Penny's home to ensure that she would identify Steven in court with absolute certainty. He asked how sure she was that Steven had done the crime. She replied 90 to 95%. Unsatisfied with a response that could have created the possibility of reasonable doubt in the jurors' minds, Vogel coached Penny to say that she was 100% certain it had been Steven.

When Penny took the stand, Vogel ran through a series of questions that he had helped her to rehearse answers for. "This is important now, Penny. At any time did Deputy Kusche suggest to you any of the features that might appear on your assailant?"

"No, no, not at all," Penny said.

"Were you the one making the suggestion to him as to what the features look like?"

"Yes."

"In other words, the changes he may have made on that drawing, how were those changes directed, by himself making those decisions or by you telling him to make the changes?"

"No, by me telling him to make the changes."

Vogel asked Penny to walk over to an enlarged photo of Steven Avery. "Is this the picture that you picked out in that photo line-up without anybody telling you what your assailant would look like or that he might be in the line-up, that sort of thing?"

"Yes, that's the picture."

"Did you have a picture in your mind, Penny?"

"Yes, I remembered very clearly," Penny said. "It's as if there's a photograph in my mind."

"Would you recognize the person that attacked you if you saw that person today?"

"Yes."

"Is that person in the courtroom right now?"

"Yes, he is."

"Can you please tell me where?"

"Yes. He's seated next to Mr Bolgert in the tan suit."

"The record will reflect identification," the judge said.

"Looking at Mr Avery today, the defendant," Vogel said, "do you understand that your ability to be positive about your assailant is important in this case?"

"Yes, I do."

"Have you thought about that from the time when this case began, when you actually became involved in the process until today's trial? Have you thought about how important that is?"

"Yes, I have."

"Penny, is there any question in your mind as to whether or not the person you picked out for us today is in fact the person that attacked you?"

"There is absolutely no question in my mind."

Up against Penny's dramatic and convincing testimony, Steven's lawyer didn't stand much of a chance. "Ms Beerntsen, did your attacker have brown eyes?"

"I originally said he had brown eyes, but when I picked him out of the photo line-up, I handed it to the sheriff and said, 'He's got blue eyes. I was mistaken.'"

"And you also told Deputy Dvorak two days later that he had brown eyes. Is that correct?"

"That's correct."

"And you are speaking from your memory when you told Deputy Dvorak that?"

"Yes."

Steven's lawyer had already told the jury that Steven's hands were perpetually greasy from working on cars. He asked Penny if her attacker's hands were greasy.

"No. They were clean."

Steven's lawyer challenged Deputy Dvorak. "You stated after that statement was signed that Penny changed her description of the eyes from brown eyes to blue, isn't that right?"

"Yes," Dvorak said. "It was not noted on the statement."

"Did that happen the same day or is that on your interview of August 1?"

"I believe this is what she told the sheriff, possibly that first evening."

"Did she ever tell you the attacker had blue eyes?"

"Yes, after I had taken the second statement."

"On August 1?"

"Yes."

"So, the first time she told you about the blue eyes was on August 1, three days after the assault?"

"Yes."

"Deputy Dvorak, did you specifically ask Ms Beerntsen whether the attacker's hands were dirty or greasy?"

"Yes, I did, and she did not include any mention of them being greasy or dirty."

Penny's testimony was believed over multiple alibi witnesses who stated that Steven was at the salvage yard pouring concrete, and later had travelled to Green Bay with Lori and the children.

Steven even had a receipt for paint he'd purchased in Green Bay at 5:13 pm, rendering it impossible for him to have been at the crime scene. The checkout clerk had told the police that she remembered Steven and the twins.

When court is theatre, the constraints of time and the laws of physics are easily overcome by dishonest witnesses. For this purpose, Kocourek employed Detective Fred Nicholson.

To escape from the crime scene at 4:05 pm and show up at 5:13 pm to buy paint in Green Bay required sixty-eight minutes. In that time, Steven would have needed to have run half a mile from the crime scene to the nearest car park, driven ten miles back to the salvage yard, packed Lori and the kids in the vehicle and driven thirty miles north to Green Bay.

To testify in court that this was feasible, Detective Nicholson replicated the journey, while adding techniques of his own that condensed time. It took Nicholson thirteen minutes to get from the crime scene to the car park. By speeding at 10 to 15 mph over the limit, Nicholson managed to drive to the salvage yard, continue to Green Bay and purchase paint in forty-four minutes. The complete journey had taken fifty-seven minutes. By speeding and omitting the length of time it had taken for Steven to get five children into and out of his truck, Nicholson's estimate was eleven minutes below what Sheriff Kocourek needed.

On top of Nicholson's generous calculation, the prosecution used a witness that devastated the timeframe for Steven. Donald Cigler's cement truck had been at the Avery property on the day of the assault on Penny. When questioned by the police, the Avery family members all stated that the cement truck had been there when Steven came inside after *Divorce Court* ended at 3:30 pm – thus Steven didn't have enough time to attack Penny and escape from the crime scene at 4:05 pm.

But Cigler's memory differed. "Well, they poured a slab for a sheep barn and then they had some small odd pours around the building. I must have left around 2:30 [pm] I'd say – somewheres in there. Then I went back to the pit. It's about five or six miles back to the pit. When I got back to the pit, I washed up the truck with some water in there and then dumped that, parked it and shut it off. It takes about ten minutes or so to wash the truck, so I estimate it was half an hour after I left the Averys' that I checked out and went home. We have timecards that we fill out ourselves, and on that date I entered seven and a half hours, so since I began work at 7:30 [am] and worked right through noon without a lunch hour, that means I checked out at 3 [pm]. So, I'd say it was around 2:30 [pm] when I left the Avery place."

Under cross-examination, Cigler acknowledged working irregular hours each day, and that he recorded his hours in a notepad, not with a timeclock. But the damage had been done. His testimony had made it seem as if the Averys had been lying about the timeframe to support Steven. It also provided Steven an opportunity to have attacked Penny at 3:50 pm.

Years later, a private investigator ascertained that upon leaving the courtroom that day, Cigler had been overheard saying, "I think I'd gypped myself out of an hour."

Suspecting something was amiss with Kusche's sketch of Steven Avery, Steven's lawyer requested to suppress Penny's identification of Steven as her assailant. In court, the lawyer questioned Sheriff Kocourek, Gene Kusche and Deputy Judy Dvorak about the methods they had used to identify Steven as the culprit.

Vogel's next witness identified himself as "Eugene Kusche, Chief Deputy Sheriff for Manitowoc County." His expertise as a police artist had come from participating in a course at the FBI only one month prior to Penny's assault. "I attended a course in what's called rapid visual perception. It's on how to train individuals, such as bank clerks or what-have-you, on what to look for in facial characteristics. Part of the course was also on how to prepare the drawing, the composite comparisons."

"In this particular case," Vogel said, "did you have any suspects in mind before you made the drawing for Penny Beerntsen?"

"Did I have in my mind?" Kusche said.

"Yes."

"Visually?"

"Yes, visually or any other way."

Kusche paused. "I was told a name earlier, but I did not know the person."

"So, you had no preconceived ideas of your own of any particular feature or any drawing or any descriptions of anybody prior to talking to Penny Beerntsen? So, you're saying you didn't see any photographs and neither did the victim. Is that correct?"

"I did not, and to my knowledge the victim did not."

"At any time during your interview of Penny, did anyone come in and suggest to you a name or a description?"

"Not a description. I know a name was stated to me. But I don't know if she was within earshot at the time it was stated to me."

"Now, once you had the victim at ease and began the interview, did you suggest any features of a face to the victim?"

"No, sir. You ask them to tell you, then you draw what you think they mean, and if it is not, like I said, they will correct it. And one of the important portions of the training is not to be suggestive, like you don't say, 'Did the person have a round face?' Instead, you ask 'What was the shape of the face?' So, that way, you're not putting anything in their mind."

"I show you what's been marked as Exhibit 26," Vogel said, "and I ask if you recognise it?"

"This is my original drawing, the charcoal drawing."

"Is Exhibit 26 the final product?"

"It is," Kusche said. "This was the original and final drawing."

Steven's lawyer cross-examined Kusche. "You mentioned that the mug shots for the photo line-up had been pulled before the composite was done. Is that standard practice?"

"Apparently from the description prior to me arriving at the scene or at the hospital, the officers had some idea of who it might be. Therefore, it would not be unusual that photographs would be pulled."

"Did she give you a description of eye colour?"

"I can't say that I asked, so I don't remember that."

"That wouldn't be part of your standard procedure, to ask eye colour?"

"It would probably be, but in this case, I can't recollect having asked her. I may have, but as I did not do this in colour, I didn't make any representation in colour."

Vogel called Sheriff Kocourek to the stand. "Could you please tell everyone what your occupation is?"

"Sheriff of Manitowoc County."

"And were you involved in coordinating the investigation of the incident regarding Penny Beerntsen?"

"Yes."

"When you presented the photo array to her, did you lay them out for her, or just give her a stack to finger through?"

"I just spread them out on a table and she looked at all of them at the same time."

"And did Penny Beerntsen pick out any one of those photographs for you?"

"Yes, she did."

"Which one did she pick?"

"She picked out photograph number 3746, which is of Steven Avery."

"Was there any hesitancy that you could observe about her when she was asked to pick out a photograph and when she did in fact pick out that photograph?"

"As a matter of fact," Kocourek said confidently, "I noted that she was kind of drawn to that one, and then she sort of held her hand on this one and looked at the others, but then she came right back to this one and said, 'This is the man.'"

Steven's lawyer cross-examined the sheriff. "Before July 29, did you know Steve?"

"Yes, I did."

"And that was through professional contacts?"

"That's correct."

"When you heard [Penny's] description, you suspected Steve?"

"Yes."

"And did you tell the victim that you had a suspect in mind?"

"Yes."

"And did you direct some deputies to pull some photographs?"

"Yes."

"When did you do that?"

"It would have been during the evening of July 29."

"Before the composite was drawn?"

"Yes."

"Did you have those photos before the composite was drawn?"

"They were delivered to me at the hospital."

"Before the composite was drawn, did you indicate to the artist that you had a suspect in mind?"

"Yes."

"When the composite was done, did you immediately present the photograph to [Penny]?"

"After the composite was complete and she was sure in her mind that there wasn't much more that she could offer to, you know, change the composite, the composite was set aside and the photographs were presented to her."

"Do you think she realised that those photos had been pulled before the composite was drawn?"

"I'm sure she probably did, yes."

"The other times you've seen Steven Avery, did you ever see him wearing a waist-length leather jacket?"

"No."

"That's all I have. Thank you."

Judge Hazlewood ruled, "The preparation of a composite drawing prior to showing the complaining witness a photo line-up was particularly appropriate in this case. And as noted, both the sheriff and the deputy who initially interviewed Ms. Beerntsen considered the possibility that the defendant was involved in this assault… This additional check, arguably unnecessary, provides an added assurance that Deputy Dvorak and Sheriff Kocourek's initial suspicions did not become a self-fulfilling prophecy when Ms Beerntsen selected the defendant's photograph."

With Penny coached into misidentifying Steven Avery, and Detective Nicholson ready to lie on the stand about the feasibility of the timeframes, all that remained was to get a witness to lie about seeing Steven Avery in a dark waist-length leather jacket, just like the one Penny had described her assailant had on. Three days before Steven's trial was due to start, his lawyer received a letter from Dennis Vogel:

"In speaking with three witnesses, [Deputies] Froelich, Judy Dvorak, and Ken Peterson, all three officers have had prior contact with Steven Avery, the defendant, and will be in a position to testify that they have personally seen Mr Avery wearing a leather motorcycle-type jacket, dark brownish in colour, which would be short/waist-length."

The jacket found in Steven's house didn't match the one Penny had described. Steven's uncle, Deputy Arland, who saw Steven on a regular basis, had never ever seen Steven in a leather jacket. These obstacles were overcome by Vogel not questioning Deputy Aland about the leather jacket, but instead, only questioning deputies who had been coached to lie such as Judy Dvorak, who stated that she'd seen Steven in a leather jacket identical to the one Penny had described on her attacker.

In court, Vogel asked Froelich about the jacket. "Prior to July 29, 1985, had you ever seen Mr Avery wearing any sort of a leather jacket?"

"Yes," Froelich said.

"More than one time?"

"Yes, it's a black waist-length motorcycle-type leather jacket."

"Is that an old-looking jacket to your knowledge?" Vogel said.

"Yes, old-looking."

"Are there any specific dates or time you remember specifically seeing him having that jacket?"

"Yes." Froelich handed Vogel a child safety-seat warning ticket that he'd issued to Steven on April 6, 1984.

Vogel held the ticket up. "For example, on this particular date and time, do you remember what Steve was wearing?"

"He was wearing the black, faded black motorcycle jacket. And I've seen him wearing the jacket more recently, but I just don't remember any specific dates."

Steven's lawyer challenged Judy Dvorak about the jacket. "You don't know if Steven Avery owns a leather jacket like the assailant was wearing, do you?"

"No, but I have seen him with an older looking dark leather jacket."

"When is the most recent time?"

"I couldn't be sure, but I remember last fall I had seen him wearing it several times and during the winter."

"Where did you see him?"

"Steve lives across Old Country Highway Y from where I live. Our residence is just to the east on the opposite side of the road."

"So, you would see him when you drove by occasionally. Is that when you'd see him?"

"I would see him in the yard as I walked by, or I jog frequently, or when I do walk, when I drive by. Yes."

"Was there any reason for you to take note of what he was wearing?"

"Not really. I also have the project child safe car, the safe car-seat project, and I had to pick up a car-seat from Steve once in his home also."

"He was wearing that coat?"

"I can't be sure on that, but I believe he may have."

"But you had no particular reason to remember what he was wearing, did you?"

"No, I did not."

"Did you make notes when you saw him wearing different items of clothing?"

"No, I did not. This is not a thing you generally do about your neighbours."

"I agree. Were you specifically asked whether you had ever

seen Steve wearing a short leather coat for the purpose of this case?"

"Yes. It has come out in a conversation."

The police had also been coached to state that they had heard Steven say that he had been accused of murdering a woman before Steven could have possibly known that a woman had been murdered.

"The defendant's wife came downstairs," Sergeant Peterson said, "and asked him what was going on, and he said, 'They say I murdered a woman.'"

"Did he use the word 'woman'?" Vogel said with emphasis.

"Yes," Petersen said. "Prior to that time, you hadn't mentioned the world 'woman' when you arrested him, had you?"

"No, not at all."

"Had anyone else mentioned that it was a woman?"

"Not in my presence."

Deputy Froelich described hiding in a closet until Steven Avery came down stairs, and arresting Steven in the kitchen.

"When the defendant's wife came downstairs," Vogel said, "did she ask him anything?"

"His wife asked, 'Would somebody please tell me what's going on?' And then Sergeant Petersen and myself, we just looked at each other, and Steve looked at his wife and said, 'They said I murdered a girl.'"

"When he said that, did you specifically make a note of that, a mental note that he said it?"

"Yes."

"Why?"

"Because at that point, no one had said it was a male or female."

The Wisconsin State Crime Lab provided a witness who contributed to both of Steven's wrongful convictions: Sherry Culhane. As well as botching the DNA tests in the second wrongful conviction, Sherry had used the science of hair analysis to state that a hair found on Penny Beerntsen – that belonged to Gregory Allen – could possibly have come from Steven. This was based on her examination of a hair extracted from Steven's T-shirt on the night of the assault. She opined that her conclusion was valid to a reasonable degree of scientific certainty.

Steven's lawyer did his best to pull her conclusion apart: "Is it possible to prove identification by hair analysis?"

"No."

"Is the hair of many people consistent with each other?"

"Yes."

"Is it unusual for hair from different people to be consistent with each other?"

"No, it's not."

"For example, is it unusual for the hair of white Caucasians to be consistent with each other?"

"No."

"If you take a hair from ten different people, would it be unusual to find the hair from those different people to be consistent?"

"No."

"Did you have any standards from hospital or ambulance personnel?"

"No, sir."

"Any standards from any of Mr Avery's children?"

"No, sir."

With the victim, the police and prosecutor reciting thoroughly rehearsed lies on the stand, Steven's credibility was ruined – until DNA science advanced in ways that those framing him had not anticipated.

The most compliant and dishonest witnesses to procure are informants. Those in jail will fabricate the most creative lies to get released or to receive lighter sentences. Due to the War on Drugs, there are now more informants on the streets of America than there are police. Protected by the police for providing information, they remain at large, often dealing drugs, using drugs and committing crimes.

One example is Darryl Moore. Attorney Richard Daley wanted

to incarcerate Charles Ashley, the head of a Chicago drug ring who was dying from cancer. Daley did a deal with Darryl Moore, a hit man, drug pusher, robber, rapist, junkie, parole violator and perjurer, who was facing a long sentence due to prior convictions for sexual assault and armed robbery. In exchange for testimony from Moore concerning an alleged contract murder committed on behalf of Charles Ashley, weapons and drug charges against Moore would be dropped. Moore would be paid cash, and he would be immune from prosecution for his role in the alleged murder.

In court, Moore's mother was called as a defence witness. "Do you know Darryl's reputation . . . for being truthful?" asked the defence lawyer.

"Yes," Moore's mother answered.

"Is that reputation good or is it bad?"

"Bad."

"Would you believe Darryl Moore under oath?"

"No, I wouldn't."

The prosecution alleged that Charles Ashley had paid two co-defendants to murder a suspected informant. With Moore's testimony, Ashley was convicted of murder and sentenced to spend his brief remaining life in prison. By now Ashley was so sick, he was confined to a wheelchair. The two co-defendants were also found guilty.

After being freed for his testimony, Moore went back to his neighbourhood. On February 13, 1987, he approached an 11-year-old on her way to the grocery store with $10 in her pocket. He grabbed her and asked if she had a match. She tried to escape, but he clutched her by the arm and the back of her neck. Brandishing a gun, he asked if she knew anyone who wanted to buy it. She started crying.

"Shut up or I'll blow your head off!" Moore dragged her into an alley, pushed her down, removed her pants and raped her.

The defence lawyer in the Ashley case made a statement about the attorney who'd struck the deal to free Moore: "Richard Daley is, in my opinion, as guilty, morally, as Darryl Moore of the rape of that child, perhaps more so because he, unlike Moore, is presumed to be a moral decent man of intelligence."

Richard Daley refused to comment. The man he'd incarcerated – Ashley – died not long after.

In another case, Sunny Jacobs and her husband, Jesse Tafero, were wrongfully convicted for the murder of a policeman. Facing the death penalty, the killer, Walter Rhodes, turned informant and implicated Jacobs and Tafero. As a reward for his information, Rhodes ended up serving less than 20 years. Sentenced to death, Tafero was executed by electrocution, but the machine malfunctioned, causing six-inch flames to shoot out of his head. It took him seven minutes to die and the inmates said that they could smell his burning flesh for days. After his death, Rhodes confessed, and Sunny was released in 1992.

While Steven was in prison on his first case, Sheriff Kocourek kept a document in his safe that was probably a form of insurance in case his framing of Steven was ever exposed:

AFFIDAVIT OF RAYMOND E. CRIVITZ:

I, Raymond E. Crivitz, do hereby swear and attest to the following:

1. My name is Raymond E. Crivitz.

2. As of the date of the signing of this affidavit, I am an inmate at Green Bay Correctional Institution in Green Bay, Wisconsin.

3. During a previous period of my incarceration I lived here from fall of 1988 to the summer of 1989.

4. During this period of incarceration I was housed in the North Cell Hall, C Tier, in cell C-73.

5. While I was living in C-73, I came to know another inmate who was housed in C-72 right next to my cell.

6. This inmate was Steve Avery (approximately five feet five inches tall with sandy/dirty blond hair and ice blue eyes), who also went by the nickname "Stivers."

7. During one of several conversations I had with Steve Avery (while each of us were sitting in our cells), in the spring/summer of 1989, I asked him what he was in for.

8. Steve Avery told me that he was arrested and convicted for raping a woman on a beach near Manitowoc, Wisconsin.

9. I responded that I was also in for assault (even though I wasn't) just to get his trust and so he would talk to me.

10. Steve Avery told me that he was "set up by this bitch," that he was on the beach and saw a woman jogging. He said he "wanted some." I asked him if he got some.

11. Steve Avery then told me that "yes he got some," that he "fucked the bitch" and that "she loved it."

12. I asked him if that was a small town and if he thought he would see her again. He said it was and that if he did see her again that he "Would finish what he started" because he felt he had been "set up by the bitch" and that he thought she was working with the police or was some kind of policewoman.

13. About three weeks later I was transferred out of Green Bay Correctional Institution.

When a new sheriff took over from Kocourek in 2001, Kocourek's safe had been emptied except for the above affidavit. The standard procedure should have been for Kocourek to have added it to a police report and sent a copy to the district attorney. Prosecutor Griesbach has speculated that the affidavit might have been Kocourek's trump card, that if the case against Steven collapsed then at least Kocourek could have pointed to the affidavit as one more piece of evidence that had made him believe in Steven's guilt.

In Steven's second case, the prosecution procured statements from jailhouse snitches, who claimed that Steven had told them that he planned to build a torture chamber when he got out. They described how Steven intended to assault, torture and murder young women.

On March 9, 2006, a prisoner who was no longer incarcerated made a statement to a Calumet County investigator, who documented the interview:

Rieckhoff indicated he had seen the news in which inmates had been telling the police that Avery had shown them a torture chamber on a piece of paper. Rieckhoff indicated he was in prison with Steven Avery in Stanley Prison in the Wausau area and had spoken to Steven approximately 20 times. Rieckhoff indicated he was in Unit 3 and Avery was in Unit 2, but he would talk to Steven Avery in the recreation field and in the prison library. Rieckhoff indicated Steven hated all women, and would resort to the saying about women, find them, feel them, fuck them, forget them.

As approximately 3:30 pm, I [Investigator Gary Steier] again had telephonic contact with Ronald Rieckhoff. Ronald stated he had been in prison with Steven Avery since 2001 and had spoken with Steven approximately 20 times while he was in prison. Rieckhoff stated he was a paralegal and from time to time Avery would ask him questions. Rieckhoff stated Steven Avery had told him he wanted to kill that young bitch that had set him up for the rape when he got out. Rieckhoff again stated he would talk to Steven Avery in the recreation field or in the prison library. Rieckhoff again indicated in Rieckhoff's words, he hated all bitches, he hated all women. Rieckhoff again reiterated Steven's comment to him, I'll find them, feel them, fuck them, forget them.

In terms of the trial, the strategy of employing jailhouse snitches failed for the prosecution: Judge Willis – who was not known for his kindness towards Steven – ruled that the informants' statements were inadmissible. Years later, the statements were resurrected by Steven Avery detractors like Griesbach, in a weak attempt to show that Steven had made violent plans towards women while he was incarcerated. Griesbach went so far as to say that because Rieckhoff was a free man at the time he gave his statement, he had nothing to gain from the police. Griesbach would have us believe that Rieckhoff volunteered information to the police out of the kindness of his heart. But there are more informants outside prison than there are inside, so Griesbach's claim is unfounded. Informants remain free by providing information.

Griesbach has authored two books about Steven: The Innocent Killer: A True Story of a Wrongful Conviction and its Astonishing Aftermath and Indefensible: The Missing Truth about Steven Avery, Teresa Halbach, and Making a Murderer. He is also on the advisory board of the Wisconsin Innocence Project.

After DNA evidence came to light in Steven's first wrongful conviction, Griesbach was instrumental in Steven's exoneration. In his books, Griesbach bravely exposed the corruption at the top of law enforcement that helped to frame Steven the first time around. He lambasted the prosecutor Dennis Vogel and Sheriff Kocourek for incarcerating Steven for the attack on Penny when they knew that Gregory Allen was the culprit.

Although Griesbach's analysis of the first wrongful conviction provides excellent supplemental material to *Making a Murderer*, his analysis of the second wrongful conviction has outraged *Making a Murderer* viewers. His books were slaughtered at the Amazon reviews and his life was threatened. Many viewers bought Griesbach's *The Innocent Killer* due to its title in the mistaken belief that Griesbach was on Steven's side, only to be disappointed by his Trojan horse approach.

In his books, Griesbach claimed that his conclusions are based on hard cold objective science, which was true for the first wrongful conviction. For the second conviction, Griesbach contradicted his reliance on science by stating in *Indefensible* that the most solid evidence of Steven's guilt is Brendan Dassey's confession. On page 134, he referred to Brendan as a cold-blooded killer, undeserving of leniency.

It is apparent from both of Griesbach's books that his opinion of Steven is based on hearsay, not science. His books quote police reports and even jailhouse snitches as if they are infallible. Years working as a prosecutor seems to have instilled Griesbach with a belief in his own omniscience, like the God complex that occurs in some physicians and surgeons.

In his books and interviews, Griesbach loves to quote the cat incident as evidence of Steven's psychopathy. He has claimed that *Making a Murderer* left details out to maintain sympathy for Steven. His basis for this is a police report that quotes one of Steven's friends, who claimed that Steven poured oil on a cat, threw it into a bonfire, watched it jump out of the fire, caught the cat, poured more oil onto it, threw it in the fire again and watched it burn until it died.

All animal cruelty is despicable, and this incident occurred during a difficult time in Steven's life when he was involved in petty crime. Steven's own account was that he and his friends were drunk and sat around a fire. With them encouraging each other, they doused the cat with fuel and tried to see how close to the fire they could toss it over without lighting it. They probably underestimated how much energy is in a little fuel and assumed that the cat would only get singed. Having being raised with cats, I find it hard to believe that the cat jumped out of the fire and Steven threw it back in. It's hard enough to catch a frightened cat, especially for a drunken person.

Griesbach and others have pointed out that serial killers sometimes have a history of animal cruelty. But those killers usually had multiple incidences over many years. Steven's horrific mistake with the cat was an isolated incident, which laid the groundwork for the bias against him. There is also the possibility that Steven took the fall for his friends with the cat. He has shown a pattern of doing that, such as trying to protect Jodi when she was in trouble for drunk driving. One such friend that Steven may have been protecting is Jerry Yanda, who on September 2, 1982, provided a written statement claiming that he had thrown the cat on the fire because Steven had told him to.

Prison makes you mature fast. During the 18 years of his first wrongful conviction, Steven would have deeply regretted the cat incident. He would have thought long and hard about being a free, useful, good person if ever given another chance. This forged Steven into the man who could hug Penny and not hold anything against her, recognising that she was a victim in his prosecution. His actions demonstrated that any residual of the person he was during the cat incident had become non-existent.

Even worse is Griesbach's overreliance on the words of one of the people responsible for stirring up so much local hatred against Steven: the wife of the deputy sheriff who lived near to Steven. According to her, Steven was stalking her with field glasses and running out onto the road naked when she was driving to work at 5:30 am. Supposedly, Steven had a habit of rubbing himself on the hood of her car, while wearing nothing but his shoes. Griesbach offers no scientific explanation as to how a person standing in a road can possibly rub themselves against the hood of a moving car. The lies she spread incensed Steven so much that he did run her off the road and pull an unloaded gun on her. Steven was arrested and released on $2,000 bail.

Griesbach's faith in the coerced confession of Brendan Dassey is matched by his belief in phoney evidence. In one interview, he explained the absence of blood splatter and DNA at the crime scene because some assaults don't leave as much DNA as crime shows portray. His faith in Lenk and Colborn is unwavering. He described them as two of the most honest cops you could find.

The absence of DNA evidence caused many Steven Avery

detractors to latch onto things that are insignificant and to blow them out of proportion, such as answering the door in a towel, which is not uncommon, and certainly not an indicator for psychopathic tendencies. Whenever I order a special delivery, I can spend hours waiting. Then the minute I step into the shower, there's a knock at the door. Rather than suffer the inconvenience of having to pick my package up from the post office, I tend to rush to the door in a towel.

Kratz manufactured a story about Teresa stating that Steven had creeped her out by once answering the door in a towel. Steven had answered the door in a towel, but not to Teresa. It had been to the woman assigned that photo route before Teresa. Kratz also claimed that Teresa told her boss that she didn't want to go to the Avery property anymore. Her boss was deposed and this was a false claim. Kratz and other detractors still use this story in the court of public opinion.

Both Kratz and Griesbach have cited Steven's *67 calls numerous times. In America, dialling *67 before a number prevents callers' names and phone numbers from being displayed on the receivers' screens. To protect his identity, Steven used *67 quite often. Having been in the news over the years and still embroiled in a hotbed of controversy because of the civil suit at the time Teresa went missing, Steven valued his privacy. Due to his unusual circumstances, pressing *67 before making a call had become a reflex action.

Detractors have cited the *67 calls Steven made to Teresa before her arrival as proof of an ambush. Teresa had dealt with Steven over a dozen times in the previous year. Working in the salvage business, Steven was a large and cherished repeat customer. Teresa knew where she was going and whom she was meeting. She even left a message at the office that she was going out to the Avery property to take photos.

Detractors have claimed that Steven's call to Teresa at 4:30 pm without using the *67 function was his attempt to camouflage his crimes by supposedly leaving a voicemail along the lines of

"Where are you? You never showed up." This is pure speculation. It could have been Steven calling Teresa to come back, so that he could list another car. At that point, he might have wanted Teresa to know it was him. In any case, when Colborn went to the Avery compound on November 4, Steven never hid the fact Teresa had arrived, disproving the theory that the 4:30 pm call was to establish that she had never showed up.

The *67 calls combined with Steven taking the afternoon off work and booking the appointment with Teresa in his sister's name, "B. Janda," led Griesbach to conclude in *Indefensible* that there was no doubt in his mind that Steven had lured Teresa there with the intent to rape her. So much for solid cold scientific evidence.

Griesbach loves to Tweet about the Avery case:

@MCGriesbach Jan 7 [2017] Did You Know... (first in a series)

That Steven Avery argued with his sister Barb about selling her van?

@MCGriesbach Jan 8 Did you know ... that Steven Avery invited his nephew's girlfriend over the night before he raped and murdered...

@MCGriesbach Jan 9 Did you know ... that SA told his brother Chuck the photographer never showed up that day? What's up with that?

I responded:

@shaunattwood Jan 9 .@MCGriesbach non-sequitur, B doesn't follow A, nor does Steven's sex drive or any of the ad hominem fallacies cited in your books #avery

@MCGriesbach stop with the non-sequitur sequence, you sound like @kenkratz I'll expose the full extent of your errors soon

@MCGriesbach where's the proof of torture/murder/rape in Steven's home? why didn't Brendan go home covered in blood? #makingamurderer

Lying on the stand is perjury, which is defined as "the offence of wilfully telling an untruth or making a misrepresentation under oath." People who lie on behalf of the prosecution are rarely held accountable, and they are often rewarded. Police who lie on behalf of the prosecution become known as team players. They are more likely to receive career advancements. An example is Sergeant Ken Peterson, who arrested Steven for the assault on Penny and lied about seeing Steven in a leather jacket that matched Gregory Allen's. Peterson rose through the ranks to become the Manitowoc County Sheriff.

A local TV station asked Sheriff Peterson whether the Manitowoc County Sheriff's Office had planted evidence to incriminate Steven in the Teresa Halbach case.

"If we wanted to eliminate Steve, it would've been a whole lot easier to eliminate Steve than to frame Steve... or if we wanted him killed, it would be much easier just to kill him," Petersen said in the calm self-assured way of a Mafia don.

After watching Peterson make the statement about killing Steven, Dean Strang commented, "This is insane. This is completely insane."

STRATEGY 9: HIRE SOCIOPATHIC PROSECUTORS

Two definitions of a sociopath:

1: A person with a psychopathic personality whose behaviour is antisocial, often criminal, and who lacks a sense of moral responsibility or social conscience.

2: Someone whose social behaviour is extremely abnormal. Sociopaths are interested only in their personal needs and desires, without concern for the effects of their behaviour on others.

Sociopathic prosecutors are ideal for framing innocent people because they have no qualms about the suffering of the wrongly convicted or about the actual murderer or rapist being at large and committing more crimes. They can look in the eyes of a victim's family members and guarantee with confidence that the culprit is incarcerated. Their only concern is what is in it for them: promotions in high-profile murder cases, media attention, accolades from colleagues and associates. The most cunning sociopaths try to parlay wrongful convictions into political capital. That's why high-profile convictions and executions rise just before elections – when the power hungry are portraying themselves as being tough on crime.

This book has already detailed the sociopathic behaviour of prosecutor Dennis Vogel, who fabricated the probation-officer alibi for Gregory Allen, who roamed free for years, sexually terrorising more women. Interested only in convicting Steven Avery, Vogel had no concern for Allen's future victims.

During and after Steven's second wrongful conviction, Ken Kratz took sociopathic and narcissistic behaviour to a whole new level. Revelling in the limelight, he lambasted Steven Avery at every opportunity, while maintaining the strategy of triggering emotional reactions. With the help of sociopathic TV personalities such as Nancy Grace, he attempted to turn public opinion against Steven and Brendan.

Kratz protested that the *Making a Murderer* filmmakers had never given him a chance to answer the defence attorneys' allegations. He said the documentary ignored up to 90% of the physical evidence that linked Steven to the homicide. He wants Netflix to give him an opportunity to tell his side of the story.

While prosecuting Steven and Brendan, Kratz was abusing prescription pills and sexually harassing vulnerable women with whom he had met in the court system. *Making a Murderer* mentioned Kratz's sexting, but left out that Kratz had been accused of sexual assault by lawyer Thomas Basting, who filed eleven charges against Kratz for the Office of Lawyer Regulation (OLR):

After various phone conversations, Kratz asked to visit JW at her apartment. JW asserts that Kratz arrived at her apartment and after threatening JW, forced her to have sex... On September 28, 2010, JW provided the information about Kratz to her probation officer at the Department of Corrections (DOC). The DOC reported the issue to the DOJ. The DOJ interviewed JW who provided a statement. The statement JW provided alleges that Kratz, while District Attorney of Calumet County, had forcible sex with an emotionally vulnerable woman after previously prosecuting the woman.

Kratz denied the charge and it was eventually dropped, but other less serious sex charges stuck:

7. Of the six counts of misconduct to which Attorney Kratz pled no contest, three counts concern SVG.

According to the OLR's complaint, on August 12, 2009, Attorney Kratz, while serving as Calumet County District Attorney, filed a felony criminal complaint against SRK of Kaukauna, Wisconsin. According to the complaint, SRK beat and strangled SVG, a former live-in partner and mother of SRK's child. The complaint charged one felony count of strangulation and suffocation... and one count of disorderly conduct...

8. Shortly after the preliminary hearing in this matter, SVG met with Attorney Kratz alone in a conference room at the district attorney's office. SVG requested the meeting, exercising her right to consult with the district attorney "concerning the disposition of a case involving a crime of which he or she was a victim..."

9. During the meeting, SVG volunteered personal information to Attorney Kratz, stating that she did not have a current boyfriend, that she suffered from low self-esteem, that she lived with her mother, and that she was struggling as a single mother.

10. According to SVG, she understood during her meeting with Attorney Kratz that he would be prosecuting SRK. SVG also relayed details of her relationship with SRK, and indicated that SRK had previously abused her, including beatings and strangulation. Attorney Kratz asked SVG if she objected to reducing the felony charge to a misdemeanour. SVG objected to the suggestion. At the conclusion of the meeting, Attorney Kratz and SVG exchanged cell phone numbers.

11. After SVG left Attorney Kratz's office, Attorney Kratz began texting SVG from his personal cell phone.

Attorney Kratz sent her three messages on October 20, 2009, the same day they met, his last message stating, "I wish you weren't one of this office[']s clients. You'd be a cool person to know!"

12. On October 21, 2009, Attorney Kratz sent SVG 19 messages, including asking her: "Are you the kind of girl that likes secret contact with an older married elected DA [district attorney] ... the riskier the better? Or do you want to stop right know [sic] before any issues?"

13. On October 22, 2009, Attorney Kratz sent SVG eight more messages, telling her that she was "beautiful," "pretty," that "I'm the atty [attorney]. I have the $350,000 house. I have the 6-figure career. You may be the tall, young, hot nymph, but I am the prize! Start convincing," and that "I would not expect you to be the other woman. I would want you to be so hot and treat me so well that you'd be THE woman. R U that good?"

14. According to SVG, Attorney Kratz's personal over-tures were unwelcome and offensive, and she was concerned that if she failed to respond to Attorney Kratz, he might take action with respect to the case against SRK that could potentially adversely affect SVG.

15. On October 22, 2009, SVG reported Attorney Kratz's text messages to the Kaukauna Police Department.

16. After photographing the text messages on SVG's telephone and taking SVG's statement, the Kaukauna Police Department referred the matter to the State of Wisconsin Department of Justice (DOJ).

17. After reviewing the text messages and the report of the Kaukauna Police Department, the DOJ determined that there had not been any criminal activity. Nonetheless, DOJ representatives strongly suggested to Attorney Kratz that he step aside from the prosecution of SRK and self-report his conduct to the OLR.

18. Attorney Kratz facilitated the appointment of a special prosecutor to take over the SRK case. Attorney Kratz also agreed to resign as chairman of the Wisconsin Crime Victims' Rights Board.

19. In a December 4, 2009 letter to the OLR that included the transcribed messages to and from SVG, Attorney Kratz admitted that he sought a personal "friendship" with SVG. He expressed regret and embarrassment for his conduct and admitted that he had violated SVG's trust. Attorney Kratz also noted that he was undergoing therapy "to answer why a career prosecutor, with a spotless record and sterling reputation, would risk his professional esteem on such a disrespectful communication with a crime victim."

20. On September 15, 2010, the Associated Press published a story regarding Attorney Kratz's text messages to SVG. Attorney Kratz issued a statement admitting that he sent the texts and was embarrassed at his lack of judgment.

21. On September 17, 2010, the executive committee of the Wisconsin District Attorneys Association issued a letter to Attorney Kratz calling for his resignation.

22. After then-Governor James Doyle initiated removal proceedings against him pursuant to Chapter 17

of the Wisconsin Statutes. Attorney Kratz resigned his position as Calumet County District Attorney on October 4, 2010.

23. Two counts of the OLR's complaint involve Attorney Kratz's verbal statements to SS, a social worker with the Calumet County Human Services Department.

24. In October of 2009, Attorney Kratz prosecuted a termination of parental rights case in which SS was a witness. Prior to testifying, SS commented to Attorney Kratz that she was nervous about testifying. In response to SS's concerns, Attorney Kratz stated to SS that he "won't cum in your mouth." Later that day Attorney Kratz remarked to SS that he wanted the trial to be over because he was leaving on a trip to Las Vegas, where he could have "big-boobed women serve me drinks."

25. One count of the OLR's complaint involves Attorney Kratz's verbal statement to RH, also a social worker with the Calumet County Human Services Department. During a court proceeding, Attorney Kratz commented in court to RH that a reporter had "big beautiful breasts."

26. On the first day of the scheduled disciplinary hearing in this matter, Attorney Kratz entered pleas of no contest to six counts of misconduct stemming from his behaviour toward SVG, SS, and RH. The referee found that an adequate factual basis existed on each of the six counts and accepted the no contest pleas...

34. In its post-hearing brief, the OLR argued that Attorney Kratz's license should be suspended for six months. The OLR emphasized that Attorney

Kratz's conduct involved multiple women, all of them in vulnerable or subordinate positions. The OLR argued that Attorney Kratz did not intend to remove himself as prosecutor in the SVG matter until DOJ officials asked him to do so after SVG reported his actions to the police. The OLR also argued that Attorney Kratz refused to take responsibility for his offensive statements to SS and RH. The OLR further argued that because Attorney Kratz blamed his misconduct on various addictions yet offered no competent medical testimony that he had recovered from his addictions, a six-month suspension would be appropriate given that it would require him to petition the court for reinstatement...

35. In his post-hearing brief, Attorney Kratz argued that a public reprimand was warranted. In support of his argument that a license suspension was not warranted, Attorney Kratz downplayed the seriousness of his misconduct toward SVG, SS, and RH.

36. Regarding his texts to SVG, Attorney Kratz admitted they constituted wrongful behaviour, but "disagree[d] with the OLR's characterization that the messages contained 'sexual overtones' (as no message included one single sexually explicit term, nor was any sexual conduct or sex act ever suggested)." Attorney Kratz also described his conduct upon learning that SVG objected to his texts as praise-worthy. He wrote: [Upon] even the hint of a conflict of interest, or reports of unsettling reaction by [SVG], immediate steps were taken to eliminate even the perception of continued violation; timely self-report to the OLR for imposition of sanction (if required); and aggressive steps to ensure this stupidity never, ever repeated itself. That is the attorney response that this Court should praise, rather than punish.

37. Regarding his verbal comments to social worker SS that he "won't cum in [her] mouth" and [he] looked forward to having "big-boobed women serve [him] drinks," Attorney Kratz wrote that he "recognized the disrespectful phrase used, and apologized to the Social Worker at the first opportunity."

38. Regarding his statement to social worker RH that a "reporter" had "big beautiful breasts," Attorney Kratz wrote in his post-hearing brief that this comment "never occurred." Attorney Kratz argued that "the reporter referred to, although admittedly beautiful, does NOT have large breasts . . . this single important factor has been relied upon by Respondent to conclude the comment never was made, or at the very least, [was] misinterpreted by [RH]." Attorney Kratz conceded, however, that "given the posture of this case, the tribunal is free to include the facts of the [RH] comment, and provide it such weight in the sanctions recommendations as deemed necessary."

39. As a mitigating factor, Attorney Kratz wrote in his post-hearing brief that at the time of the events in question, he "suffered from the combination of Sexually Compulsive Disorder (SCD) and prescription drug dependence" – conditions for which he has sought treatment. He also claimed that he wanted "to settle the case" early in the disciplinary process, but the OLR refused to do so, in part because it is "apparently more concerned with how 'they look' in the zealous pursuit of an attorney's 'pelt,' rather than what result 'should' be reached..."

40. On July 30, 2012, the referee filed a report and recommendation. In considering the appropriate

discipline, the referee weighed various aggravating and mitigating factors.

41. The referee noted as aggravating factors that Attorney Kratz acted with a selfish motive; that SVG was a vulnerable victim; and that Attorney Kratz's misconduct was particularly inexcusable in light of his considerable legal experience and his previous leadership on issues pertaining to victims' rights.

42. The referee assigned neutral weight to Attorney Kratz's self-report to the OLR of his misconduct involving SVG. The referee wrote that "at the time of the respondent's self-report, the cat was already out of the bag, so to speak. SVG had gone to the police, the police had contacted the Wisconsin Department of Justice, and that agency urged the respondent to self-report to the OLR." The referee found that these circumstances "significantly undercut any claim of virtuousness by self-reporting."

43. The referee noted a variety of mitigating factors, which, in summary fashion, are as follows: Attorney Kratz has no prior disciplinary history; he apologized to SS for his vulgar comment shortly after making it; he has never attempted to justify or defend his conduct toward SVG; he cooperated with the disciplinary proceedings; he previously enjoyed a good professional reputation and engaged in significant volunteer activities within the legal profession; he has been diagnosed with and sought treatment for narcissistic personality disorder and sexual addiction; he was abusing the sleeping aid Ambien, the painkiller Vicodin, and the anti-anxiety drug Xanax at the time of the misconduct; he subsequently sought treatment for his substance abuse issues;

he voluntarily obtained a mentor attorney through the State Bar's Wisconsin Lawyer Assistance Program (WisLAP), who reported being impressed with Attorney Kratz's character and commitment to recovery; and he had suffered substantial collateral consequences from his misconduct, including considerable negative publicity, the loss of his district attorney position, and significant financial difficulties.

44. After weighing these aggravating and mitigating factors, the referee recommended that Attorney Kratz's license to practice law should be suspended for a period of four months. In support of his recommendation for a lighter sanction than that proposed by the OLR, the referee emphasized the number and weight of the mitigating factors in this case. The referee also suggested that a four-month suspension was consistent with the discipline imposed in two cases that he believed were particularly analogous to this case...

In the typical manner of a sociopath, Kratz feigned taking responsibility to mitigate any punishment while being unable to hide his sneering condescension towards the whole process. He knew that he would only suffer negligible consequences because Wisconsin barely punishes attorneys who break the law.

An article published in the *Journal Sentinel* in 2011 titled "Convicted attorneys are still practicing," revealed Wisconsin's relaxed attitude towards criminal lawyers. It stated that 135 Wisconsin attorneys with convictions were practising law, including some who kept their licences while serving time and others who got them back before they were off probation.

They included lawyers with felony or misdemeanour convictions for fraud, theft, battery and repeat drunken driving, as well as political corruption, drugs and sex. A child-sex offender got probation and never lost his law licence. A politician convicted of cheque kiting was reprimanded but kept his licence.

Seventy more attorneys were charged with crimes but managed to get the charges reduced or avoided conviction by completing a deferred prosecution plan. All of them kept their law licences.

"The system is run by lawyers and is for lawyers," said Michael Frisch, a national expert in legal discipline who teaches law at Georgetown University. "It's called self-regulation, and it's a pretty good system for lawyers."

Kratz breezed through the sexual assault charge because he'd chosen his victim carefully. A 2011 article in the *Wisconsin State Journal* titled "Disgraced former DA Kratz cited by regulators for alleged sexual assault," stated that the victim had a documented mental illness and had three criminal convictions: making a false representation, retail theft and disorderly conduct. Kratz knew that her allegations would lack any credibility.

"Any time you go into a prosecutorial decision, you have to look at whether a jury will believe your witnesses," said Steve Means, executive assistant at DOJ. He added that the investigation into the allegation was thorough. "Any time there's an allegation of sexual assault by a person in power, it's a serious matter and we treat it that way." He said that Kratz wasn't prosecuted because the state could not prove beyond a reasonable doubt that a crime was committed. If such an allegation had been made against Steven Avery, the State of Wisconsin would have never raised such an objection.

The *Wisconsin State Journal* article suggested that the sexual contact with the alleged victim was far from consensual. She claimed that Kratz had prosecuted her three times in Calumet County between 2006 and 2008. Then suddenly Kratz requested to visit her at home between Thanksgiving and Christmas 2009. After arriving, Kratz allegedly told the woman several times that he knew everything about her and could make trouble for her. After discussing bondage, he allegedly ordered her to perform a sex act. The victim stated that he groped her and she was quoted telling the agents that "she was a fool to have let him."

Throughout the interview with the investigators, the woman cried, trembled and blamed herself multiple times for the incident, which she described as "really scary" because Kratz had "such seniority" over her. She alleged that Kratz had bragged about hitting women who did not "submit" to him. The woman "kept stating that she had done something wrong, and she questioned whether she would be going to prison for it."

According to the DOJ report, Kratz called the woman almost fifty times after the alleged sexual assault. He also showed up at her apartment a few times, but she pretended to be absent. "He's a pig," the woman told agents. "What he did was wrong."

Fifteen women reported receiving inappropriate statements and text messages from Kratz. Three women alleged that Kratz made sexual contact with them. One of the women declined to provide any more information about an alleged 1989 incident. Another said that the sexual contact that allegedly happened in 1999 was "theoretically" consensual because she had agreed to it because Kratz had said he could help her regain custody of her children.

Kratz suffered no prison time for the alleged sexual assaults and for trading legal favours for sexual ones.

Activist Karla Boldt of Illinois was so annoyed by Kratz eluding punishment that she started a petition: "Strip Ken Kratz law license for being a sexual predator."

Karla wrote: "Based on the info in these articles I feel Attorney Ken Kratz needs to be stripped of right to practice law/disbarred due to the rape accusations and sexual harassment with at least 4 victims to which he pled no contest to some of the charges. We, as citizens nationwide, need to make an example of him that we will not tolerate this from legal workers including but not limited to police and attorneys. Attorney Kratz need to at the very least be STRIPPED OF HIS LAW LICENSE for life!!!"

Since *Making a Murderer*, Kratz has done many interviews. No mainstream TV personalities have pointed out that there is more evidence to suggest that Kratz has committed sexual assault than Kratz has presented against Steven and Brendan for the same allegation. Such shows shy away from anything more serious than the sexting scandal. Kratz even protested that it was wrong of Netflix to bring up the sexting. On Fox TV, Kratz seemed to disassociate himself from his own behaviour. He refused to take any responsibility.

His lack of remorse reminded me of the depraved paedophile priest Oliver O'Grady, who was the subject of another documentary film broadcast on Netflix called *Deliver Us from Evil*. O'Grady molested over fifty children, including one only nine months old. He spoke in the same way as Kratz: completely detached from his behaviour. The worst sociopaths find ways to justify their actions.

Nancy Grace and her cohorts have supported Kratz and given him plenty of airtime to express his views.

Shortly after Steven's second arrest, Kratz appeared on TV. "It's no longer a question, at least in my mind, of who is responsible for the death of Teresa Halbach," whom he said was the only victim in the case.

A guest host Harris Faulkner, standing in for Nancy Grace, turned to Wendy Murphy, a former prosecutor. "Wendy, if you're prosecuting this case, what does all this evidence tell you?"

"Well, this doesn't take rocket science," Wendy said. "It doesn't get any closer to a slam dunk, even without knowing yet that it is, in fact, this woman. I mean, I've got to tell you something. The sympathy for this guy, the idea that he's filed this law suit, I just want to reach through this camera and grab the guy and shake him and bang his head on the wall because I'm not convinced at all that he was wrongly convicted of the first crime!

"I will not deny for a minute that the DNA evidence that wasn't available at the time of his trial kind of affected his ability to have a fair trial. But let's not confuse this with innocence. I'm not persuaded at all that this guy was innocent with regard to that earlier rape! So, let me say this to the people who helped him get out: good job! You let the guy out by claiming he's innocent. And now look what he did. He killed a woman! Thanks a lot!"

"But he was exonerated," Faulkner said.

"That doesn't mean he's innocent," Wendy said. "I'm sick of these DNA lies. The Innocence Project and these people who falsely claim that 150 men have been exonerated and proved actually innocent with these new DNA tests on old cases is nonsense. I don't care how many shows he goes on and claims he's not the type of guy that does this sort of thing. How does he explain the bucket of blood from his body in her car?"

A strategy employed by sociopaths who are seeking society's approval is to accuse others of being sociopaths. To achieve this on Nancy Grace's TV show, they introduced an expert in forensic psychology, who stated that Teresa's murderer was "a stone-cold sociopath."

"To put a dead body in a barrel," he said, "to light it on fire, the sights, the smells, the sounds, to watch it burn, that says that this is a man who has no care for human life."

Before becoming a TV personality, Nancy Grace was a prosecutor in Georgia, who was reprimanded twice in published opinions for engaging in conduct just like that of the prosecutors in *Making a Murderer*. Nancy believes that prosecutors are always right and the fabrication of evidence justifies the means. In a 1997 arson and murder case, a conviction was overturned, and Nancy's behaviour was documented: "It demonstrated her disregard of the notions of due process and fairness and it was inexcusable." She had allowed detectives to testify falsely under oath. In 2005, an appeals court found that she "played fast and loose with core ethical rules and conduct."

Even after *Making a Murderer* had shown how Brendan was coerced, Kratz and Nancy entrenched in their position:

"That's right, Nancy," Ken said. "There's absolutely no problem at all with… this interrogation, and I never thought so from the beginning. The magistrate in this case found that it ought to be believed. That is, it was a reliable statement by this young man. That the investigators never did make any promises. In fact, there was no single statement that they could point to that led to this being involuntary.

"What you heard at the beginning of this segment, you heard Brendan Dassey's very clear, very coherent... admission about what had happened. You know, Brendan Dassey has exactly the same IQ as Steven Avery does. Steven Avery they never claimed had a problem resisting any kind of temptation or statements by the investigators... That statement was very clear, very detailed and horrific, and that's the kind of behaviour that this young man engaged in that led to this conviction.

"The totality of the circumstances is the standard for voluntariness, however, totality of the circumstances, Nancy, is put together with all of those circumstances that we talked about, and when the magistrate in this case admitted that there was no... promises that were made. In fact, the officer said, 'I can't make any promises to you.' When they absolutely did not make any threats. When they told Brendan Dassey that, 'We want you to tell the truth.' Telling the truth or imploring somebody to tell the truth is not the same as making promises or making inducements or threatening them. These are things that happen every day across this country when they take statements from people, and is absolutely not rendering this statement involuntary."

If Kratz genuinely believes that Brendan is guilty then he is the most dangerous type of sociopath: one who believes that his own evil actions are actually beneficial to society. Kratz certainly possesses plenty of sociopathic traits: narcissism, a lack of empathy, a cold calculating nature, shallow emotions, grandiosity, manipulative, authoritarian, compulsive lying...

Sadly, the sociopathic prosecutors in both of Steven's wrongful convictions will never be held accountable for their crimes due to the absolute immunity they have from prosecution and the system's propensity to protect itself.

When Steven was exonerated and Dennis Vogel was at risk of exposure for fabricating Gregory Allen's parole-officer alibi, the independent investigation was headed by Wisconsin Attorney General Peg Lautenschlager. It was a case of the State of Wisconsin investigating itself.

Initially, Peg had declined heading the independent review due to an absence of legal authority to conduct such an investigation. Within days, she changed her mind. Peg appointed two people to depose everyone involved in the Beerntsen case. Unsurprisingly, they found the Manitowoc County Sheriff's Office not liable for Steven's wrongful conviction – a result most likely due to Peg's orders.

When it comes to lawsuits, Peg is a sociopath who is willing to sacrifice justice for financial interests. Peg was against Jim Doyle, the Governor of Wisconsin, who was Steven's champion. The Avery Task Force was formed in December of 2003 at Doyle's request. It was to study the reasons for wrongful convictions to prevent them. Doyle wanted Peg to be involved with the Avery Task Force, but she wanted nothing to do with Steven whom she viewed as the enemy concerning financial liability.

In 2004, Peg was driving a state car on unofficial business. Coming home from a party, she passed out at the wheel. A Dodge County sheriff's deputy found her car in a ditch, and her unharmed inside. She refused a blood test. A breathalyser test at the scene showed that her blood alcohol level was 0.12 – 50% above the legal limit of 0.08.

Peg claimed to have fallen asleep at the wheel after consuming only two glasses of wine. She was arrested and later released to her husband. Dodge County Case Number: 2004TR001348.

A state Ethics Board investigated Peg's case and ruled that some use of the state car for personal use exceeded state-allowed limits. Peg reimbursed some of the costs and paid a fine of $784. Her driver's licence was revoked for a year. Just like Kratz, she received hardly any punishment.

Doyle used the opportunity to get her to head the Avery Task Force. Peg transformed the Avery Task Force's objective from protecting people to avoiding liability pay-outs for wrongful convictions, with special concentration on Steven's civil suit.

It's no wonder that the wrongful conviction was determined to be a consequence of poor communications between departments and that Vogel and the sheriff hadn't committed any misconduct.

According to the blog "MAM: The Political Spectrum 'The Corruption Behind Steven Avery's Make Believe Trial,'" Peg played major roles in both wrongful convictions. To help Mark Wiegert interrogate Brendan, Peg appointed DCI Special Agent Tom Fassbender. Peg approved the admissibility of Sherry Culhane's inconclusive blood contamination results into Steven's trial. Peg sent Assistant Attorney General Thomas J Fallon, third in command of the State of Wisconsin, as a prosecutor to influence a conviction with his power not only over Judge Willis in Steven's trial but also over Judge Fox as well in Brendan's trial. A seasoned veteran Assistant Attorney General like Thomas J Fallon should have known better than to prosecute Brendan on such coercion that was plainly unconstitutional.

According to the blog, in August 2005, Peg helped to start the Criminal Justice Study Commission that was to help prevent tunnel vision and other acts of wrongful conviction. In September 2005, Peg had taken on the Deer Hunting Murders – the trial of Hmong native Chai Soua Vang. Peg stated that she "has a personal interest in crimes committed against people." But when Teresa disappeared, Peg sent State Capitol agents in, who furthered the tunnel vision and set about grooming 16-year-old Brendan Dassey into a coerced false confession.

In the hierarchy of sociopaths involved in the conspiracy to frame Steven and Brendan, Peg has been a major player. She presently heads the Wisconsin Ethics Commission, a rebranded version of the Ethics Board to which she had to pay a fine for her drunk-driving incident.

The man Peg protected, Dennis Vogel, is practising law in Madison, Wisconsin. He defends organisations involved in claims of injury to dairy operations, disputes involving contracts, land, right-of-way, cooperative and utility law matters, cellular tele-communications matters, and select criminal and traffic litigation.

There is more evidence of Kratz committing sex crimes than Steven Avery, yet Kratz continues to practise law in Wisconsin, where he still receives death threats over his actions towards Steven and Brendan. After I exposed the sexual-assault allegations against Kratz, he posted online: "Shaun Attwood is a lying scumbag. How's that for my opinion!"

Juan Tescrue is the pseudonym of a *Making a Murderer* sleuth with insider knowledge of the Wisconsin political establishment who has posted a series of YouTube videos. He has generously contributed the following for this book about Peg and the bigger picture concerning Steven Avery:

What would cause numerous people from different backgrounds, professions and geographic locations to remain silent while putting two innocent men in jail? We all know about the Manitowoc County Sheriff's Office (MCSO), but what if this isn't a localized situation trying to conceal a minor mistake? This case started back in 1985. Even if whatever they're hiding happened more recently – like when Colborn took the phone call back in 1995 that could have led to Steven's exoneration – most infractions' statues of limitations would have run out by now. Some people who may have been involved are even dead. Which begs the question: what are they hiding?

It's probably something of a continuous nature. More than likely, it's drug and human trafficking. I realized this when the Wisconsin Attorney General Brad Schimel appealed Brendan's release. Perhaps he was doing a favor for his old band buddy Ken Kratz. Perhaps he was just trying to make sure all the bases were covered before Brendan's release becomes official. Perhaps he's involved. I certainly hope not.

I personally heard Brad Schimel state that Milwaukee is the number one hub for human trafficking in the US. Manitowoc was home to one of Al Capone's many bootlegging operations. It's a port town that has access to the

Great Lakes for shipments to a myriad of places including Canada and even internationally. It's smack dab in the middle of the country with an interstate highway running straight through it, so cargo can pretty much go anywhere in the US and it's a quiet little town, where quite frankly nothing much happens... or at least appears not to happen.

My guess is that the ol' mob-type operations never ceased. Drugs became a big business especially after Vietnam. During three administrations, you've had Wisconsin Attorney Generals from Victor Miller of Manitowoc, to Robert Warren who later became the Judge of the US Foreign Intelligence Surveillance Court of Review, to Bronson La Follette of the famous Wisconsin La Follette heritage who served three non-consecutive terms throughout the seventies and eighties until an ethics investigation brought him down – all with ties to these small-town Wisconsin locations and types of activities.

So, in Wisconsin there seems to be a history of corruption that dates back quite some time. For decades, the powerful have done a good job of keeping it hidden. In fact, if it weren't for two East Coast film students following a crazy headline and spending ten long years on *Making a Murderer*, no one would have ever known this atrocity took place and both Steven and Brendan would have almost certainly died in prison like so many others.

There was an investigation into Steven's first wrongful conviction. Unfortunately, that may have been the spark that ignited this conflagration of corruption that would eventually end up in a burn pit behind Steven's garage. The MCSO was investigated by Deborah Strauss, the assistant to the Wisconsin Attorney General at the time: Peg Lautenschlager. Like others before her, Peg was yet another Attorney General who had lost her last election bid due to an ethics violation. Once again, a corrupt person in power to help keep the scheme afloat. Peg also has ties with pretty much every other agency involved in this case to make sure that everything worked in tandem to put Steven and Brendan on the chopping block.

How did Peg come to power anyway? Well, she got to be Attorney General because in her prior vocation she was appointed to the position of US Attorney for the Western Wisconsin District by the newly elected President Bill Clinton. She heeded the call when he fired every single US Attorney to make sure his trafficking cabal was unquestionably loyal and complete. This occurred after his heavy involvement in Iran Contra-type CIA-sponsored drug running out of the Mena, Arkansas airport, when he was the governor of Arkansas, around which people died and there were plenty of cover-ups as the system closed ranks just like it did against Steven and Brendan – all documented in Shaun Attwood's book, *American Made*. Bill's half-brother Roger Clinton was arrested for selling cocaine and served prison time.

Is it possible that this drug and human trafficking ring has been quietly going on for decades, unnoticed, and being run by the people who make the laws? Laws that they break and profit from while ordinary people get thrown into prisons by the government that they control. What else would make people do such horrendous things to innocent people? What would cause Manitowoc family and friends of Teresa Halbach to seemingly be in on it whether she was murdered or managed to successfully skip town? What would cause local law enforcement, the Wisconsin State Department of Justice and possibly the FBI to do everything in their power to not only hide the truth but to frame an innocent man and take away the freedom of his intellectually-challenged nephew. All to cover up something that we to this day have no concrete motive for.

Why else would the State of Wisconsin appeal Brendan's release if they weren't hiding something? What would be so bad that you had to go to these lengths over this span of time and with this many transfers of people in positions of power? Why would the present Wisconsin Attorney General – two Attorney Generals and a decade removed from the case – read the Dassey court transcript and appeal Brendan's release knowing that he may be committing political suicide and lose his next election bid like most of his recent predecessors? What would an investigation, like the $36 million lawsuit that Avery was about to bring down, uncover? It must be something damning.

Like the FBI cover-up in the Franklin Credit Union scandal in the mid-eighties, where they trafficked children from all over and eventually funneled them through the largest hub for human trafficking in the entire US: Milwaukee Wisconsin.

You have local officials in "the circle," county officials, state officials including the DOJ, FBI collaborators, politicians, charity groups to mask, launder and make things legit, and other high level international organizations all working together under one umbrella. If anyone talks, there is severe punishment. Only one thing could hold that together. Something so bad that even if exposed, people may hesitate to believe it.

Perhaps one day, the case proving Avery's innocence will shed some light on this conundrum.

STRATEGY 10: RIG THE JURY

When Steven's 1985 case went to trial, the judge greeted every-body, identifying the defence and prosecution. After warning the potential jurors to not consider the charges as evidence against Steven, he read them aloud:

"Count 1: on or about the 29th July 1985, in the Township of Two Rivers, in said County and State, the defendant did unlaw-fully have sexual contact with another person without the consent of that person and by the threat of use of a dangerous weapon, to wit: by the threat of the use of a knife…"

Dennis Vogel must have been satisfied by the expressions of shock and disgust on the potential jurors as the strategy of triggering emotional reactions first took effect.

"Count 2: At the same time and place, the defendant did unlawfully attempt to cause the death of another human being with intent to kill that person…

"Count 3: At the same time and place, the defendant did unlawfully and intentionally restrain another without that per-son's consent and with knowledge that he had no lawful authority to do so…"

With the potential jury in a hyped-up state and already forming opinions against Steven, the judge added the small print: "To the charges I have just read, the defendant has entered a plea of not guilty, which means a denial of every material allegation in the information. The law presumes every person charged with the commission of an offence to be innocent. This presump-tion attends the defendant. That is, it stays with the defendant throughout the trial and prevails at its close unless it is overcome by evidence which satisfies a jury of guilt beyond a reasonable doubt. The defendant is not required to prove his innocence. The burden of proving the defendant guilty of every element of the crime charged is upon the state. Before you can return a verdict of guilty, the state must prove to your satisfaction beyond a reasonable doubt that the defendant is guilty."

The judge asked the potential jury members whether any were acquainted with or knew the defendant or any member of his immediate family. Several hands went up.

The judge addressed a female, "How long have you known either the defendant or his family?"

"About 17 years."

"And do you have regular contact with the family?"

"No."

"Or the defendant?"

"Not any longer."

"When was the last time you saw either the defendant or a family member?"

"It would have been quite a while ago. I'm a schoolteacher."

"That's how you happen to know the family?"

"Yes."

"Because of your relationship with the family – we won't probe into that in any detail – do you feel that you would tend to give great or lesser weight to one side over the other?"

"I would try not to."

"Do you feel it would be difficult for you to judge the case fairly and impartially, strictly on the evidence that is produced at the trial and excluding everything else?"

"I would try not to."

"So, do you think it would be possible for you to judge this case fairly and impartially after you have heard the evidence, without bringing any preconceived notions one way or the other into your deliberations?"

"I would hope that would be the case, yes?"

"Do you think there's a possibility that you would not be able to do so?"

"I guess I would have some question."

The judge excused Juror 8 and moved onto Juror 10. "Do you know the defendant or his family?"

"Yes, I do."

"How long have you known them?"

"Six years."

"Six years?"

"Yup."

"Do you feel it would be difficult for you to judge this case fairly and impartially because of your prior knowledge of the defendant or his family?"

"Yes."

The judge excused Juror 10.

"It doesn't have anything to do with this," Juror 26 said, "but I do know somebody who's a neighbour of the accused and I've heard that..."

"We don't want to know what you've heard," the judge said. "We'll get into that later."

One method of jury rigging by the prosecution is to get people appointed to the jury who have relationships with the members of law enforcement involved in the case. No matter what the strength of the relationship, they can remain on the jury – even when the relationships are admitted in court – by simply telling the judge that they will remain impartial.

"Are there any among you who is acquainted with or knows District Attorney Denis Vogel?"

Juror 2's hand went up.

"How long have you known Mr Vogel?"

"About five years."

"Is that a business or a personal relationship?"

"We're neighbours."

"You live right next door to Mr Vogel?"

"Same block. Three doors down."

"Do you feel that because you live on the same block, and Mr Vogel will have to go home sometime and you'll see him, that there might be cause for you to give greater or lesser weight to one side in this case over the other?"

"None whatsoever, Your Honour."

The prosecutor's neighbour was allowed to remain and so was Juror 5, a schoolteacher whom Vogel had worked with. Vogel had led a student debate at her school.

"Mr Vogel spoke at a tavern-league meeting I was at," Juror 15 said.

"Do you think that would affect your judgement one way or the other?"

"No, it wouldn't, Your Honour."

Several jurors were close to the sheriff. Juror 11 was the Maple Grove town constable.

Juror 22 had known the sheriff since 1979 when they both worked in real estate. "We spoke at church just last Sunday, Your Honour."

Juror 27 had served with the sheriff on an advisory panel for Wisconsin Public Service. A juror knew Deputy Kusche as they were both members of The Veterans of Foreign Wars of the United States. One was a member of the same church as Deputy Froehlich. One worked at church committees with Froehlich's wife. Another was Froehlich's neighbour. One's son attended a Cub Scout group of which one of the detectives was a leader.

By declaring impartiality, they were all allowed to stay.

Before Steven's alibi witnesses had even taken the stand, Denis Vogel started the strategy of neutralising them by stating early on: "Members of the jury: if one side calls more witness than the other, would you weigh that in favour of that side? As an example, if I was to call only one witness to the stand and the defence called fifteen witness, would you give the defence more weight than my one witness?"

The contamination of the jury by associates of law enforcement remained unimpeded by questions asked by Steven's lawyer: "Do any of you think just because Steve is sitting here, the chances are better than not that he's guilty? Anybody think that way? As you already know, the charges are serious: attempted murder, sexual assault. Are any of those accusations so emotional for any of you that you won't be able to make your decision rationally?

Do any of you think those accusations are so serious that you couldn't find anyone charged with them not guilty?" Of course, none of the remaining potential jurors were caught off-guard by this questioning.

The jury selection involved each side – prosecution and defence – declining six potential jurors. With twelve gone, fourteen remained. The verdict would be made by twelve jurors. Two additional jurors were alternates who would be excused at the end of the trial.

After the jury was sworn in, the judge instructed the members not to speak to anyone about the case, including what they may have heard or read about the case. The jurors were sequestered in a hotel opposite the courthouse, and banned from drinking alcohol in the daytime.

After the jury had heard all the evidence, the judge gave them their instructions:

"Ladies and gentlemen, the defendant is not required to prove his innocence. The burden of establishing every fact necessary to constitute guilt is upon the state. Before you can return a verdict of guilty, the evidence must satisfy you beyond a reasonable doubt that the defendant is guilty. If you can reconcile the evidence upon any reasonable hypothesis consistent with the defendant's innocence, you should do so and find him not guilty. Now, in reaching your verdict, examine the evidence with care and caution. Act with judgement, reason and prudence.

"The term 'reasonable doubt' means a doubt based upon reason and common sense. It is a doubt for which a reason can be given, arising from a fair and rational consideration of the evidence or lack of evidence. It means such a doubt as would cause a person of ordinary prudence to pause or hesitate when called upon to act in the most important affairs of life.

"A reasonable doubt is not a doubt which is based upon mere guess work or speculation. A doubt which arises merely from sympathy or from fear to return a verdict of guilt is not a reasonable doubt. A reasonable doubt is not a doubt such as may be used to escape the responsibility of a decision. Now, while it is your duty to give the defendant the benefit of every reasonable doubt, you are not to search for doubt. Rather, you are to search for the truth.

"The duties of counsel have been performed, and the great weight of reaching a verdict is to be thrown wholly upon you, the jurors, called to exercise this important duty. You are not to be swayed by fear, sympathy, passion or prejudice. You are to act with judgement, reason and prudence. I charge you now to exercise your duty faithfully."

Any hope of the jurors searching for the truth was thwarted by the strategies described in this book. The honest witnesses were made out to be liars. The lying witnesses, including the sheriff's deputies, were viewed as honest not only because of the jurors' trust in the police, but also because many of the jurors had relationships with the police who had lied on the stand.

The jury took six hours to reach a decision, which the judge read aloud:

"Let the record reflect – I'm not going to drag this out – the verdict of the jury with regard to the charge of first-degree sexual assault: guilty. With regard to the charge of false imprisonment: guilty. With regard to the charge of attempted murder in the first degree: guilty."

Steven's conviction was a career steppingstone for some of the players involved. Dennis Vogel parlayed his success as a prosecutor – including Steven's conviction – into a high-paying job.

On July 25, 1986, Steven's new lawyer filed a motion for post-conviction relief. He requested a new trial on the basis that Vogel had not turned some exculpatory evidence over to the defence. Exculpatory evidence is evidence favourable to the defendant that tends to exonerate the defendant of guilt.

Judge Hazlewood denied a new trial:

"None of the evidence characterised by the defence as exculpatory, neither individually nor collectively, materially affected the question of whether the defendant committed the assault...

At this point, there is no reason to believe that testimony will produce anything other than what has already been demonstrated by way of the affidavits and file. The only interest of the defence that might be served by taking additional testimony would be to have an additional crack at the prosecution witnesses."

Steven's next hope was the Wisconsin Court of Appeals. In making a case for a new trial, his lawyer cited evidence that had been withheld from the jury, including the concealment of other suspects:

"While the state's evidence consisted primarily of the complaining witness' identification of the defendant as her assailant, the defendant called sixteen alibi witnesses and testified categorically denying any involvement in the crime. His alibi is consistent with the story he told the sheriff at the station house right after he was arrested. However, the jurors were not told that Kathy Sang, the last person to have seen Penny Beerntsen jogging before the assault, had seen another man on the beach near the time of the assault. Nor were the jurors told the police had conducted a canvass near the crime scene showing pictures of [Steven's] vehicle to people in the area, and none of them identified him. Also, they did not know that officer [Arland] Avery had seen cement on Steve's clothing at the time of his arrest.

"All of this evidence is exculpatory. And regardless of whether it's characterized as evidence improperly withheld by the state, newly discovered evidence or evidence not presented due to the failure of defence, defence counsel's investigation, this evidence warrants the granting of a new trial."

On August 5, 1987, the Wisconsin Court of Appeals denied Steven a new trial. People are convicted with great urgency, but appeals take years because the system has a vested interest in keeping people incarcerated regardless of innocence or guilt. Private prisons get millions in taxpayers' money to house people like Steven Avery.

On July 30, 1996, Anita Lynn Matthews – the scientist who had performed new DNA tests on behalf of Steven testified at a hearing for a new trial, conducted by Judge Hazlewood:

"As human beings, we share many physical traits: we all have hair and eyes and skin, for example, so we have many similarities in our DNA. But there are regions on each strand of our DNA called loci, where the number and the order of chromosomes vary from one person to another. It's these regions that scientists examine to identify the source of a particular specimen of DNA."

Asked how scientists test DNA, she said, "Police submit a questioned sample or specimen of biological material – blood, skin, hair, semen, saliva, that sort of thing – along with a known sample that was collected from the suspect. DNA testing is simply a comparison of the DNA patterns between the questioned sample and the known sample. If the DNA profiles are consistent with each other, then they could have originated from the same source, and we assign a statistical likelihood of that, such as 1-in-2 billion Caucasians, or 1-in-5 billion Hispanics... On the other hand, if the DNA profiles are different from each other, then they could not have originated from the same source."

"What did you find in this case?" Steven's lawyer asked.

"In this case, there were two questioned samples: fingernail scrapings and a pubic hair – and the two known samples, one purported to be from Penny Beerntsen and the other from Steven Avery."

"Specifically, how did you analyse the pubic hair and the fingernail scrapings in this case?"

"The DNA testing performed in this case involved first puri-fying the DNA in one-half of the evidentiary sample to remove cellular debris, resulting in a clean DNA solution. Then I used the polymerase chain reaction (PCR) technique to amplify the DNA at the specific regions or loci where variability is generally noted. PCR essentially copies the DNA until there is enough to analyse. Then a detection method is applied to visualize the different alleles or forms of DNA, which are present at each locus, permitting a comparison of the DNA in the evidentiary sample with that from the known samples." She concluded that the source of the fingernails' scraping had to be someone other than Steven or Penny.

As usual, the new prosecutor, Jim Fitzgerald, was as disinterested as Vogel in unearthing the truth or for justice to prevail. All he cared about was keeping Steven incarcerated, and the State of Wisconsin never being held accountable or having to pay Steven millions in compensation.

Fitzgerald argued that the DNA could have come from anyone, including Penny's family members. "The only new evidence the defendant really has is that some of the DNA underneath the victim's fingernails came from somebody else, Judge, and that's not enough for this court to grant a new trial."

On September 23, 1996, Judge Hazlewood, yet again, denied Steven a new trial because he did not believe that the newly discovered evidence would generate a different result on retrial.

Steven's lawyer took Judge Hazlewood's decision to the Wisconsin Court of Appeals with this argument:

"Given the extent of her injuries and the blood on her hands, one source of the DNA underneath the victim's fingernails was certainly the victim herself. Likewise, given her clawing at the assailant and his forcing her to stroke his penis with her right hand while grabbing that hand with his own, another source was almost as certainly the assailant. While the DNA results themselves could not show whether there were only two sources, the most likely conclusion on the facts in this record is that there were only two: the victim and her assailant.

"It was the perpetrator whom the victim clawed at with such force as to break her own fingernails, and it was the perpetrator who forced her to stroke his penis with her right hand. The state's assertion that the DNA could have originated from some sort of casual contact with someone else is wholly speculative on this record.

"Evidence that the sheriff's department had identified an alternate suspect in the next county who matched the description of the perpetrator is material and exculpatory. This was an extremely close case, and the withheld information goes directly to the sole contested issue at trial: that of identification. There was a strong case on Mr Avery's side in terms of alibi, and no physical evidence tied him to the crime. Under these circumstance, evidence that someone else from a nearby county who resembled the assailant was suspected by the police creates a reasonable probability of a different result on retrial."

On September 3, 1997, the Wisconsin Court of Appeals denied Steven a new trial.

Three years after the decision, Steven's father Allan urged him to apply to the Wisconsin Innocence Project. In 2001, they accepted Steven's case. Two students from the project asked prosecutor Fitzgerald to authorise the retesting of the physical evidence for DNA. He said that there was no physical evidence connecting Steven to the assault on Penny, so there was nothing to retest. He told them to read the trial transcript, over 1,000 pages, and to highlight any references to physical evidence.

The students responded:

Dear Mr Fitzgerald,

We have reviewed the trial transcripts as you requested. Enclosed please find those parts of the state's case which address the issue of microscopic hair evidence.

The hair found "consistent" by Ms Culhane (from the Wisconsin State Crime Lab) was the only physical evidence tying Mr Avery to the victim in this matter. Testimony by Ms Culhane about that hair consisted of approximately twenty-five pages. Testimony by three other witnesses was offered solely for the purposes of establishing a chain of custody and/or emphasising the importance of the "consistency" testimony by Ms Culhane.

Please let us know what else, if anything, we can provide for you.

Fitzgerald never responded.

On March 22, 2002, a motion filed by the Wisconsin Innocence Project was heard in Judge Hazlewood's court. Fitzgerald objected to retesting the evidence. Twelve days later, Judge Hazlewood granted the motion and asked both sides to reach a stipulation as to which evidence should be tested.

A month later, Steven received a letter from two new students at the Wisconsin Innocence Project:

We have spoken with the district attorney regarding the evidence you would like retested. As you may know, the labels have fallen off the exhibits, and it has now become necessary to arrange a time with the DA to relabel the evidence. Hopefully, once the pertinent evidence has been identified, we will be able to get the DNA testing process underway shortly thereafter.

On September 16, 2002, six days after Fitzgerald lost at the election, he authorised the transportation of the evidence to the crime lab, which took another year to test it. Sherry Culhane ended up re-examining the thirteen pubic hairs she had looked at eighteen years earlier. Steven Avery was excluded. The DNA profile from a single hair matched Gregory Allen, who was serving 60 years for sexual assault.

Getting released from prison is never a simple process. The authorities held onto Steven for another year. As his release drew closer, the attorney general's office issued a press release:

Upon receipt of the new DNA evidence, this office conducted an exhaustive review of the original investigation, earlier crime lab reports and the complete court record. Based upon this review, it is clear that Steven Avery did not commit this crime. It is tragic that Mr Avery spent eighteen years in prison for a crime he did not commit, but the DNA identification technology that has exonerated Mr Avery was not available when this case was investigated and prosecuted in 1985. Now that technological advances have established that Mr Avery did not commit this crime, justice requires the dismissal of the charges, and it is my duty to see that Mr Avery is immediately released from prison.

On September 11, 2003, TV crews and journalists formed a mob outside Steven's home for almost two decades: the Stanley Correctional Institute in Wisconsin. Behind a chain-link fence, Steven led a group of people towards the final locked gate, holding his sister on one side and his daughter on the other, his parents and lawyers behind him.

"I'm out!" Steven announced, wearing a red and white checked shirt, his long pale beard getting tossed around by the wind. "Feels wonderful." Asked about the role Penny had played in his wrongful conviction, Steven said, "It ain't her fault. They [the Manitowoc County Sheriff's Department] put it mostly in her head... They wanted somebody real bad. And I was the one." Although relieved that his daughter was there, Steven expressed sorrow over his incarceration resulting in a divorce from his wife and the estrangement of his twin sons. "There ain't no way I can make it up," Steven said about the time he had lost with his family. He urged other wrongfully convicted prisoners to keep the faith: "There's always miracles going around. Hopefully, they can get out just like me and get the guilty one in."

WISN 12 News reporter Nick Bohr interviewed Steven:

Asked what comes next, Steven said, "I don't know. Probably get up and eat breakfast or something." Steven laughed.

"Try to have a regular day, huh?"

"Yeah. I have to try a little bit. It will be different sleeping in a good bed."

Steven admitted that there came a time in prison when he tried to distance himself from his family. "Sometimes I had to cuss them out a couple of times, you know. 'Don't come up no more.' Sometimes it was pretty tough."

"And you did that because it was too hard to be that close to them?"

"Yeah. It was just too hard. They had to leave [the prison] and I had to go back. It was pretty tough." Steven nodded, his clear blue eyes filling with sadness.

In the past eighteen years, Steven had suffered tremendously. His wife had divorced him. A grandmother he loved had died. His nephew had been killed in a car accident. Steven hadn't been allowed to go to their funerals. After spending that long in prison, adjusting to society was hard. He was used to being told what time to wake up, eat, exercise, go to sleep... As a free man, he was offered no mental-health assistance. Large open spaces intimidated him, so he ended up living in an ice-fishing shanty.

Penny wrote Steven a letter, which included:

There are no words sufficient to express how deeply sorry I am for what happened. Your wrongful conviction has taken away eighteen years of your freedom, something that can never be given back to you. I wish it was in my power to restore those years, but it is not. The only thing I can offer now is a sincere apology that I identified you as my assailant when you were not. I am also aware that after eighteen years of imprisonment, these words must sound inadequate in the face of your tremendous losses...

My prayer these past eighteen years was that justice would be done in this case. That prayer was answered on September 11, 2003, when you were reunited with your family. Ultimately, no one can give you back time you lost. My hope is that in the years ahead, many good things will happen for you and your loved ones and that something positive will come from this incredible tragedy.

When I testified in court, I honestly believed you were my assailant. I was wrong. I cannot ask for, nor do I deserve, your forgiveness. I can only say to you, in deepest humility, how profoundly sorry I am. May you be richly blessed, and may each day be a celebration of a new and better life.

When they first met, Steven hugged Penny and assured her that he did not hold her responsible. Penny described Steven as extremely gracious.

Steven's exoneration came just in time to save Penny from Gregory Allen again. Penny had been a regular speaker at Green Bay Correctional Institution. Allen had enrolled in her September 2003 class called Challenges and Possibilities. After learning that she had come within weeks of encountering Allen, Penny said, "I can only imagine the jollies this horrible man would have gotten from that experience."

With Steven's second wrongful conviction, the odds were stacked steeply against him by the incendiary press conference hosted by Ken Kratz. Due to a tainted jury pool, 129 out of 130 potential jury members stated during jury selection that they believed in Steven's guilt. Even so, after the trial was over, the jury initially voted 7 to 5 in favour of acquitting Steven. But over the course of three days of deliberations, some of the jurors who had sided with Steven started to get pressured by jurors related to law enforcement.

After watching *Making a Murderer*, Juror 11 – Richard Mahler – revealed why he left the jury: "Family emergency and [I] felt threatened by the father of the sheriff's deputy [who was on the jury]. He knew I was swaying to not guilty based on the fact I wanted to review the evidence which 98% of it you saw in the documentary. The other 2% I do not recall."

On December 20, 2015, Juror 11 posted details on his Facebook wall:

There was a father of a Manitowoc County officer on the jury, also the husband of a woman who works in the Manitowoc County Clerk's Office, whom should have never been on the jury. I was juror #11. The .22 in Steven Avery's trailer was never dusted for prints, Steven's DNA was tampered with and other things that were not adding up to me. I was excused for an emergency. My gut feeling after looking at all the evidence is that the killer is still out there. I talked to another juror after the trial. I asked him why they found him guilty and he told me, 'Think of all the things he did when he was younger.' If they, after I left after four hours of deliberation, convicted him on that basis then most of us should be locked up for the stupid shit we did when we were younger. After I watched this, my feeling of his innocence is stronger. I am not saying the police did this terrible crime and my heart goes out to Teresa's family, no family should have to go thru what they did. But my heart also goes out to the Avery family. And it worries me that the real killer may still be out there while once again an innocent man is put back in prison. Many jobs and reputations were on the line with Steven suing for $36 million. And who found that key in Avery's trailer, one of the Manitowoc deputies that should have not been there in the first place and had a lot to lose from Steven's civil suit against Manitowoc county and this officer and other officers.

During a TV interview in January 2016, Juror 11 added more information, "I would have voted not guilty... When we got into the jury room, the father of the Manitowoc County Sheriff Deputy sat there with his arms folded and says, 'He's guilty as all hell.'" Commenting on another juror who came forward after watching *Making a Murderer* with allegations of illegal vote trading, Juror 11 said, "This person feels relieved that they got it off their chest. I talked to this person and they are scared."

The *Making a Murderer* documentary producers – Laura Ricciardi and Moira Demos – talked on TV about the frightened juror who had contacted them.

"The juror contacted us directly," Ricciardi said, "and told us that the verdicts in Steven's trial were a compromise. That was the actual word that the juror used and went on to describe the jurors ultimately trading votes in the jury room and explicitly discussing,

'If you vote guilty on this count, I will vote not guilty on this count.' So, that was a significant revelation."

"That's a very serious charge obviously, Moira," the presenter said. "Obviously, one that could turn this case on its head. Have you been able to independently verify that with another juror?"

"We have not spoken to other jurors at this point," Demos said. "This juror reached out directly to us. They told us really that they were afraid that if they held out for a mistrial that it would be easy to identify which juror had done that and they were fearful for their own safety. And what they explained to us was they believed that if there was a split verdict like this that that would send a message to the appellate courts, and they thought that Steven would get a new trial. That was sort of their plan, but obviously, it didn't work out that way."

Juror 11's family emergency that had caused him to quit jury duty was described by his daughter on Facebook:

I was leaving a family member's house in Howard's Grove...
I was driving perfectly fine doing the speed limit, with a van quite aways ahead of me. The van all of a sudden slammed on their brakes to turn (with signal on at last second) and I had no reaction time. They ended up not turning and I rear-ended them. I was pretty hurt as I was not wearing a seat belt... but that wasn't even the weird part. I did not call 911 and [n]either did the people in the van so I don't know who did. But the cops (mind you there is no police station in Howard's Grove) were there within 2 minutes or less... and I got an inattentive driving ticket because I hit them. I am not by any means saying that it was set up or anything like that... Just kinda weird.

How convenient that Juror 11 had to leave at such a pivotal moment. He posted, "I would have stayed if it were not for my daughter having a car accident. I have a very hard time accepting that I was not there and could have made a difference. I have to live with that as the 12 remaining have to live with their decision."

In both of Steven's wrongful convictions, the juries were tainted by the presence of people related to or loyal to members of law enforcement involved in Steven's cases. Juror 11 provided a glimpse of the tampering, which is the crime of attempting to influence a jury through other means than the evidence presented in court, such as making threats. It seems that Steven would never have been convicted in the second case if the father of the Manitowoc County Sheriff's deputy hadn't intimidated other jurors.

WHO KILLED TERESA AND PLANTED EVIDENCE?

Writing for the *Daily Mail*, Chris White referenced a Facebook poll of more than 1,200 people: 62% thought that Teresa's ex-boyfriend was guilty of her murder and 17% blamed Manitowoc law enforcement for the crime. If Steven and Brendan are innocent, then who killed Teresa and how was the evidence planted? I put that question to some sleuths and here is a plausible scenario written for this book by Kilauea:

Criminal profilers would note this as a heinous crime, committed by someone with extreme deviant thoughts, in a furious, savage, sexual rage, absolutely out of control. To take the time to burn the body at the quarry site and transport it to Steven's burn pit, the murderer would have to be comfortable with the entire compound and would not be out of place if seen. This eliminates law enforcement. No one seems to fit this description until you take drugs into consideration. The crime screams of crystal meth and was probably a crime of opportunity.

My theory is that two local meth users stopped Teresa shortly after she had left the Avery compound and kidnapped her. They raped and killed Teresa, put her body in the back of her own car and took her to the burn site next to the quarry. Beforehand, the meth users had probably partied together, and while really messed up on drugs had expressed some dark sexual fantasies. This is one of the things meth can do. It should be noted that in all the searches of Steven's place, no drugs were found.

After raping and killing Teresa, the murderers tried to figure out how to cover their tracks. Their reasoning was probably along these lines: *Well, heck, let's burn her up to get rid of our DNA. And to boot, we'll put Teresa's car somewhere obvious on the lot – as we don't want to take a chance of being seen driving it on the county roads – and move Teresa's ashes to Steven's place with this here barrel. The cops already have it out for Steven, and would jump at the chance to pin it on him just like in his first case.*

After just experiencing an intense rape and murder, the meth users' minds would have been going a million miles an hour. The degree to which Teresa's body and bones were reduced shows meth-like determination.

How did law enforcement get involved? Enter Pam Sturm and Mike Halbach. Pam is a private investigator, Teresa and Mike's aunt. Mike is Teresa's half-brother. Mike grew up friends with Blaine Dassey, and had spent time at the Avery salvage yard as a kid. Mike also grew up with Ryan Hillegas, Teresa's ex. Being a private investigator, Pam would have known local law enforcement and was probably on a first name basis with Deputy Colborn.

Auto Trader was the first to notice that Teresa had gone missing after she did not show up for work for a couple of days. They had called Teresa's parents, who reported her missing on Thursday November 3rd around 4 pm. They most likely also called their relative Pam Sturm, possibly even before law enforcement.

According to *Auto Trader*, the Avery compound was one of Teresa's last appointments. Pam, knowing Mike Halbach was familiar with the Avery lot, asked him to go with her for a look-see. She probably called Colborn (the first bridge to law enforcement) and mentioned her and Mike's plan. Colborn probably couldn't resist and met them out there. This was on the 3rd, the same day Teresa was reported missing.

The sun set on the 3rd around 5:45 pm, with Teresa being reported missing at 4 pm. They were a bit spread out during the search, with Colborn coming across the RAV4 first. Knowing that he didn't have a warrant, he called dispatch on his cell phone instead of his official radio. At the moment dispatch said Teresa's name, you can hear Pam in the background exclaiming "The car is here!" as she walked up to it.

Colborn didn't realize his 911 call had been recorded. You can see how surprised he was on the stand when they played back his call. He hadn't expected to hear himself, and was unprepared to explain why he had described the vehicle as a '99 after reciting the license plate, indicating he was in the presence of the RAV4.

The next day, Friday the 4th, knowing Teresa's car was on the compound, Colborn approached the Averys and first spoke with Steven's parents. At some point, Steven was questioned about meeting Teresa. Steven gave them an unabashed account of Teresa's visit. He let Colborn do a cursory check of his residence without a warrant. Colborn was fishing. Steven let him search his place, but Colborn found nothing.

Colborn admitted to Lenk that he had found Teresa's car on the 3rd without a warrant. Lenk, not asking to be, was now complicit. He wasn't going to rat out Colborn, and still had it out for Steven.

Once Lenk realized he was complicit in an illegal search, he was more inclined to do other illegal things to protect himself. He was already complicit with Colborn for covering their butts in 1995 about the Gregory Allen tip for which he was about to be deposed. Knowing there was nothing out of place according to Colborn's search of Steven's home, Lenk decided to plant blood evidence and remove the license plates the evening of the 4th. This helped to distance Colborn from the RAV4 regarding the plates.

Lenk did this alone. No one else had to know about the blood. Lenk and Colborn in good faith at that time were sure beyond the shadow of a doubt that Steven had done it – just like the meth users had anticipated.

Why would Lenk cross to the dark side? Judge Fred Hazlewood, who had presided over the Penny Beerntsen case, upon learning of the exoneration of Steven through DNA evidence showing Gregory Allen had raped Penny, showed no sympathy for Steven or Penny and was only concerned with whether Gregory Allen could be tied to him. Allen had appeared before Hazlewood on a sexual-assault case in 1984, so Hazlewood should have put two and two together in 1985 with the Beerntsen case. Both Hazlewood and Lenk were about to be deposed in the civil trial within weeks where the connection to Hazlewood and Allen probably would have been made. Hazlewood and Lenk would have spoken regularly, and after Colborn found Teresa's car on the 3rd (weeks before they were to be deposed) Hazlewood probably implored Lenk to do whatever he could to nail Steven, getting both him and Lenk off the hook. It worked. It wasn't just about the $36 million. Lenk took the risk for Hazlewood's and the Manitowoc County Sheriff Department's reputations.

Law enforcement had the problem of legally finding Teresa's car. Enter Teresa's ex Ryan Hillegas, friend of Mike Halbach. Mike came up with a plan to have Ryan involved. Ryan didn't have to know that Pam or Colborn were involved. Mike – to distance himself from the illicit discovery of the RAV4 – told Ryan about the vehicle and had him organize search parties.

Mike had Ryan send Pam to the Avery property to supposedly have an initial look-see. Ryan gave Pam a map and a camera, perhaps not knowing that she had already been out there. Most of the Averys were gone. Pam got permission from Steven's brother Earl to have a poke around the compound. Heck, why not? Earl knew Steven hadn't done it. Steven had let Colborn search his house the day before on the 4th. Pam was not a cop. Earl didn't even know that she was Teresa's aunt nor that she was a private investigator or that she had been there before.

At this point, Mike and Ryan were complicit, which explains their suspicious and animated behavior. Mike slipped, accidentally referring to Teresa in the past tense.

Manitowoc County Sheriff's Office botched the exhumation of Teresa from Steven's burn pit. This was not on purpose to hide anything they had done, but afterwards it was impossible to tell whether Teresa was incinerated there, or possibly the other burn site next to the quarry. The exhumation of the pit was headed by an arson investigator, Pevytoe, and not by a coroner. Too bad. If they could have proven that Teresa had not been moved, and Steven's burn pit was definitively where Teresa was incinerated, my narration falls apart.

Mike Halbach in good faith believing Steven had killed his sister, had gone through Teresa's room at some point early on and found her spare key. He gave it to Colborn, who gave it to Lenk. Now Mike was totally committed. He was the only non-law enforcement wildcard, knowing eventually that the key was planted.

The key was a valet key. The lanyard it was on – with only Steven's DNA – was linked to Teresa by her sister. But, this wasn't the key that Teresa would have carried, and you can't open the back door with it where her blood was found. Lenk didn't know that when he dropped it in Steven's room. Who carries around their extra key with the main one? You'd lose them both.

As for the bullet: there is a tremendous amount of blood everywhere whether someone is stabbed or shot. The presence of Steven's blood in the RAV4 is the strongest evidence that he did it, but the finding of the bullet in the garage with no blood spatter points to law enforcement dropping the bullet, and casts doubt on all the other evidence. Law enforcement could easily have taken a slug from a fencepost or fired that rifle after confiscating it, rubbed the bullet on Teresa's steering wheel, and voila, instant DNA evidence. This opens the possibility that law enforcement – either Lenk or Colborn, but probably Lenk seeing how he's got a few more marbles upstairs – planted Steven's blood in the RAV4, and removed the plates at the same time on November 4.

The eleven shell casings found in Steven's garage were definitively linked to the Marlin .22 calibre rifle found in Steven's room by machine tool marks or the unique marks a specific firearm makes when the firing pin strikes a shell. Fassbender and Wiegert, after pulling Brendan from school with no warning, got Brendan to parrot their story. Fassbender and Wiegert's agenda was to get Brendan to say that Steven had shot Teresa in the garage, twice in the head, eight or nine times in the torso. Teresa's skull fragments contained two .22 calibre-sized holes. The supposed confession would legitimize the physical evidence of the eleven shell casings, the holes in the skull and the garage as the kill zone. Four months later, the day of Brendan's supposed confession, they went back again and found the magic bullet. Lenk had probably coached Fassbender and Wiegert on what they needed Brendan to say, and he had a doped bullet ready to drop that day.

The slug with Teresa's DNA – supposedly, via a test that at best should have been regarded as inconclusive – was not definitively linked to the rifle that came from Steven's room. The best was testimony that the bullet had come from that specific model of Marlin, but the bullet was too deformed to do a lands and grooves comparison (that which we loosely refer to as the ballistic test) that might have linked it specifically to the rifle in Steven's room. So, the bullet was forensically, but not ballistically tied to the rifle in Steven's room, surmising that the slug had to have come from one of the eleven shell casings that had been linked to the rifle in Steven's room. The rifle was not Steven's. Prosecution could not come up with anyone who ever saw Steven handle that rifle, and none of Steven's DNA was found on it. And shouldn't another nine or ten bullets have been recovered from the burn pits or the barrel?

The consensus now is that Brendan's confession was coerced. I believe that Fassbender and Wiegert set out that day to get Brendan to implicate himself at any cost. Brendan was Steven's best alibi as to the comings and goings of the compound on Halloween. Setting Brendan up as an accomplice not only discredited him as an alibi, it also set the stage for Kratz to give that insane press conference which tainted the chance of Steven ever getting a fair trial.

What they did to Brendan was witness tampering with malice aforethought, which is a felony. It should have been grounds for a new trial for Steven.

I don't blame the jury for finding Steven guilty. It was the only narrative that made sense at that time from beginning to end. Kratz kept repeating that if the Manitowoc County Sheriff's Office had planted evidence, then they had killed Teresa as well. I don't believe that Manitowoc County Sheriff's Office would have killed Teresa over a lawsuit. I believe the whole thing to be split into three sequential narratives. Firstly, the meth users raping, killing, covering their tracks. Secondly, Pam, Mike and Colborn finding the RAV4 during an illegal search on the 3rd, and setting the stage for a fiction on how the car was discovered on the 5th. And thirdly, the planting of the key, bullet and blood.

As for conspiracies? Not something they called a meeting for and voted on. Just the opposite: everyone would have kept things as compartmentalized as possible. The killing of Teresa was most likely a spontaneous violent act of opportunity followed by a series of micro-conspiracies. People doing what they thought was right, and/or protecting themselves.

WHAT YOU CAN DO FOR STEVEN AND BRENDAN

Sign Brendan's mother's petition: Please Pass Juvenile Interrogation Protection Law In Wisconsin

If you live in Wisconsin, you can vote out Governor Scott Walker @ScottWalker for vowing that he will never pardon Steven Avery and Brendan Dassey.

If you don't live in Wisconsin, you can Tweet #whereistheblood #makingamurderer to @ScottWalker and the Wisconsin Department of Justice @WisDOJ

Visit our official support site unmakingamurderer.co.uk with the latest case news, ways to show your support, how to write to Steven and Brendan, how to send them things in prison and our newsletter signup.

Join Facebook Pages:
Un-Making a Murderer Community
Un-Making a Murderer Book
Official Family Discussion Page: Steven Avery
& Brendan Dassey Project
Official Family Support Group: Justice and
Freedom for Brendan Dassey
Largest Group: Steven Avery Project

You can contribute to Steven's and Brendan's legal fees:
Kathleen Zellner: Avery Legal Defense Fund
Laura Nirider: Center on Wrongful Convictions of
Youth – Action Agenda

Support the work of the Innocence Project

Help spread the word about this injustice on social media and by leaving Amazon reviews for Un-Making a Murderer. The more reviews Amazon receives the more it promotes this book to its other customers. You can also leave reviews at Amazon platforms in other countries, using your same log-in and password. Here are the English-speaking platforms:

Amazon USA
Amazon UK
Amazon Canada
Amazon Australia

Thank you for taking the time to support Steven and Brendan!

GET A FREE BOOK

Sign Up For Shaun's Newsletter:

http://shaunattwood.com/newsletter-subscribe/

SOCIAL-MEDIA LINKS

Email: attwood.shaun@hotmail.co.uk
Blog: Jon's Jail Journal
Website: shaunattwood.com
Twitter: @shaunattwood
YouTube: Shaun Attwood
LinkedIn: Shaun Attwood
Goodreads: Shaun Attwood
Facebook: Shaun Attwood, Jon's Jail Journal,
T-Bone Appreciation Society

SHAUN'S BOOKS

English Shaun Trilogy
Party Time
Hard Time
Prison Time

War on Drugs Series
Pablo Escobar: Beyond Narcos
American Made: Who Killed Barry Seal?
Pablo Escobar or George HW Bush
We Are Being Lied To: The War on Drugs (Expected 2017)
The Cali Cartel: Beyond Narcos (Expected 2017)

Life Lessons

Two Tonys (Expected 2017)
T-Bone (Expected 2020)

SHAUN ATTWOOD'S TRUE-LIFE JAIL EXPERIENCE

Hard Time 2nd Edition Chapter 1

Sleep deprived and scanning for danger, I enter a dark cell on the second floor of the maximum-security Madison Street jail in Phoenix, Arizona, where guards and gang members are murdering prisoners. Behind me, the metal door slams heavily. Light slants into the cell through oblong gaps in the door, illuminating a prisoner cocooned in a white sheet, snoring lightly on the top bunk about two thirds of the way up the back wall. Relieved there is no immediate threat, I place my mattress on the grimy floor. Desperate to rest, I notice movement on the cement-block walls. *Am I hallucinating?* I blink several times. The walls appear to ripple. Stepping closer, I see the walls are alive with insects. I flinch. So many are swarming, I wonder if they're a colony of ants on the move. To get a better look, I put my eyes right up to them. They are mostly the size of almonds and have antennae. American cockroaches. I've seen them in the holding cells downstairs in smaller numbers, but nothing like this. A chill spread over my body. I back away.

Something alive falls from the ceiling and bounces off the base of my neck. I jump. With my night vision improving, I spot cockroaches weaving in and out of the base of the fluorescent strip light. Every so often one drops onto the concrete and resumes crawling. Examining the bottom bunk, I realise why my cellmate is sleeping at a higher elevation: cockroaches are pouring from gaps in the decrepit wall at the level of my bunk. The area is thick with them. Placing my mattress on the bottom bunk scatters them. I walk towards the toilet, crunching a few under my shower sandals. I urinate and grab the toilet roll. A cockroach darts from the centre of the roll onto my hand, tickling my fingers. My arm jerks as if it has a mind of its own, losing the cockroach and the toilet roll. Using a towel, I wipe the bulk of them off the bottom bunk, stopping only to shake the odd one off my hand. I unroll my mattress. They begin to regroup and inhabit my mattress. My adrenaline is pumping so much, I lose my fatigue.

Nauseated, I sit on a tiny metal stool bolted to the wall. *How will I sleep? How's my cellmate sleeping through the infestation and my arrival?* Copying his technique, I cocoon myself in a sheet and lie down, crushing more cockroaches. The only way they can access me now is through the breathing hole I've left in the sheet by the lower half of my face. Inhaling their strange musty odour, I close my eyes. I can't sleep. I feel them crawling on the sheet around my feet. *Am I imagining things?* Frightened of them infiltrating my breathing hole, I keep opening my eyes. Cramps cause me to rotate onto my other side. Facing the wall, I'm repulsed by so many of them just inches away. I return to my original side.

The sheet traps the heat of the Sonoran Desert to my body, soaking me in sweat. Sweat tickles my body, tricking my mind into thinking the cockroaches are infiltrating and crawling on me. The trapped heat aggravates my bleeding skin infections and bedsores. I want to scratch myself, but I know better. The outer layers of my skin have turned soggy from sweating constantly in this concrete oven. Squirming on the bunk fails to stop the relentless itchiness of my skin. Eventually, I scratch myself. Clumps of moist skin detach under my nails. Every now and then I become so uncomfortable, I must open my cocoon to waft the heat out, which allows the cockroaches in. It takes hours to drift to sleep. I only manage a few hours. I awake stuck to the soaked sheet, disgusted by the cockroach carcasses compressed against the mattress.

The cockroaches plague my new home until dawn appears at the dots in the metal grid over a begrimed strip of four-inch-thick bullet-proof glass at the top of the back wall – the cell's only source of outdoor light. They disappear into the cracks in the walls, like vampire mist retreating from sunlight. But not all of them. There were so many on the night shift that even their vastly reduced number is too many to dispose of. And they act like they know it. They roam around my feet with attitude, as if to make it clear that I'm trespassing on their turf.

My next set of challenges will arise not from the insect world, but from my neighbours. I'm the new arrival, subject to scrutiny about my charges just like when I'd run into the Aryan Brotherhood prison gang on my first day at the medium-security Towers jail a year ago. I wish my cellmate would wake up, brief me on the mood of the locals and introduce me to the head of the white gang. No such luck. Chow is announced over a speaker system in a crackly robotic voice, but he doesn't stir.

I emerge into the day room for breakfast. Prisoners in black-and-white bee-striped uniforms gather under the metal-grid stairs and tip dead cockroaches into a trash bin from plastic peanut-butter containers they'd set as traps during the night. All eyes are on me in the chow line. Watching who sits where, I hold my head up, put on a solid stare and pretend to be as at home in this environment as the cockroaches. It's all an act. I'm lonely and afraid. I loathe having to explain myself to the head of the white race, who I assume is the toughest murderer. I've been in jail long enough to know that taking my breakfast to my cell will imply that I have something to hide.

The gang punishes criminals with certain charges. The most serious are sex offenders, who are KOS: Kill On Sight. Other charges are punishable by SOS – Smash On Sight – such as drive-by shootings because women and kids sometimes get killed. It's called convict justice. Gang members are constantly looking for people to beat up because that's how they earn their reputations and tattoos. The most serious acts of violence earn the highest-ranking tattoos. To be a full gang member requires murder. I've observed the body language and techniques inmates trying to integrate employ. An inmate with a spring in his step and an air of confidence is likely to be accepted. A person who avoids eye contact and fails to introduce himself to the gang is likely to be preyed on. Some of the failed attempts I saw ended up with heads getting cracked against toilets, a sound I've grown familiar with. I've seen prisoners being extracted on stretchers who looked dead – one had yellow fluid leaking from his head. The constant violence gives me nightmares, but the reality is that I put myself in here, so I force myself to accept it as a part of my punishment.

It's time to apply my knowledge. With a self-assured stride, I take my breakfast bag to the table of white inmates covered in neo-Nazi tattoos, allowing them to question me.

"Mind if I sit with you guys?" I ask, glad exhaustion has deepened my voice.

"These seats are taken. But you can stand at the corner of the table."

The man who answered is probably the head of the gang. I size him up. Cropped brown hair. A dangerous glint in Nordic-blue eyes. Tiny pupils that suggest he's on heroin. Weightlifter-type veins bulging from a sturdy neck. Political ink on arms crisscrossed with scars. About the same age as me, thirty-three.

"Thanks. I'm Shaun from England." I volunteer my origin to show I'm different from them but not in a way that might get me smashed.

"I'm Bullet, the head of the whites." He offers me his fist to bump. "Where you roll in from, wood?"

Addressing me as wood is a good sign. It's what white gang members on a friendly basis call each other.

"Towers jail. They increased my bond and re-classified me to maximum security."

"What's your bond at?"

"I've got two $750,000 bonds," I say in a monotone. This is no place to brag about bonds.

"How many people you kill, brother?" His eyes drill into mine, checking whether my body language supports my story. My body language so far is spot on.

"None. I threw rave parties. They got us talking about drugs on wiretaps." Discussing drugs on the phone does not warrant a $1.5 million bond. I know and beat him to his next question. "Here's my charges." I show him my charge sheet, which includes conspiracy and leading a crime syndicate – both from running an Ecstasy ring.

Bullet snatches the paper and scrutinises it. Attempting to pre-empt his verdict, the other whites study his face. On edge, I wait for him to respond. Whatever he says next will determine whether I'll be accepted or victimised.

"Are you some kind of jailhouse attorney?" Bullet asks. "I want someone to read through my case paperwork." During our few minutes of conversation, Bullet has seen through my act and concluded that I'm educated – a possible resource to him.

I appreciate that he'll accept me if I take the time to read his case. "I'm no jailhouse attorney, but I'll look through it and help you however I can."

"Good. I'll stop by your cell later on, wood."

After breakfast, I seal as many of the cracks in the walls as I can with toothpaste. The cell smells minty, but the cockroaches still find their way in. Their day shift appears to be collecting information on the brown paper bags under my bunk, containing a few items of food that I purchased from the commissary; bags that I tied off with rubber bands in the hope of keeping the cockroaches out. Relentlessly, the cockroaches explore the bags for entry points, pausing over and probing the most worn and vulnerable regions. *Will the nightly swarm eat right through the paper?* I read all morning, wondering whether my cellmate has died in his cocoon, his occasional breathing sounds reassuring me.

Bullet stops by late afternoon and drops his case paperwork off. He's been charged with Class 3 felonies and less, not serious crimes, but is facing a double-digit sentence because of his prior convictions and Security Threat Group status in the prison system. The proposed sentencing range seems disproportionate. I'll advise him to reject the plea bargain – on the assumption he already knows to do so, but is just seeking the comfort of a second opinion, like many un-sentenced inmates. When he returns for his paperwork, our conversation disturbs my cellmate – the cocoon shuffles – so we go upstairs to his cell. I tell Bullet what I think. He is excitable, a different man from earlier, his pupils almost non-existent.

"This case ain't shit. But my prosecutor knows I done other shit, all kinds of heavy shit, but can't prove it. I'd do anything to get that sorry bitch off my fucking ass. She's asking for something bad to happen to her. Man, if I ever get bonded out, I'm gonna chop that bitch into pieces. Kill her slowly though. Like to work her over with a blowtorch."

Such talk can get us both charged with conspiring to murder a prosecutor, so I try to steer him elsewhere. "It's crazy how they can catch you doing one thing, yet try to sentence you for all of the things they think you've ever done."

"Done plenty. Shot some dude in the stomach once. Rolled him up in a blanket and threw him in a dumpster."

Discussing past murders is as unsettling as future ones. "So, what's all your tattoos mean, Bullet? Like that eagle on your chest?"

"Why you wanna know?" Bullet's eyes probe mine.

My eyes hold their ground. "Just curious."

"It's a war bird. The AB patch."

"AB patch?"

"What the Aryan Brotherhood gives you when you've put enough work in."

"How long does it take to earn a patch?"

"Depends how quickly you put your work in. You have to earn your lightning bolts first."

"Why you got red and black lightning bolts?"

"You get SS bolts for beating someone down or for being an enforcer for the family. Red lightning bolts for killing someone.

I was sent down as a youngster. They gave me steel and told me who to handle and I handled it. You don't ask questions. You just get blood on your steel. Dudes who get these tats without putting work in are told to cover them up or leave the yard."

"What if they refuse?"

"They're held down and we carve the ink off them."

Imagining them carving a chunk of flesh to remove a tattoo, I cringe. He's really enjoying telling me this now. His volatile nature is clear and frightening. *He's accepted me too much. He's trying to impress me before making demands.*

At night, I'm unable to sleep. Cocooned in heat, surrounded by cockroaches, I hear the swamp-cooler vent – a metal grid at the top of a wall – hissing out tepid air. Giving up on sleep, I put my earphones on and tune into National Public Radio. Listening to a Vivaldi violin concerto, I close my eyes and press my tailbone down to straighten my back as if I'm doing a yogic relaxation. The playful allegro thrills me, lifting my spirits, but the wistful adagio provokes sad emotions and tears. I open my eyes and gaze into the gloom. Due to lack of sleep, I start hallucinating and hearing voices over the music whispering threats. I'm at breaking point. Although I have accepted that I committed crimes and deserve to be punished, no one should have to live like this. I'm furious at myself for making the series of reckless decisions that put me in here and for losing absolutely everything. As violins crescendo in my ears, I remember what my life used to be like.

OTHER BOOKS BY SHAUN ATTWOOD

War on Drugs Series Book 1
Pablo Escobar: Beyond Narcos

The mind-blowing true story of Pablo Escobar and the Medellín Cartel beyond their portrayal on Netflix.

Colombian drug lord Pablo Escobar was a devoted family man and a psychopathic killer; a terrible enemy, yet a wonderful friend. While donating millions to the poor, he bombed and tortured his enemies – some had their eyeballs removed with hot spoons. Through ruthless cunning and America's insatiable appetite for cocaine, he became a multi-billionaire, who lived in a $100-million house with its own zoo.

Pablo Escobar: Beyond Narcos demolishes the standard good versus evil telling of his story. The authorities were not hunting Pablo down to stop his cocaine business. They were taking over it.

War on Drugs Series Book 2
American Made: Who Killed Barry Seal?
Pablo Escobar or George HW Bush

Set in a world where crime and government coexist, *AMERICAN MADE* is the mind-twisting true story of CIA pilot Barry Seal that the Hollywood movie starring Tom Cruise is afraid to tell.

Barry Seal flew cocaine and weapons worth billions of dollars into and out of America in the 1980s. After he became a government informant, Pablo Escobar's Medellin Cartel offered a million for him alive and half a million dead. But his real trouble began after he threatened to expose the dirty dealings of George HW Bush.

AMERICAN MADE rips the roof off Bush and Clinton's complicity in cocaine trafficking in Mena, Arkansas.

"A conspiracy of the grandest magnitude." Congressman Bill Alexander on the Mena affair.

War on Drugs Series Book 3
We Are Being Lied To: The War on Drugs

A collection of harrowing, action-packed and interlinked true stories that demonstrate the devastating consequences of drug prohibition.

War on Drugs Series Book 4

The true story of the Cali Cartel, who took over Pablo Escobar's cocaine business with the help of the Colombian government, the CIA and a death squad called Los Pepes.

After Pablo's death, the cocaine entering America increased in large part due to the Cali Cartel.

Party Time

In *Party Time*, Shaun Attwood arrives in Phoenix, Arizona a penniless business graduate from a small industrial town in England. Within a decade, he becomes a stock-market millionaire.

But he is leading a double life.

After taking his first Ecstasy pill at a rave in Manchester as a shy student, Shaun becomes intoxicated by the party lifestyle that changes his fortune. Making it his personal mission to bring the English rave scene to the Arizona desert, Shaun becomes submerged in a criminal underworld, throwing parties for thousands of ravers and running an Ecstasy ring in competition with the Mafia mass murderer "Sammy The Bull" Gravano.

As greed and excess tear through his life, Shaun experiences eye-watering encounters with Mafia hit men and crystal-meth addicts, extravagant debaucheries with superstar DJs and glitter girls, and ingests enough drugs to kill a herd of elephants. This is his story.

Hard Time New Edition

"Makes the Shawshank Redemption look like a holiday camp" – NOTW

After a SWAT team smashed down stock-market millionaire Shaun Attwood's door, he found himself inside of Arizona's deadliest jail and locked into a brutal struggle for survival.

Shaun's hope of living the American Dream turned into a nightmare of violence and chaos, when he had a run-in with Sammy the Bull Gravano, an Italian Mafia mass murderer.

In jail, Shaun was forced to endure cockroaches crawling in his ears at night, dead rats in the food and the sound of skulls getting cracked against toilets. He meticulously documented the conditions and smuggled out his message.

Join Shaun on a harrowing voyage into the darkest recesses of human existence.

HARD TIME provides a revealing glimpse into the tragedy, brutality, dark comedy and eccentricity of prison life.

Featured worldwide on Nat Geo Channel's Locked-Up/Banged-Up Abroad Raving Arizona.

Prison Time

Sentenced to 9½ years in Arizona's state prison for distributing Ecstasy, Shaun finds himself living among gang members, sexual predators and drug-crazed psychopaths. After being attacked by a Californian biker in for stabbing a girlfriend, Shaun writes about the prisoners who befriend, protect and inspire him. They include T-Bone, a massive African American ex-Marine who risks his life saving vulnerable inmates from rape, and Two Tonys, an old-school Mafia murderer who left the corpses of his rivals from

Arizona to Alaska. They teach Shaun how to turn incarceration to his advantage, and to learn from his mistakes.

Shaun is no stranger to love and lust in the heterosexual world, but the tables are turned on him inside. Sexual advances come at him from all directions, some cleverly disguised, others more sinister – making Shaun question his sexual identity.

Resigned to living alongside violent, mentally-ill and drug-addicted inmates, Shaun immerses himself in psychology and philosophy to try to make sense of his past behaviour, and begins applying what he learns as he adapts to prison life. Encouraged by Two Tonys to explore fiction as well, Shaun reads over 1000 books which, with support from a brilliant psychotherapist, Dr Owen, speed along his personal development. As his ability to deflect daily threats improves, Shaun begins to look forward to his release with optimism and a new love waiting for him. Yet the words of Aristotle from one of Shaun's books will prove prophetic: "We cannot learn without pain."

ABOUT SHAUN ATTWOOD

Shaun Attwood is a former stock-market millionaire and Ecstasy supplier turned public speaker, author and activist, who is banned from America for life. His story was featured worldwide on National Geographic Channel as an episode of Locked Up/ Banged Up Abroad called Raving Arizona (available on YouTube).

Shaun's writing – smuggled out of the jail with the highest death rate in America run by Sheriff Joe Arpaio – attracted international media attention to the human rights violations: murders by guards and gang members, dead rats in the food, cockroach infestations…

While incarcerated, Shaun was forced to reappraise his life. He read over 1,000 books in just under six years. By studying original texts in psychology and philosophy, he sought to better understand himself and his past behaviour. He credits books as being the lifeblood of his rehabilitation.

Shaun tells his story to schools to dissuade young people from drugs and crime. He campaigns against injustice via his books and blog, Jon's Jail Journal. He has appeared on the BBC, Sky News and TV worldwide to talk about issues affecting prisoners' rights.

As a best-selling true-crime author, Shaun is presently writing a series of action-packed books exposing the War on Drugs, which feature Pablo Escobar and the Cali Cartel.